Developing as an
EDUCATIONAL LEADER
and MANAGER

I would like to dedicate this book to my friend and mentor Marianne Coleman, without whose support this book would never have been finished. Her wise comments were greatly appreciated.

Developing as an
EDUCATIONAL LEADER
and MANAGER

MEGAN CRAWFORD

Los Angeles | London | New Delhi
Singapore | Washington DC

Los Angeles | London | New Delhi
Singapore | Washington DC

SAGE Publications Ltd
1 Oliver's Yard
55 City Road
London EC1Y 1SP

SAGE Publications Inc.
2455 Teller Road
Thousand Oaks, California 91320

SAGE Publications India Pvt Ltd
B 1/I 1 Mohan Cooperative Industrial Area
Mathura Road
New Delhi 110 044

SAGE Publications Asia-Pacific Pte Ltd
3 Church Street
#10-04 Samsung Hub
Singapore 049483

Editor: Marianne Lagrange
Assistant editor: Rachael Plant
Production editor: Nicola Marshall
Copyeditor: Peter Williams
Proofreader: Caroline Stock
Indexer: Judith Menes
Marketing manager: Dilhara Attygalle
Cover design: Naomi Robinson
Typeset by: C&M Digitals (P) Ltd, Chennai, India
Printed in India at Replika Press Pvt Ltd

First edition published 2014

Library of Congress Control Number: 2014930799

British Library Cataloguing in Publication data

A catalogue record for this book is available from the British Library

ISBN 978-0-8570-2922-5
ISBN 978-0-8570-2923-2 (pbk)

MIX
Paper from
responsible sources
FSC
www.fsc.org   FSC® C016779

Contents

Acknowledgements

I would like to thank my publishers, my family, especially Philip, and my colleagues at the Faculty of Education, University of Cambridge for their support of this endeavour. I am also grateful to Roy Lilley for granting permission to include his '7 Things to Think About' for NHS leaders. Special thanks to Sonia Ilie for sorting out my formatting and to Peter Barnes for helping me get to grips with that difficult chapter. As this book suggests, people and context are vitally important, not just for leadership in the abstract, but for getting things done.

Preface

This book is woven around the idea of a personal narrative. My own narrative is based, as yours will be, on a unique set of experiences in particular contexts. I have been involved in educational leadership in universities and in primary and secondary schools. If I were to tell you the complete story and engage in autobiography, this would engulf the entire first chapter of this book. Instead, I will concentrate on my own leadership narrative, a concept that I will explain more fully in Chapter 1. The story of how I have moved from working in schools to working in universities relates to how I have come to understand the relationship between theory in practice and educational leadership, which was the motivation to write this book. My story can be seen as the underlying narrative of this book. I started my career as a primary teacher and moved into the higher education sector after eleven years but retained my interest in schools by becoming a governor. In schools, I rapidly (in retrospect too rapidly) moved from being a classroom teacher to a year group leader, to a deputy head teacher. When my children were small, I pragmatically took a part-time administrative post in higher education, having recently finished a Masters degree, in order to spend more time with my family. This moving in and out of jobs reflects what is known about many women's career patterns. I was encouraged by a valued mentor to move into writing and lecturing, and became part of a highly motivated team of people whose experience, warmth and intelligence made me want to continue with this new career, something that I had never planned to do. When I reflect back upon it, the need to stay true to my values as a teacher was at the heart of this move. Whether in primary schools or in university, I have always wanted to teach and discover more about working with others in organisations. Ex colleagues might suggest that 'nosey' would be a better description. At the same time, I was keen to keep up with the daily realities in primary schools, so in 1990 I became a school governor, a role which I thought would be short term but has continued up to now. Over 20 years I have had the privilege of being involved in five different schools in England, with age ranges from 4 to 18. A unique part of my leadership narrative is that I have been able to be involved in starting three new schools from the very beginning (Crawford, 2007). All these governing body experiences were diverse: from being asked to chair a school board in severe difficulties, to a tiny village primary, to setting up a large secondary school from a greenfield site. This has enabled me to see the way that theory and practice work together in leadership, and perhaps become more adept at understanding the viewpoints of other governors whose backgrounds are not in education. The role of governors in England is 'complicated, demanding, and goes on largely unnoticed' (James et al., 2010: 1), but I have found it particularly useful as an academic to be able to continually reflect on the reality of schools and understand the impact policy changes have in particular contexts. I have also spent parts of my life living in other countries. Eagled-eyed readers will spot references to life in the USA. Within the university sector, I have been privileged to teach leaders and potential leaders from around the world, and have learnt a great deal from those Master's and Doctoral students, not only about context in leadership, but also about their personal commitment to reflective practice (Schön, 1983) and the future of young people in those countries. All these instances make up my narrative and, as I examine it, several threads become apparent to me that concern people, values and a love of teaching. There are, of course, many more, and more of my own story will become apparent as you read on. Reflecting on my career as a narrative allows me to own difficult periods where certain critical events either changed my story entirely or took me in a new direction. My personal journey has caused me to reflect on the interface between research and practice in education, and particularly in educational leadership. In a sense, then, this book aims to bridge some of the gap between what academics write about and what practitioners 'do'. It draws upon both theory and practice. There is a firm emphasis throughout that the best educational leaders are dynamic and adaptable and are most effective when they draw upon understandings developed from theory. Your own narrative forms a very particular story which, I will argue, you can use to inform lived lives in schools and other educational organisations. My narrative and examples of the stories of others, discussed in this book, are there to help you develop as a leader and manager, by allowing you space to think more clearly about yourself as a leader and manager.

The author

Dr Megan Crawford is a Reader at the University of Cambridge. Her background is in primary schools, where she was a deputy head teacher. She is on the Executive of the British Educational Leadership, Management and Administration Society (BELMAS: www.belmas.org.uk.), and was its Chair from 2009 to 2011. She has been visiting Professor at a number of international universities.

Megan is very involved in governing schools, and was the Teaching Awards Governor of the Year, East of England, in 2009/10. She has been a governor of five schools, and is Chair of Governors at Oakgrove School, Milton Keynes. Her research encompasses principal preparation, teacher development, and emotion and leadership. Her previous book *Getting to the Heart of Leadership* was published by Sage in 2009.

Section 1

Evolving as an educational leader and manager

1

Becoming and staying an educational leader

In this chapter I will:

- explain the structure of the book;
- discuss and define the idea of a leadership narrative and how it could be useful to you;
- suggest that you may wish to consider a reflective journal, or companion, as a tool for development so that you can continually reflect as you read through the book.

Near and far

This book is about educational leaders, and specifically about those who lead schools, both in England where I live and in other countries and international contexts. There are also, I hope, aspects of the book which offer useful insights for those of you who work in educational settings other than schools. This book is based around the idea of a reflective journey into your own development and aims to make you think about how your past learning as a leader relates to your present needs as a professional. Inevitably, I will draw upon my own experiences, which will be contextually and time bounded. However, you will also be offered many opportunities to compare and contrast my experiences, and those included in the vignettes, with your own professional learning journey. This journey is captured for me in the phrase 'personal leadership narrative'.

The book is divided into five sections. The first three sections and the final one, focus on the ideas and issues that concern educational leaders, and the fourth reframes the role of the leader within the context of research. Throughout the book, but especially in Section 4, I will discuss some of the dilemmas and discussions that educational leaders have around theory and practice, touching on definitions, debates and controversies. I will discuss the extent to which leaders can use their experience to work with theory and vice versa, covering areas that I think leaders and potential leaders will find most useful and sometimes difficult. The book thus differs from others that are about leadership development generally, as it adopts the individual perspective so that the leadership roles in the organisation can be examined more clearly. In that, the perspective I adopt is rooted in the organisational, in both social and psychological aspects. Chapter 17 goes into more detail about my own personal approach.

Other perspectives are also introduced and examined because I will argue that very capable leaders can articulate their own perspectives clearly and know that research and practice are intermingled. Although there will be reference to practical processes that leaders may have to deal with, this is not the main focus of the book. Instead, the book is more akin to an inner, intellectual journey to illuminate leadership and management for you as a developing educational leader. Your written reflections in the companion will augment this journey.

The personal

In previous writing, I have noted that we should take as a starting point the fact that leaders lead from themselves as people, albeit within particular organisational and policy contexts (Crawford, 2009). Educational leaders globally share many of the same dilemmas and challenges because they are all dealing with people while dealing with dilemmas and challenges specific to their own contexts. The commonalities of those who choose to take up leadership roles all over the globe are often to do with their own values such as concern for young people and the life-enhancing side of education. Three different aspects of leadership – the person, the place and the policy context – make up a narrative that is woven together over time. As in all good stories, there are times when the plot thickens and out of it may come an effective educational leader, while at other times an ineffective educational leader may appear. The complex issues involved are something that any aspiring educational leader needs to understand, because such understanding can determine whether a leader succeeds at the task in hand, but is also able to sustain themselves and their organisation over time.

Policy context

Any policy context for education has its challenges, as changes and external mandates bring with them difficult choices for educational leaders as well as new opportunities. It may be going too far to suggest that policy-makers in some countries seem to assume that school leaders can change course, make policy implementation quickly and without strain, and have a work ethic which puts students, parents and the community ahead of the leader's own family. Leaders can be offered leadership courses but few clear opportunities to sustain themselves as they try to balance their life and work. I argue that educational leaders need to sustain themselves before they can help others to work together creatively, and need to grasp this need for reinvigoration early in their careers before they are completely overtaken by the demands of the job. This is especially true of the job carried out by head teachers/principals. To give you an example, regular annual surveys have highlighted the decline in applications for senior posts in England and Wales, particularly in primary schools (Howson and Sprigade, 2011). The figures for your country may be similar or radically different. Whatever your context, there is no doubt that the woman or man at the top has many stakeholders holding them to account, with all the attendant pressures that brings. Inevitably this leads to what Gronn has called 'greedy work' (2003b: 147). MacBeath and Townsend (2011) quoted one school leader who articulated what many, certainly in England and Scotland, feel: 'We now seem to be responsible for a lot of society's well-being, as well as education issues, and in many ways it is becoming an impossible job' (p. 106). Leaders in schools are not responsible for the whole of society's well-being, but they do need to attend to their own-well being, and I will look at this more closely in Chapters 9 and 17.

Whenever a book on leadership comes out, it is usually in the midst of some educational change or other, whether you are in England, Scotland or elsewhere in the world. This makes it challenging to write a book on developing as an educational leader because of the importance of context in leadership. However, because my foremost intent is to write a book for and about the individual, I hope it will be relevant to any reader who is either thinking about or beginning to think of themselves in some kind of leadership role in an educational organisation. Parts of the book may also be relevant if you are a more experienced leader, but its key focus is on developing leaders. Instead of looking at the process of leadership as an individualist concept, the book is focused on working with others and challenges you to be dynamic as an individual leader enhancing your own practice by reflecting on your self-development at each stage of your career.

Leadership as a narrative

Why people become educational leaders and how they sustain that commitment and energy over months and years is of interest to both policy-makers and to individual schools intent on growing and sustaining their own leadership teams. In a fast-moving educational world, the challenges for leaders are great and the policies ever changing. This book does not intend to proselytise, suggesting everyone should aim to become a principal or head teacher, because there are many facets of leadership which are worthwhile in themselves and which may or may not lead to that particular 'top' post. Leadership is a term that will run through the book rather than leaders per se, because leadership should be seen, I will argue, as part of an understanding of organisations (Ogawa and Bossert, 1997) and not just as a personality trait of an exceptional individual. I regard leadership as an organisational quality but, at the same time, I ask each reader to consider the personal leadership qualities they can bring, or develop, so that their organisation is able to adapt and change over time in whatever their particular context. As you read through the book, you will see that the view promoted sees leadership and the organisation as woven together. A key assumption I make is that one of the roles of leaders is to see that the people that make up the organisation are valued and recognised. This assumption can be interpreted in many ways, some of which I will return to later, but it focuses on the centrality of people and the leadership of people to any well-run organisation. Valuing people could mean helping an individual towards promotion or, in a more difficult sense, helping them move with dignity out of their role if leadership is not for them. In this, the book takes a humanistic perspective on leaders and leadership. This comes from my own leadership narrative.

Your resource

This book can also be viewed as a resource that can be used at different times in an evolving leadership journey. In fact, my aim is to set out a book that prospective, developing and current educational leaders can dip in and out of. If there were a book to compare it with, my suggestion would be my one of my favourite fictional travel books, *The Hitchhiker's Guide to the Galaxy* by Douglas Adams. If you have read this, you may remember that the Guide had inscribed on the back, 'Don't panic', and its alien guide, Ford Prefect, suggested you always carry a towel as well. This book agrees with the sentiment, but instead of asking you to bring along a towel for your journey, I will be asking you to instead take with you: an open mind, a questioning voice and the desire to learn more about yourself as an educational leader. Like the Guide, the way you use this book will be different for each person, as life will be for you as a leader. If I were to be a coercive leader, I might suggest that you read this book from cover to cover but, realistically, parts of it will be used more at some times than others. So, read the first and second chapters and then plot your course through the chapters that are most relevant to you.

Narratives

This chapter highlights the centrality of your own narrative to your personal development and by thinking of your life as a story you can begin to examine more closely your own leadership style and your relationships with others. I will suggest that developing yourself over time involves you not only becoming more aware of your strengths through this kind of narrative, but also allows you to learn from critical incidents that take place in your life as you develop to your fullest potential as a leader. Developing such self-reflection is crucial to enriching your own leadership. This chapter, then, serves as an introduction, establishing the idea of your career as a story you tell to yourself and others, and which you can use to reflect on as you move forward – a leadership narrative. Initially it may seem strange to think of storytelling as something that can help with both personal development and organisational analysis, but storytelling is very powerful.

> Many [accounts] ... are highly charged narratives, not merely recounting 'events', but interpreting them, enriching them, enhancing them, and infusing them with meaning ... such accounts can be seen as an attempt to re-create reality poetically. (Gabriel, 2000: 31)

School leadership takes place in a myriad of contexts around the globe and some of the examples in this book are drawn from that rich international context. There are many opportunities in the book to compare and contrast your experiences with that of others. Engaging with the personal meaning of your story – and, importantly, the stories of others – can be very useful for you in understanding more about how and why leaders make meaning for their organisations.

A view of leadership or management

For me, leadership is at once an organisational quality and a personal quality. This is true for leaders at whatever stage in their career they find themselves. As you read this, I have no idea whether you are an experienced educational leader in Hong Kong looking for inspiration, a teacher in rural Canada or a newish year head in England wondering what the future may hold. Crucially, this book aims to promote critical thought and constructive analysis about what it means to be a leader in schools, over time, in different contexts and with radically different government accountability structures. Later in the book, I will look at whether there is any difference between being a leader or a manager, and if there is, why it may not matter. For now, I will be using the terms interchangeably because I see them as creatively entwined and complementary. Different terms are used at different times because of the recent emphasis by many policy-makers on leadership as a 'magic bullet'. This will be discussed in Chapter 3. For now, it is worth bearing in mind any differences that you see between the two and noting them down in a journal.

The importance of reflective writing

As a way to begin to understand your own narrative while reading the book, whether you read it through sequentially or in chunks, I suggest you start a companion for your travels in the form of a journal. This could be a notebook or a virtual space somewhere. Whatever you choose, there are specific activities in the book where I will suggest that you spend time, maybe even just a few moments, with your journal. I am assuming that you are reading this book in the first place because you see yourself as someone on a leadership journey, who is willing to be reflective in order to best benefit from the professional development opportunities that the book affords. To start you off, here is your first opportunity to tell your own story, in writing.

Activity 1

Briefly sketch out your educational journey, starting with your own schooling. Then, look back over your career so far and note down significant people, places and events. Note the nature of their significance to your leadership journey. Were they significant because they moved your ideas and career on positively, or were they difficult and/or traumatic and made you change your own thinking about leadership? At this early stage, try to identify one event of each kind, and what it taught you about yourself, as a person and professionally. In the following section, I will ask you to add to this activity.

I introduced the idea of a personal leadership narrative in a previous book (Crawford, 2009). This has also been called the 'personal interpretative framework' (Kelchtermans et al., 2011). Both of these similar concepts invoke the way that leaders and their ideas develop over time: they take into account retrospective views of experiences as well as the importance of the here and now in personal development. Your identity as a leader is formed partly through such narratives. Just like schools as organisations use narratives to manage meaning, communicate core values and negotiate social order and identity (Armstrong, 2011), so leaders use them to do similar things at the personal level. Narratives can help express emotions and help the reader begin to understand the current organisational context or lived reality of schooling. At the same time, narratives help construct new ideas, not just for the leaders themselves but for those they work with.

Telling your story

Narrative is linked to leadership in many significant ways, through past events, through talk, through the personal sense of self, and in the culture of schools and schooling. For each person, this narrative will be different and personal. Roberts (2002) sums up this process of recalling events and putting them in a particular personal context:

> In our own personal conceptions of our biographical time we are aware of our own mortality but not our actual end; we also remember the 'past' but cannot live it again except in the imagery of recollection. (p. 171)

In particular, he suggests that an individual life is full of events never completed – interpretations that lie within the consciousness of the interpreter. Interpretation and consciousness together make up a key frame for the way leaders see their own narrative. This will inevitably be full of ambiguity about the past, present and future.

Recognising the role of memory is important to this book because the personal *leadership* narrative involves what Briner (1999) calls 'our history, present and anticipated future', and memory will be shaped by other forces. So leadership narratives are not memories per se, but much more about the stories that people use to make sense of situations. Several authors (Pascal and Ribbins, 1998; Southworth, 1995) have over time given very clear accounts of leaders in action, speaking in their own words. You might like to read some of these accounts yourself.

Sparrowe (2005) has a useful idea to think about, which relates to the activity that you have just completed. He suggests that using the idea of a narrative crystallises the fact that the self changes and moves through time and events. 'The narrative self is not a constant self, identical through time, but the subject that experiences change, reversal, and surprise' (p. 426). Change, reversal and surprise are very important parts of the educational leadership narrative. Sparrowe also usefully outlines how a narrative works in practice. To make sense of our lives we use different kinds of stories to tell others about events and to relate each event in our lives to the ones that have preceded it and will come after. He notes:

> One way to do that is to recognize an event as the outcome of an intention – this happened because I intended it to. Another way is to construe the event as the effect of the intentions of some other individual, entity, or contextual factor. Put another way, when we think about ourselves in relation to our actions, we often do so in small plot segments [...] Plot is the organizing theme of a narrative. It weaves together a complex set of events into a single story.

It could be argued that recognising the plotline becomes easier as you become an experienced leader, partly because there are only so many plots, but also your self-awareness will be more developed. Sparrowe suggests that self-awareness can be aided in many ways, and work, such as writing your own life story and keeping journals, can be seen as the most common form of accessing narrative (Bush and Glover, 2003; Crawford, 2004). It also offers a space to reflect. Sparrowe suggests that writing your own obituary can help you see the plot of your life, but perhaps this should only be attempted when you are in the right frame of mind! Other activities build on the basic reflection in Activity 1. One such is 'The Reflective Best Self Portrait' (Dutton et al., 2006) where people get feedback on their unique strengths as individuals from significant others, not just by listing them but by relating three stories of when they feel they were at their best. Sparrowe calls this 'the narrative construction of an esteemed self'. Adding this idea to your journal could be a useful extra exercise. He also advocates engaging leaders in understanding what Luthans and Avolio (2003) refer to as trigger events. In Activity 1, consideration of these may have informed your understanding. These events, like a denouement in a soap opera, represent transitions in the plot of your narrative identity. He notes: 'Enriching the variety of alternative but positive plot lines enables developing leaders to find in others new ways of being.' For me this is important. A book that was totally introspective about the leader and his/her own narrative would not be very useful, I believe. The leadership narrative should not be viewed in isolation, as others are very much engaged in the process, from students, to staff, to the wider community. Later in the book I will look more closely at the role of the wider community in such engagement.

Writing or telling a narrative is all about reframing situations in order to understand them better. The reframing process is ongoing in a career. One of the theoretical structures that you may find useful in your leadership development is to frame your choices and opportunities in different ways, using some of the resources given in the book. When I work with education leaders on postgraduate courses, I have found that the concept of reframing has proved very useful to students of leadership, especially when applied to organisations (Bolman and Deal, 2003) as well as to your own narrative. I will return to Bolman and Deal's conception of framing later (in Chapter 5), because frames are a useful starting point for analysing any particular management problem that is concerning you, perhaps starting with the one of the four frames that you feel you use least often in order to give yourself a new viewpoint. You may want to briefly scan that part of the book now.

The idea of story and narratives is one that most of us are familiar with, and the personal leadership narrative is complex, many layered and ever evolving. It chimes in with much of contemporary leadership theory and practice that describes authenticity. Although authenticity can be seen as a contested concept (Fineman, 2000), as an idea it can be useful if it is viewed in relation to self-awareness of one's fundamental values and purpose rather than what others judge to be authentic. Leaders' sense of self will be framed by government policy, parents and the community, students and teachers and their own life experiences. Awareness that this is so is vital, and one of the most helpful aspects of personal leadership development to understand from the start if educational leaders are to become more resilient and less reluctant to take up challenging leadership positions. In terms of narrative, the plot of your leadership story may be at the beginning, or at the end of Act Two. Wherever you are in the plotline, this book will endeavour to help you make sense of your narrative, and look at ways of enhancing your knowledge of both theory and practice.

Of teaching and learning

Teaching and learning is at the heart of all that education is about and should be central to why you want to lead and manage effectively. Your personal leadership narrative will draw upon both your own experiences as a learner at school and beyond, and on your ability to work with others. The book will discuss how school leaders can develop and nurture talent in curriculum leadership, and foster a climate for professional development for all staff whether they are teachers or not. There is not a specific section in this book that deals with leading teaching and learning. That is because my own core values assume that the educational leader is a leader of teaching and learning, and this is the key core function of a school leader. I take this for granted because I believe that the best educational leaders come from a background that is enriched by their own work with young people on teaching and learning. This experience offers them real pedagogical insight, which makes them able to identify and tackle key learning and teaching aspects of schools. This insight comes from their training, from experience of being a teacher in the classroom and from professional development opportunities pertinent to the classroom. My viewpoint means I have difficulty with policies that suggest it should be otherwise. For example, it is part of English government policy currently to suggest that those from a non-teaching background, e.g. school business managers, ex army officers, etc. can take up headship. Such people may have many of the skills required to lead a school, but at the heart of the job, I would argue, is someone that is passionate about learning and helping young people develop both their knowledge and their skills. I would probably argue that a non-teacher head would need a teaching deputy, who would have a very important role as regards curriculum management and delivery. Before you read on, add the following notes to Activity 1.

Activity 1 (cont'd)

Do you agree with my viewpoint concerning teaching and learning experience? Note why, or why not. Add one example of how this viewpoint might influence your own journey through leadership.

Becoming and staying a leader

Teachers are socialised into their profession, and moving into more formal leadership roles can require a period of re-socialisation as the expectations of colleagues, parents and children change. This process of socialisation leads to the establishment of occupational identity both in teachers and in leaders (Weindling and Earley, 1987; Draper and McMichael, 1998). The path to leadership is situated in long-term and informal socialisation, with many transitions between different facets of leadership (Duke, 1987: 261). It is worth looking more closely at what this process of socialisation entails, and this is covered in Section 1. Classroom teachers also have leadership roles, some of which are informal and may be the start of their own personal story towards more formal leadership roles. This complex interplay means that becoming an educational leader is a complex business, and is dissimilar for each person, but there are also many similarities in the paths people take to leadership roles (Cowie and Crawford, 2008). Some of the major differences may be due to the cultural context in which the leadership role is developing and the book will reference several as the major practical and theoretic issues are discussed. Throughout, you are asked to apply what you read to your own contextual specifics, and ask: 'What is it that is different here and now for me and the people I work with?'

Any educational library is replete with books and articles about leadership theory. A casual reader might observe that there appear to be fashions in theory. For example, many articles have looked at how schools both in England and the US have distributed leadership. Distributed leadership has also been the focus of a great deal of research and debate (Spillane, 2006; Harris, 2008). It is worth noting that in countries with high accountability regimes, such as England, these discussions about a more flexible, distributed pathway of leadership have occurred at a time when the final accountability of the head teacher has never been greater. In other countries, where there is more local accountability and autonomy through a district or province system, such as Canada, it could be argued that there is still some flexibility in the structures for principals to work in and through their organisation by a distributed leadership framework. Chapter 3 will discuss these theoretical debates about leadership in more detail.

Your role

Another factor, if formal leadership roles are your aim, is how leadership roles are described and constructed in your particular context. In some countries it would seem that both systemic and personal factors might be stopping people becoming 'formal' educational leaders. Kelly and Saunders (2010) suggested that developing people for headship is a complex process which is a mixture of on the job informal learning and more formal courses. The traditional route in many countries is to become a deputy then a head so that you can take advantage of such developmental opportunities. However, if you wish to become a head teacher or principal, the number of deputy posts available may affect your pathway, both in terms of how many are available, and also how many are filled at any one time. For example, in England, the annual survey of leadership posts by Howson and Sprigade (2011) noted a decline in the number of advertised deputy posts and they worried that this would reduce the number of candidates for headship in the future. We also know from Howson that in England in particular, record numbers of primary school headship vacancies were seen during the 2009/2010 school year. He points out that the annual readvertisement rate for heads in primary schools reached 40 per cent, the highest in the 26-year history of the survey. The secondary rate rose by a smaller amount, 28 per cent. For the first year in the survey Scotland was included and its vacancies levels rose slightly but remained lower than in England and were mostly in rural areas. So, becoming a head teacher is not as easy as one might first assume, certainly in parts of the UK. There is developing evidence that in other countries, such as Ireland and parts of Canada, some middle leaders and deputies are also reluctant to move upwards (Anderson et al., 2011). What is the situation in your context? I will return to leadership qualifications and development programmes specifically in Chapter 9, as well as addressing specific contextual challenges.

To travel hopefully

Nothing in the world of educational leadership stands still, whether you are in Chile, Botswana or elsewhere, and change is ever present. The purpose of this book is to help any potential or current leader in education to develop practical strategies and a developing ability to articulate ideas that will aid them through the differing contexts that will arise over the length of a professional career. By asking you to read and reflect, I hope that the book will have a useful part to play in your own continuing professional development planning. It aims to help you think and research ideas and practices, and tailor your development to the particular context that is uniquely yours.

I have stressed that this book views leadership in education as an evolving journey over time, set within a personal leadership narrative. Although it could be argued that the journey narrative is hackneyed and overused in education and elsewhere, it does sometimes serve a useful purpose. When we travel we have a choice of routes and transport – we can take the shortest route to our destination, usually by plane, or take the train and admire the landscape, or cycle in teams for charity, or a plethora of other options. All of this assumes of course that we have a destination in mind when we set out. I would argue that many teachers set out to work with children and young people, and often only gradually do they realise that their journey is taking them towards leadership positions. So your journey and that of your contemporaries will be different in the ways that travel is different – mode, destination, purpose, equipment levels and so forth. I have argued in this introduction that this journey is actually only partially about an external mode of travel through some sort of educational landscape, and more a journey through relationships with others and a continuous reflection on self – a narrative journey. The narrative journey this book takes will draw on concepts from the educational leadership and management literature, personal narratives from around the world, and my own reflections from my experiences as a teacher, lecturer, governor, parent and student. I will invite you to examine and illustrate some of the routes that you have discovered. The next chapter will look at values and frameworks of meaning, so that you can begin to position yourself as an educational leader.

2

Values

In this chapter, I will:

- argue that at the crux of your development as a leader is an ongoing commitment towards examining your values towards leadership and education;
- ask you to examine your own leadership narrative in terms of the values you bring to the task of leadership;
- think about the values that you may intentionally or unintentionally promote.

Introduction

The subject of values is a complex one on which countless words have been written. Your values will be examined and re-examined over time and related to your developing knowledge and experience. Greenfield and Ribbins tell us: 'The school is a crux of values and for values [...] schools are a reflection of the culture that they exist within but they are also a prime instrument for shaping and developing that culture' (1993: 213). Thus developing as an educational leader means that one is constantly reflecting on what is important to you.

Leadership is concerned with values specifically because thinking about values concerns basic beliefs about education, and how you as a leader relate to the organisational structures you find yourself in and the values of the people you work with. They are the ideals that you view as important and which influence not only how you think about leadership, but also how you act in the classroom, in the school and in the community. Drawing upon the work of Haydon (2007) and others this chapter asks you to examine your own leadership narrative in terms of the values you bring to the task of leadership and the values that you may intentionally or unintentionally promote. This will then be taken up in later chapters where I discuss the school ethos and culture and the school as an educational community.

In leadership and education literature, a great deal has been written about values, far more than this chapter could possibly cover in the allotted space. Hodgkinson (1991), a key figure in educational administration, wrote that administrators 'must know two things: where the values are and where the power lies' (1991: 6). In terms of the context of this book, he also suggested that the aspiring leader should study values:

> By doing so, he or she may gain self knowledge and self understanding [...] it should lead to a better understanding of one's fellows thus enhancing the possibility of greater empathy, sympathy and compassion [...] The leader is one who can best perceive and best resolve value conflicts. If there are no value conflicts then there is no need for leadership. (p. 11)

The term 'values' is often used at the same time as words such as 'ethics' and 'morals'. Begley (2012: 40) argues convincingly that this can lead to confusion, so for the purpose of this chapter, the discussion will be confined to his definition of values as 'the umbrella term under which other specialised forms of values can be subsumed'. Begley uses Hodgkinson's (1978) definition of values 'as conceptions of the desirable' and notes that all forms of values can be thought of as 'conscious or unconscious influences on attitudes, actions and speech' (p. 41). The idea of 'conceptions of the desirable' seems a useful definition for the purposes of reflection.

Activity 2

In your journal, reflect upon your own ideas about 'conceptions of the desirable' or guiding principles. Values are influenced by many factors and you may want to reference examples such as your childhood, your parents or your own schooling as such values are deep-seated. How does this idea relate to your own personal values? How much do these personal values align with the values of your current workplace? Try to write down what these values are, and say something about the relationship between the two.

This is not an easy activity, but beginning to think about your values and the idea of shared values is crucial to leadership. This chapter will only look at a small part of the writing that is particularly pertinent to school leaders at whatever career stage, and will also make a case for why thinking about values is important for leadership in education more generally. It should be thought of as an introduction so that you can follow up the references and ideas that are particularly useful for you. If you are already a trained educational philosopher, you may wish to move through this section more quickly! I am expecting, however, that most readers will be looking at this area, for the first time, or with only limited background knowledge. Gill (2011: 162) argues that the successful leader should be able to 'identify, display, promote and reinforce shared values that will inform and support the vision, purpose and strategies [...] we evaluate aspects of existence [...] on the basis of our values.' Begley's (2012) argument is that the primary way values relate to leadership is the way in which such values influence the cognitive processes of individuals and groups and, in turn, reflect people's underlying motivation. These values, he suggests, determine where we put our efforts. I will return to this later in the chapter.

There are also many different ways of classifying values. The values that you emphasise as a leader will be different to those in other professions and even other educational organisations in different countries. Multicultural and cross-cultural contexts mean that leaders need to be able to examine those things that are common values across societies, and those that are heavily influenced by cultural situations. One useful classification of values given is that developed by Rokeach (1989, cited by Bloisi 2003: 167). Rokeach describes instrumental values as those that are concerned with beliefs about behaviour and what kinds of behaviour may be used to reach desired goals and ends, e.g. honesty. He describes terminal values as those which are about 'desirable ends that are worth striving to reach', e.g. a happy, well-run school. This is not always possible. Starratt (2003: 29) suggested that a key thing to learn as a leader is to:

> Recognise that most of the time you do not know what you are doing, and that you are probably, however unwittingly, often doing some harm or hurt to somebody. Be assured that there is always someone in the community who does not appreciate or benefit from your leadership.

If there is one idea that recurs in the leadership literature, and when talking to leaders in schools, it is that of vision. Sometimes it is used to exhort colleagues to some future place, and sometimes it is found purely in statements in school documentation. What is usually clear if you look closely enough is that, however a vision is encapsulated, it is closely and inevitably tied to values. In all cases, it is usually useful to ask the questions 'Whose vision?' linked closely to 'Whose values?' Fullan (2003) wrote about the moral purpose of the leader in their school, and how s/he needs to 'visualize and then create the conditions' (p. 29) in which every child can flourish. This idea of moral purpose is a driving force behind many initiatives that seem to have gone well (Crawford, 2002), and can be seen not only seen at the school level but in the community more widely as well.

Of ideals and instances

I have found Haydon's definition of values, based originally on that of the sociologist Kluckhohn, and on the work of Begley and Johansson (2003) very useful:

> Values are conceptions, explicit or implicit, distinctive of an individual or characteristic of a group, of the desirable which influence the selection from available modes, means and ends of action. (2003: 3)

Begley and Johansson suggest that defining values in this way brings to the fore the role of values in the making of choices, which is clearly an important part of leadership roles in schools. They also note that it is 'important to establish a balanced appreciation of the relationships between personal values, professional values, organizational values and social values.' One of the focuses of this book is, of course, on the first two. Haydon makes an important distinction when he reminds us that values may be explicit or implicit. If you say that one of your values is honesty you are making this value explicit. In your day-to-day life, your choices and actions may well be influenced by this value, even if you don't make this explicit in day-to-day interactions. Others will make inferences of your values from your actions, and as a leader these may be about other values that you implicitly take to be important, whether or not you spell out to yourself or to anyone else exactly what ideas are influencing you. In the extract above, no doubt you made explicit connections to the faith-based values that may or may not be held by the head teacher concerned. I think Haydon also makes a useful distinction around the word desirable. If values are *conceptions* of what is desirable, he argues that this means something like 'worthy to be desired', and this may be different from what actually is desired. So if you have an addiction of some kind (food, alcohol or smoking) you know that it is desirable to lose this addiction, even though you may still desire cream cakes, for example. Haydon argues that being free of such a habit is one of your values – one of your conceptions of what is desirable – and links values and motivation.

Decision-making

Leaders draw on values in decision-making. In this example, I introduce Simon, who needs to reflect on his personal values to make a decision about his future. The free school which he is considering is a particular type of school set up in England. Such schools are funded by government but are set up by groups of parents, teachers and other people interested in schooling. These groups can set up a school after making a case to the government and are then funded directly from central government money. The school is also directly accountable to central government. This new kind of school has been welcomed by many people in education, but it has also been criticised as a policy for allowing inexperienced people to set up schools and as a waste of public funds at a time of overall shortages. All of this background is known to Simon.

Vignette

Simon Jackson went to school in a small English town, and all his educational experience, both as a pupil and a teacher, is in the state sector of education in small communities. He started out as a teacher of small children, and his particular area of expertise is literacy, especially reading. He is a now a very capable middle manager in a primary/elementary school in England, looking, at 28, towards his future career direction. He has already studied for a Master's degree in his own time and is looking for a new challenge, having been in his current school for five years. He loves the area in which he lives, where he is settled with his wife and small child. Because it's not a heavily populated area, there are not that many schools to which he could apply for promotion. He has been contemplating looking for a deputy post in a large town, which would mean a house move. He notices in the local newspaper that a new 'free school' is being set up and is advertising for a head teacher. Reading the advert, Simon is struck by how much of what is being said about this new school resonates with his own views on primary schooling. He notes that the person in charge of setting up the school is not from an educational background and has been involved in local business ventures including farming.

Should he apply? What do you think might influence his decisions and how might these relate to values, if at all? The answer to this depends on many factors of course, not all of them to do with Simon's educational values. However, whether he believes that the free school model is a suitable one for education locally, based on his values about what constitutes good education and how strongly he believes in these, will play a part. You may like to consider in more detail what particular values might influence his decision as you read this chapter.

Personal value systems and the context

Simon's case illustrates how our personal value system is important and will inevitable shape the way you behave in certain contexts. Haydon

(2007) suggests that although educational leaders need to look at their own individual values, they also need to look beyond this to the values that are embodied in a particular institution or community context. Different cultural values will also shape which values are viewed by society as important. Schools will have their own values which are part of the culture of that particular organisation, and any newcomer entering that community needs to be aware of the power of the organisational culture on the individual's behaviour and loyalty to its organisational values. Furnham (2006) notes that: 'Values relate to a wide variety of features at work: how one is rewarded, how one responds to authority, how proud one is of the organisation' (p. 300). Leadership has a key role to play in how the values of an organisation are discussed, made explicit and promoted. Developing shared values and pride in an organisation is an important part of shaping the culture of a school, and is not an easy task. As Simon discovered as he rejected the idea of applying to the free school position, there are some values that are very important to you personally that remain relatively constant and inform decision-making.

The situational context outside the school is also crucial to understanding the way values are part of the educational picture. Schools in an emerging post-conflict state, such as Kosovo, will be very different in terms of cultural context to schools in Edinburgh, Scotland. Within countries, the cultural context of the school will also be very different, especially in large countries with huge variations in local conditions. Both Canada and the USA offer examples of countries that have similar cultures, but different local contexts. In business, this offers challenges to leaders of multinational companies. Lencioni (2002), writing for the business market, suggests that these need to embrace values and contexts for successful business can lead not only to cynical behaviour by employees, but also real confusion in business as to what values are all about. He distinguishes between *core values* that often follow the values of the founder; *aspirational values* which companies use to point towards future success; *permission-to-play values* such as teamwork and customer satisfaction which are common to most companies but don't make them distinctive; and *accidental values* which reflect the common values of those in the company, perhaps as expressed by a dress code, for example. For the reflective educational leader, this is also a complex area, full of subjectivity, and Lencioni's definitions of values could, I would suggest, be seen in schools, colleges or other places involved in education. You may want to note down in your writing companion whether any of those definitions struck a chord with you and why. For me, it raises a question about the transition of core values as the organisation changes and develops to meet new needs. It prompts me to try and think about the core values I have in mind when I think about schools, and in particular one school in which I worked. On reflection, part of the difficulty I found about 'fit' into the organisation is that one of my core values, trust, did not seem to be very prevalent in a climate of suspicion and mistrust.

Communicating your values

There are many occasions where leaders have to make their values explicit through the way the work, communicate and deal with difficult decisions. Before you read the next section, reflect on the following vignette.

Vignette

Sister Katherina is the very experienced teacher and head teacher of a medium-sized secondary school in Africa. Run by an order of teaching nuns, the school is in the middle of a country that has had an on-off civil war for over a decade. Periodically, the fighting has caused the closure of the school, but most of the time, the education continues for the young people in the school, who are drawn from an area very local to the school.

What are your first thoughts about Sister Katherina and her values? You might imagine that Sister Katherina's values will be shaped both by her personal religious beliefs (moral purpose) and those of her order. The community of nuns might also be expected to have certain key values in common. So, Sister Katherina might exhibit both group values and personal values that are distinct to her as a person and head teacher. Her vision for the future of the school may be based on these.

If you want to be an educational leader or manager, you will come across values influencing all aspects of what you do. Begley and Johansson (2003: 4) remind educators that leaders tend to speak of ethics or morals as an overarching term for anything in education that is values-related, and this can cause particular problems in societies that have a different ethical framework to the one you know. They note: 'As a practical consequence, administrators naturally tend to opt for employing rational consequences and consensus with grounded values as guides to action and decision-making whenever that is possible.' Sister Katharina in the vignette came from a particular religious background and a European one, but she was now working in an African country with two major religions. Haydon also suggests that we are more likely to talk about our values when there is something important at stake. Given what you have inferred about her values, how would you expect her to handle the following dilemma?

Vignette

On one of the occasions when fighting raged around the school, staff and students stayed overnight and for several days in the school compound. The caretaker ventured out on the second day to see what was actually happening and was killed. His body was thrown into the school compound to be seen by Sister Katharina as she looked out the next morning.

You may immediately be drawn to the practicalities of the incident, once you have got over the sheer horror of it. What would you do next? I will come back to what she did in a moment, but think about how what you are suggesting may or may not be related to your own values. Gill (2011: 172) points out that leaders can lack 'the ability, moral courage or energy to act in accordance with their values'. He defines this moral courage as 'standing up for a set of beliefs and values when the sands are shifting beneath one's feet'. In the particular context above, both moral and physical courage may well be needed. The head teacher's concern was with the dignity of the deceased, as well as the need to make sure that it was a safe situation to deal with. She wanted, she told me later, to look after the body as soon as possible, for both spiritual and pragmatic reasons due to the heat and the distress to staff and children. She had to balance some deeply held values about human dignity with her overarching task to keep everyone safe. So she had to wait until she was sure all danger was passed before attending to the rites of burial.

This is an extreme example to make you think about what leaders value in a different way and to introduce the idea of moral courage in a particular dilemma. Leaders will be consistently faced with dilemmas, and ask to act swiftly and decisively. Their value base informs these decisions on a daily basis, without necessarily being made explicit. Moral courage is about acting in accordance with these values. You might like to consider whether moral courage is a core value for leaders in education as they face day-to-day dilemmas, mostly thankfully less extreme than the one above. Personal values will also play a major part in terms of how individuals handle challenges and changes in their careers, as the Simon Jackson example suggested.

Shared values

The vignette above highlights how values and practice fit together. In less extreme circumstances, there are also challenges for educational leaders. When we view a leader as authentic, it could be that we attribute the motivational effects of leadership to the consistency of a leader's values and behaviours. At the same time, we make a judgement about how this aligns with our own values, and the values of other potential followers. So when we think about authenticity it is not just an individual process, achieved by self-awareness of one's own inner values or purpose. It can be viewed as an emergent, evolving framework from the narrative process in which others play a hugely important part. In educational leadership contexts of course, the 'others' have many differing attributes. Haydon carefully points out that a great deal of lip service may be paid in education to the idea of values, where the rhetoric is that something is important but the actions don't seem to match this. He cites an example of a male head teacher who says that gender equality is important but actually takes no action to prevent practices that discriminate against girls and women. The question then to ask, Haydon notes, is: 'Does he, then, recognise the importance of gender equality at all?' Haydon concludes that in fact maybe he does, because it is far too easy to judge, without further details, whether such a teacher is neglecting the value of equality altogether. So he concludes that the idea of a connection between values and actions is correct, but it can be a complex connection. This complexity is part of the intellectual challenge of leadership, and one which you may explore in more detail in the literature in the educational leadership field.

Gill (2011), notes that the values of business leaders matter to the organisation and the same would be true for education. His key values for leaders are honesty, truthfulness, integrity, trust and trustworthiness, and he argues that the best leaders have values that closely match those of the organisation that they are leading. He also notes that 'shared vision, purpose and values in an organisation or nation constitute a strong positive culture' (p. 176). This again reminds us of the importance of local and nation contexts. A democratic leadership approach may seem like an ideal way to put values into practice. Woods (2005) contrasts instrumental reasons for valuing democracy with intrinsic reasons. As an approach to educational leadership democracy may be difficult to achieve and, of course, will not solve all problems. Haydon says that democratic leadership chosen for intrinsic reasons

> may even be the most difficult of all approaches to realise its full potential. It is not something that can be laid superficially over the existing structure or ethos of a school; it has to go deep, affecting the whole life of the school. Working out its practical implications is bound to be complicated.

Challenges for leaders

The educational leader is faced with huge challenges when s/he considers values. They underpin almost everything that is part of educational life, from the government's policies to the aspirations of parents and staff. Gill suggests that a helpful idea is that of 'transcendent' values that are able to accommodate different wants and needs of these various groups. Transcendent, shared work values would seem to be at the heart of effective leadership. In your reflective journal, make notes on the following activity.

Activity 3

Look back on what you wrote about your own ideas about 'conceptions of the desirable' or guiding principles. Given your current leadership role, how do you implicitly or explicitly translate these principles into shared work values? Can you identify one important thing that you did that has transformed an aspect of your work?

Shared work values in teaching and learning seem like a given but of course they are much more complex than that. The ethos of a school or other educational workplace reflects the values and beliefs of all those who work there. Leadership strategies are a large part of helping to build or sustain an ethos. The next chapter will look at how such strategies are also built around your own understanding of leadership and leadership styles, and I will also return later to the connections between values and organisational culture.

Summary

Personal values underpin educational leaders' actions. The task then is to understand more clearly where those values help build a great school and how the role of the leader is to identify ways in which teams and individuals can explore and shared their experiences of working together in order to build those transcendent values. At the same time, leadership is contextually based in a particular culture, whether that is local or national. Building on your knowledge of personal values and shared values means that you are more able to understand both the culture of the locality and the culture of the organisation.

Ways of thinking about leadership

This chapter will cover:

- some of the theoretical discussions that have influenced both policy and practice;
- ways of discussing or conceptualising leadership;
- distributing leadership;
- gender and equity issues relating to leadership;
- ways of developing better leadership.

As we have seen so far, there are many ways that leadership can be conceptualised and in this chapter ways of considering leadership in education are discussed. It may seem like rather an intellectual pursuit that has no immediate relevance to your own work in practice, but in this chapter I hope to show you how research about leadership and practising leadership do relate. Not only is it interesting and helpful to look at ways of considering leadership in its own right, but research in this area has influenced educational policy in the UK and elsewhere – impacting on the work of individuals and institutions. You may like to follow up some of the references to enable you to follow up particular areas of interest.

As a newcomer to leadership in education, it may seem that if you look at the number of works available it is difficult to know where to start. As MacBeath and Townsend describe it: 'The qualities of leadership have proved harder to pin down than the less elusive functions of management, but have, nevertheless, provided a rich and growing seam of literature' (2011: 3). Some of the more academic discussions about leadership and/or management can help leaders think more critically about their own practice. This chapter will again draw upon examples from international contexts to highlight issues and ideas, with a particular emphasis on the cultural context as being important.

Terminology can also confuse. Some countries, such as the USA and Canada, put both leadership and management together under the heading of educational administration, but in the UK the term most often used is leadership. It is also useful to note now that in many countries, notably England and the United States, particular discourses of leadership practice have shaped the way that policy has been formed and implemented. Many of these Anglo-centric leadership perspectives have also been very influential in very different contexts worldwide, but the assumption that they can automatically be applied cross-culturally is now more widely challenged in the literature (Dimmock and Walker, 2005).

In this chapter I encourage you to take a critical or questioning stance. This is where you ask yourself questions about what is behind the ideas you are being asked to consider by colleagues, policy-makers or other interested stakeholders in your particular context. Looking behind the ideas can often give you insight into the context and arguments that underlie a policy. You can draw upon your own values and sense of purpose to begin to decipher the key issues that are behind any model of leadership that is being suggested to you. These discussions will be returned to later in Chapter 9. I want to start by considering some of the ways that leadership theory has been used in education, and in particular how it relates to policy and practice. I will also briefly introduce the notion that we should pay more attention to organisational theory, which will be covered in more detail in Chapter 5. This chapter then should be seen as a starting point to the huge area that is leadership theory.

Before looking at some of the theoretical discussions that have influenced practice in schools, try the following activity.

Activity 4

This chapter is called 'Ways of thinking about leadership' but it could have been called 'Ways of thinking about leaders' as this is often what people feel most comfortable discussing when beginning to study leadership. Consider someone who you regard as an effective leader. Putting aside the issue that effectiveness may mean different things to different people for a moment, note down why you believe this to be so. Is it to do with personal characteristics, particular contexts or something else entirely? How would you distinguish between the idea of leader and leadership?

This activity should make you think carefully about how you use the language of leadership. Often, when people talk about leadership, they are thinking about the personal characteristics of 'people as leaders'. Much has been written about great leaders generally and whether they are born or made. Chapter 9 will consider this conundrum in more detail when discussing leadership development. The leader you picked for the activity may have been someone whose values were in close alignment to your own, or they may have been someone who was particularly skilled in getting teams to work together in order to move an organisation forward. They could also, of course, be someone who, seemingly by sheer force of personality, got the tasks completed that were necessary for the organisation at the time. Bearing in mind your thinking so far, what immediately comes to mind when you are asked to write down styles or types of leadership? Probably you refer once again to the personal characteristics of the person you have in mind as an effective leader.

Another aspect of considerable importance in the leadership literature is that of context. Your answer to the previous activity may very well depend on your actual school/organisational context, and how the person fitted into the structures and culture of that particular institution. Sorenson et al. (2011) talk about a 'quest' for a general theory of leadership and the language of leadership is replete with people searching for this in grail-like terms. Sorenson et al. suggest that because leadership is operating within human groups, it is supported by influence and power (p. 32), and is 'a phenomenon focused on vision, challenge, collaboration, process and product'. All of these are in turn influenced by the context of the particular institution and also the culture outside the school. Different countries have different historical contexts and cultures. For example, it has been argued that education in England is disproportionately influenced by the 'public school', which is private education, to the detriment of the success of the state sector.

Another contextual aspect to leadership in any institution is whether any powerful organisation in your country has espoused a particular form of leadership as being more effective than some other type. The solo, charismatic leader who sweeps all before them may have come to mind when you were completing the activity (Crawford, 2002), as the idea of a leader who can solve all the dilemmas of an organisation is a recurring one, both in the literature and particularly in discussing organisations that are deemed to be failing. You may also have noted that you are looking for 'what works' or solution-based forms of leadership, which may be one of the reasons that solo leaders hold such sway, perhaps being seen as more effective in the popular imagination. Leaders who offer solutions in unstable situations have been seen as able more easily to transform organisations towards a new ideal and to be able to do it quickly. In the US and the UK, the idea of distributed leadership, has been very much invoked in the public policy discourse. This idea moves away from the solo leader and suggests that there is room for more voices in the leadership debate – we will be moving on to discuss this later in the chapter. Conger (2011) draws particular attention to the notion of context and situational factors, noting how a great deal of what passes for knowledge in this area can actually be rather speculative. Conger, however, suggests that a study by Roberts and Bradley (1988) gives some clues as to the importance of context and charisma that is slightly different to that of the popular imagining. A field study is cited where one person moved from being a very successful leader, known for her charisma, to a very different situation. The field study took place in America and concerned a school superintendent, who was well liked and in charge of several schools in a district. Because she was so successful in that particular context, she was promoted to the position of state commissioner of education. Her personal charisma did not appear to transfer to her new post, and she had many difficulties leading reforms in the state. The two contexts in which she worked were in some ways similar but in fact were very different. The first post gave her ample opportunity to work on a much more personal level than the second did. It may well be significant that the earlier context was one of crisis while the second was not.

Activity 5

Jot down what it might have been about the two differing contexts that caused this change in perception, and note down any commonalities with situations you have been in.

There are many factors that could have changed people's perception of her as an outstanding leader that were due to the very different contexts. For example, her ability to change the situation was much more circumscribed in the new post because she lacked the detailed control and autonomy she would have had as superintendent. There were also political factors to be taken into account and all her decisions had to go through to a higher authority. Before, she had much more personal autonomy. The study also points to another interesting factor: the lack of personal loyalties in the second post, partly due to the very number of personal relationships that were involved in the larger post. This last factor emphasises the stake that followers have in leadership. Smaller numbers of followers in her first post allows Conger to conclude that 'less geographically dispersed and more limited numbers of stakeholders fostered deeper working relationships at the district level and also inspired affection and trust in her leadership. These in turn heightened perceptions of her charisma' (p. 95). This idea of a perception of charisma emphasises the connection between what the leader is seen to do and how the followers view it. As the superindent's story shows, any immediately simple solution belies the complexity of any given situation. I am sure you can think of other examples from your own experience. This brings into focus the intellectual or conceptual arguments that you will find in the wider educational leadership literature which you may like to follow up for yourself.

Situated knowledge

In the educational leadership literature, there are many voices that suggest that no matter the amount of reading we do, there is still a long way to go in understanding leadership. For me, a useful way of thinking about this area is the idea of 'situated knowledge' (Gronn, 2003b). This knowledge comes from our own frameworks that we use to understand leadership. To begin to think of leadership in a more theoretical fashion, it is often useful to have some sort of framework to work with. Western (2012) has argued that there are three main normative, or 'how things ought to be', leadership discussions. Becoming aware of these discourses, he suggests, helps individuals to frame 'the boundaries and norms in which we all act' (p. 16). He characterises these types of discussion as:

- the leader as controller – where a leader uses a system of coercion and rewards to get the job done;
- the leader as therapist – particularly prevalent in western societies where the leader is more concerned with relationships among people and achieving meaning and purpose from the workplace;
- the leader as messiah, aka the charismatic leader – where, faced by difficult times, the leader provides vision and purpose to those he (usually a he!) leads.

The last type we have begun to discuss with the activity regarding the superintendent. I have also noted above that for many countries, there is a fourth, the shared leadership perspective, often focused on one particular kind of shared work, known as distributed leadership. Bolden (2011) notes that there has been a huge growth in various kinds of shared leadership perspectives, of which the idea of 'distributed leadership' is but one, but as an idea it has been very influential in education, perhaps because it draws on parts of all the discourses that Western suggests. This is because even the idea of shared or distributed leadership may only be 'allowed' by a forceful, charismatic-type leader. Bolden wonders whether shared leadership perspectives are about offering to school leaders a genuine alternative to past ideas or whether they are something else entirely. He even suggests that they may in fact be a chimera to describe a nonexistent way of leading which seems to respond to the profession's demands for equity and purpose in the practice of leadership (p. 254). It is worth taking a moment to look at a few of these debates in more detail.

Distributed leadership

There are many studies about the distribution of leadership (DL), both in the UK and the USA, which have been very significant to practices in those countries (Spillane et al., 2011; Spillane, 2006; Harris, 2008), many of them very theoretical. In fact, Spillane et al. (2011) argue that DL has 'effortlessly entered the conversation about school leadership and management [. . .] often with simplistic and unwarranted mantras such as "everyone is a leader" or "the more leaders the better"' (p. 159). As Bolden noted, these seem to have an appeal towards a more democratic view of leadership altogether (Woods, 2005), which has not always worked out as such in practice, partly because of the accountability which still often lies with the most senior leader in the organisation. Woods and colleagues (2004) noted the similarities in any DL discussion to the work carried out on teams and collaboration in education. In order to try and differentiate, they argue that distributed leadership has three fundamentals:

- It highlights the emergent property of leadership as groups of people working together.
- It opens up the boundaries of leadership.
- It suggests to organisations that expertise can be found across the many and not just the few.

Similar to Bolden, Woods et al. discuss the degree of control and autonomy that individuals might have within such a framework. They noted that:

- Distribution is framed within a culture of ideas and values which attaches to different people different measures of value and recognition and indicates where the limits are to what is open to discussion and change.
- These constraints may come from an organisation itself or from within the national context within which a school operates.

Activity 6

Looking at these last comments, note down whether you work now or have ever worked in a distributed leadership environment. What were the culture and values that framed that workplace, and why?

Most countries operate within a system of strong accountability mechanisms to central government. If school leaders are accountable to external agents for externally mandated targets, distributed leadership may have distinct limits on its uptake in the organisation, even if it is rhetorically part and parcel of practice. Woods et al. suggested that truly democratic leadership is concerned with much deeper philosophical values. So, senior leaders in a school can conceive of and work towards a workplace where leadership is delegated, social relations are strong and trust is high but, as they point out, 'Ideas and ingrained assumptions about whom to trust, who is legitimately able to influence decisions and so on, condition the possibilities for widening the boundaries of leadership' (p. 450). It was partly this kind of problem that has led recently to more trenchant criticisms of distributed leadership as something that might help either in understanding practice or altering practice for increased effectiveness of schooling.

Activity 7

It could also be that the idea of distributed leadership is far removed from the educational practices of the country in which you work. In that case, note down why this might be, and whether this idea of a wider distribution of leadership is helpful or not in improving the leadership of schools in your particular culture.

For example, I have already mentioned the work of Peter Gronn who was, in Gronn (2000), one of the first academic authors to look at distributed leadership. However, over time, he has changed his views (Gronn, 2009, 2011). He argues that studies in distributed leadership may have contributed to our understanding of situated knowledge but argues that this is only part of the entire picture. Partly this is because it seems that there is no getting away from the role of the individual in leadership. Gronn notes (2009: 383) that 'solo leaders continue to figure prominently in accounts that purport to be distributed and that distributed leadership apologists have not adequately clarified the role and contribution of individuals as continuing sources of organizational influence within a distributed framework.' He now suggests that what we know about leadership in education is that it is a hybrid, with many differing configurations. Gronn suggests that a key benefit of the discussions around distribution is that it has allowed scholars to recognise the importance of activities performed by hybrids in organisations and gets discussions away from 'well-rehearsed binaries, such as leader-follower, leadership-followership, superior-subordinate and leader-manager' (Gronn, 2011: 442). Distributed leadership as a concept, he suggests, doesn't fully explain what is happening on the ground, because there are different forms of leadership that may be at work at any one time, from concentrated solo leaders working in one part of an organisation to much more dispersed forms of networks or collaborations within the very same organisation.

Configurations of leadership

Gronn makes a case for the concept of leadership as a configured one, that is we need to look at leadership as built around parts that fit together. This means that for the educational leader the most useful thing to know about leadership is how to think about differing configurations of leadership practice. In other words, different kinds of leadership actions may need to be put together by the nominated leader in a particular context.

Activity 8

Following on from the last activity, can you identify different leadership configurations in your current setting? What are the important factors where this appears to work well?

I will return to this idea later, because as an idea it has tremendous practical implications for a school leader as well as even more theoretical considerations for those who wish to study the theory of leadership further. First though, let's look briefly at the organisation itself, whether a school, a college or something else entirely.

Beginning to think about the organisation and leadership

In Chapter 6, we will look in more depth at this issue, but I think it's important to bring the organisation into play when thinking about leadership theories. Each organisation is unique with its own internal and external history. Parry (2011) and others clearly argue that attributing organisational success or failure to leadership is a 'romantic oversimplification' (p. 53). Bearing this in mind, and the activities you have carried out concerning the ideas of shared leadership and configurations, undertake the following activity.

Activity 9

Drawing on an educational organisation that you have known well over a number of years, jot down the factors that you see as contributing to its success or failure. If you believe leadership has been in some way key to this, try to relate the idea of leaders and leadership to other aspects of the organisation, such as structures, teams, size of the organisation or context. There may also be other organisational aspects that you can identify. Note them down. Then, attempt to arrange them in order of importance, relative to the success or failure that you have identified. This may take more time than you think! Where do types of leadership figure if at all? We will return to this activity in Chapter 6, but in the rest of this chapter, we will focus on leadership.

This activity may highlight the fact that a specific kind of leadership was influential or it may show the role of an individual or teams. In fact, the idea of configurations of leadership, or parts that fit together in a specific context, may have particular resonance when looking at specifics within an educational organisation. Consider the following case.

Vignette

A new school was being formed in Greece. The principal tried to employ teachers who had the same teaching and student discipline culture, and for many it was their first post. It soon became clear to the principal that the teachers had different criteria for assessing students which caused problems with both students and parents. She decided to move away from the grading system used in many schools in Greece to a common student evaluation criteria and a vision for an alternative student evaluation more than grading. She had to convince the teachers of the necessity and the importance of this innovation. What are the leadership and organisational issues that she would need to focus on?

This case study has been included because it shows a very particular case, yet broader issues can also be seen, including leadership configurations.

There are many advantages for a leader in this situation – a new school with new teachers offers many possibilities, not least because most of the staff will be motivated to try out new ideas. It may well be quite easy for such a principal to persuade the staff to adopt a very different approach to the norm for the area. This particular case involves a collaborative leadership style, but also the leader and the group leaders needed to train in the skills of running such groups. Using intense group work, the teachers exchanged ideas and became collaborative groups with common student evaluation criteria. They also evaluated as they went along, and changed practice as necessary. The next step of course was how the change was received by parents and students, which was one of the key things the principal had to take into account, and how this should be managed.

Management and leadership

Notice that the work 'manage' has assumed great importance at the end of that last case study. Often, the ideas of management appear to have been subsumed beneath the all-embracing idea of leadership when educational issues are being discussed. In many ways this distinction may not really matter. However, the idea of management does focus in on the 'how' of leadership. If leadership is usefully viewed as a configured one in any educational organisation, then management is the key skill that makes the configurations work. So, in terms of the Greek school, there was solo leadership from the principal about an issue she felt was important, but this was then configured as the other parts of the organisation, plus parents and students, began to understand and take ownership of the issue. This was achieved through those configurations managing the processes as they went along. Management was the key to running the discussion groups effectively and involving parents. In fact some writers have suggested that leadership is part of management rather than the other way around (Mintzberg, 1990). This popularity of leadership brings the discussion back to the leader as messiah, aka the charismatic leader, who has everything under control (Crawford, 2002).

There are many other factors which are involved in successful leadership of a team or an organisation, and the next section is one that most leaders have some understanding of, in practice, but maybe unaware of the leadership literature.

Leadership and diversity

In the educational leadership literature, many writers (Coleman, 2002, 2012; Hall, 1996) have drawn attention to issues that relate to gender and leadership, and more recently, to more general issues of diversity and leadership. I will return to my own personal view on diversity in Chapter 17, and in Chapter 7 I will discuss such issues in relation to culture and power. Here it is important to note that leadership has a key role to play in our diverse world because leaders often come across discrimination either personally or as part of their leadership role. When discrimination occurs it takes many forms and can be both direct and indirect. Many of us will have, perhaps without knowing, carried stereotypical ideas with us of particular groups or roles. Coleman (2012) draws attention to the key relationship between leadership and diversity issues, and on 'how difference impacts on becoming a leader and how that difference impacts on the practice of leadership' (p. 600). She suggests that there are many issues to be taken into account when considering diversity and leadership including 'equal opportunities, equity, equality, social justice, inclusion and discrimination' (p. 597). Coleman's work on gender and leadership has made her realise more acutely the role of the outsider in leadership:

> Issues identified in relation to gender and leadership are largely the same as those that apply to any 'outsider' who aspires to leadership or to leading a diverse community. (p. 600)

Coleman suggests that there is a stereotype of who is appropriate as a leader in any culture. Usually that person is male, from the dominant ethnic group, of middle age and from a reasonably privileged background. In the UK, that leader might be viewed as male, middle-aged, middle-class and white. Coleman argues that the dominance of the stereotype over time makes it difficult for anyone who does not conform (i.e. an outsider) to become any sort of leader, even within a distributed type of leadership. Carli and Eagly (2011) suggest that 'leaders can be effective only if other people accept and value their leadership (p. 111), so particular contexts will give different values to the idea of women or other 'outsiders' as leaders. This may also then affect the way the structure of an organisation either impedes or helps leadership in all its diversity to take place, by inadvertently placing barriers in the way of 'outsiders', because the consequences of management decisions have not been thought through, e.g. having hastily arranged meetings in the evening for all staff. As well as being a bad idea in general, this may also make it difficult for those who work part-time, job share or have any sort of caring responsibility to attend without good notice. Although women have increased their numbers in leadership positions, they are still under-represented in most school systems in leadership positions. However, it is often difficult to find international statistics. Coleman notes that: 'There are often assumptions that it will be relatively easy to access information about gender or ethnicity of educational leaders, but in practice this is rarely the case' (ibid.). Whatever the exact figures, there is still much to debate in gender and leadership and other diversity issues. Carli and Eagly note that 'women's leadership opportunities do not appear blocked because of poor education, preferences for careers that lack potential for advancement or lack of commitment to careers, so these variables cannot be responsible for the gender gap in leadership' (p. 107). This would only be true of course of those countries where both sexes have equal access to education. They make a point that has resonance to many women, however, in that they suggest that women 'may make more accommodations in their careers to fulfil family obligations' (p. 107). All of these debates are wide-ranging, and even as the ideal of leadership moves to a team focused one in the literature, the issues raised in relation to diversity become even more relevant. As an area of exploration, leadership and diversity also has the potential to reveal more about specific organisations and the individuals within them. I will draw upon this in the Chapter 5.

Activity 10

This activity allows you to explore your own views about diversity and leadership, by focusing particularly on one context. If you are able to find comparative figures for your own context, you may also want to look at those as a contrast.

Coleman (2012) notes that:

> In England at present despite there being a large proportion of children from black and minority ethnic (BME) backgrounds (up to 75 per cent of primary school children in some areas of London) the proportion of BME teachers is small and the proportion of educational leaders is smaller. At least 95 per cent of head teachers are white British, with only 0.7 per cent from black Caribbean or black African communities [...]. In higher education there are only 50 black professors in the UK out of a total of 14,000 [...]. 35 per cent of secondary head teachers are women although 60 per cent of teachers are women, while 33 per cent of principals of further education colleges and 14 per cent of university vice chancellors are women. [...]

What would you give as an explanation for these figures and why?

Keep a note of your thoughts in your journal, as there is a linked activity in Chapter 7 once culture and power have been discussed in more detail.

Thinking about leadership

This chapter has underlined that leadership is itself a contested concept. In the mainstream educational literature, there are many ways of thinking about leadership, and the ways seem to continually grow over time. For the individual, it is often easier to think about leaders, types of leaders and contexts. They are easier initially to get a fix on. The concept of leadership is much more conceptual and can be confusing to a new reader. However, I would argue that beginning to get to grips with major theories, and how such theories might inform practice, is very important to anyone who aspires to a leadership position. Theorists are also quick to point out different ways of considering leadership, and how leaders may, or may not, also be managers. The debate about what is leadership and what is management has been the focus of many discussions and writings and often the terms are used interchangeably. Managers are often depicted as systems driven. These distinctions may not be that helpful to the actual practice of leading. Fullan (1991: 157–8) adds a very helpful definition in suggesting that leadership 'relates to mission, direction, inspiration' and management 'involves designing and carrying out plans, getting things done, working effectively with people'. Even that distinction is oversimplifying, as I would suggest that working with people is also essential to leadership.

For those who are working in educational settings around the world, the importance of context is crucial: the context of their particular organisation; its pupils and parents and its past; diversity issues; and the context of the country where it is located. Later in the book I will return to several of the themes in this chapter. You may find it useful to note down two areas you would want to know more about and follow them up in the references. Certainly, there are many ways of thinking about leadership and they can be intellectually stimulating. These ideas can also help leaders in schools to articulate their own values and ideas more clearly. Leadership studies are a lens through which individual and group functions can be discussed. However, the institution itself rests within a policy climate which affects the role of the educational leader, both in their responses, and also in terms of who they are accountable to. It could be argued that accountability frames everything leaders do and the next chapter considers the issues that arise from that for their leadership.

Evolving as a leader – working with what you have

> This chapter will:
>
> - outline professional learning and evolving as a leader;
> - give an overview of the key areas that leaders may want to focus on in terms of personal development;
> - use vignettes and research evidence to promote thinking about professional learning and development;
> - look at national leadership programmes;
> - discuss the evolving leader as a framework for personal learning.

This chapter has its roots in your own personal learning and experience and, as you read through it, you will be asked to bring together your own strengths as a leader and the areas that you need to look at in more detail. Evolving as a leader happens for every leader at different stages of an educational career. Your long-term development may occur both inside and outside your particular organisation. This chapter builds on the idea of a journey and argues that, as an adult learner and aspiring leader, you need to be aware of your own strengths and weaknesses. Your own professional expertise will be built up over time, utilising your skills and knowledge in whatever context in which you find yourself in the world of education, as educational leadership is a job that 'must reflect long-term development as well as formal pre-appointment training, emerging from the complex interplay of prior and ongoing professional experience and reflection' (Kelly and Saunders, 2010: 5). Your own personal and professional background will have formed your leadership strategies both consciously and unconsciously. Some of the latter you may be able to access as you think about your leadership, but it is not the role of this book to look deeply into your psychological states, although there are suggestions for reading in those areas. Although a leader's main focus is on the learning of young people, s/he should not neglect their own continuous professional development (CPD). Such development will build on past learning and continue throughout a career.

It is also important for the personal development of any leader to remember from the start that organisations are hardly ever run effectively by one leader, as was discussed in the last chapter. The complexities of schools, for example, require a more nuanced approach. A leader who is committed to their own professional learning influences formal and informal practice in the organisation, whether they are the principal or a newly qualified classroom teacher (NQT). The new teacher may not have the leader 'label', but may well be committed to working towards a formal position or have specific expertise in a certain curriculum area in which they could take a lead.

Professional learning in leadership

This chapter views development in leadership as a process of evolution over time. Evolving as an educational leader suggests that the process of professional learning in leadership involves change as well as development. Some professional learning will be focused on specific areas of leadership development skills, such as managing people or strategic planning, and other learning may focus on creating a culture for professional learning. Often, the focus of leaders' professional learning is about preparing themselves to work on some aspect of school improvement. This is often the area in which leaders feel they need to develop because of the obvious impact on their school and school improvement generally (Bush, 2009). Less often, the personal side of leadership development will take more precedence, as leaders look to develop themselves intellectually or in specific areas of proficiency. Research into head teacher appraisal in England (Coldron et al., 2014), for example, suggests that senior leaders are much less likely to look at their own developmental needs. Instead their key aims for the year are much more likely to be concentrated on the school as a whole. Neglect of personal development needs can mean that educational leaders don't use as much of their own knowledge as they might (Nestor-Baker and Hoy, 2001), and don't give themselves the same sorts of opportunities that they would other leaders in the school.

Leaders in schools have many roles to play. A key role is to support other teachers in making the most of opportunities that arise and supporting them through changes that occur, whether these are curricular, contextual or personal. Through the systematic process of creating a climate for what Guskey calls 'professional learning' (Guskey, 2000), leaders can enable others to move forward in their pedagogic development. Timperley (2011) identifies the key role of leaders in helping teachers meet ever changing demands in teaching and learning. The argument of this chapter is that for a leader to be able to carry out this demanding role effectively, they need always to keep in mind their own professional learning, and not only build teachers' competency in practice, but also continue to build, extend and deepen their own leadership knowledge and skills.

A second role that leaders assume is responsibility for the whole climate of the school. Southworth (2011) issues a potent reminder that schools are also learning environments for adults, 'holistic learning organisations' (p. 83), and suggests that school leaders have a major role to play in developing and improving this learning environment for others. This wider school climate influences all staff, and if the head teacher is a 'lead learner' he or she has to demonstrate in practice their own orientation towards learning. Ingvarson (2005), writing about professional learning in the Australian context, suggest that the most important changes that schools can make are not about structural change or reorganisation but are changes that help build teacher capacity and a professional culture. One of the defining facets of leadership is the ability to build and grow a professional culture in the school. A leader's ability (at all levels in a school) to focus on teacher capacity and professional culture helps build confidence so that change can take place individually, in the classroom practice of an individual.

There are also specific times in a career that may require specialised professional learning support. This could be for the NQT mentioned above or for someone stepping into a leadership role. New leaders also have to bring their own skills and work on enhancing and developing them. For example, they could need to build practical skills in managing and leading different groups. For this kind of opportunity to be meaningful they also need the opportunity to learn from experienced mentors or through coaching activities. Often forgotten in terms of development are opportunities that allow them to enhance their theoretical knowledge of leadership; these can be informal as well as formal learning described later in the book.

The personal

Evolving as an education leader is a personal journey and has personal characteristics. Vermunt and Endedijk (2011) argue that teachers, like students, will have major individual differences in how they learn. They note: 'These individual differences may reside in the constituting elements (i.e. individual beliefs, motivations, way of regulation, and learning activities used), as well as in the relationships between these elements' (p. 300). The relationship between these elements will vary from person to person, thus making it an interesting but challenging area for any leader. It is challenging because understanding the constituting elements of groups of staff requires significant individual knowledge both of the people themselves and some of the concepts that lie behind motivation etc. Vermunt and Endedijk also noted that most of the research in this area has been conducted in western countries, which may mean that some of its findings are not transportable to other parts of the world. They urge more work to be done in terms of widening the research base. For the purpose of this chapter, it is important for readers from non-western countries to be aware of this gap. As part of a major research study in England, Opfer et al. (2010: 451), found that 'Whether or not a teacher learns and then engages in a form of professional change is influenced by their beliefs, practices and experiential context.' Importantly for leadership learning and development, they go on to say that:

> Beyond individual influences, teachers' learning is also influenced by organisational conditions. What we report here is only one part of a complex process that teachers experience while learning. Until we understand how characteristics of individual teachers and their schools interact to enhance and constrain professional learning, we will be unable to explain how professional development can be made more effective.

Elmore's (2008: 58) viewpoint brings the discussion back to a focus on people. He noted that leaders should see this process as 'a human investment enterprise' because, after all, the staff of a school are its biggest financial investment. This is not always as easy to carry out in practice as it sounds.

Now have a look at the following vignette.

Vignette

Cara was the newly appointed vice principal of a small elementary school in a town in provincial Maritime Canada. Apart from herself, all the other teachers and the principal had been at the school for over ten years. In fact she discovered that the principal attended the school as a child. She wanted to develop a professional learning culture, rather like the one she wrote about in her Master's thesis, featuring collaboration, improvement of practice and on-the-job learning. She was wary of setting the agenda for the

(Continued)

(Continued)

discussions herself, reasoning that the experience of the staff would aid planning and moving forward. Full of enthusiasm, she organised several events. Although the staff dutifully turned up, it was noticeable that there was a lack of enthusiasm to engage in dialogue or discussion. Cara had hoped that her own enthusiasm for some new ideas would carry them through exciting new possibilities, but instead she was left feeling demotivated and perplexed. She wondered if she needed more or different skills in order to progress the work in the school.

Cara's situation is not a unique one, and some aspects of this have a great deal to do with the issues discussed in Section 2 of this book, that is concerned with the particular context of the school. Note down three things that might have helped Cara be more effective as a constructor of organisational climate for learning. Note them in your journal if you wish and return to them after you have read Section 2. For the moment, however, see if any of your three are to do with her personal development as opposed purely to organisational development. What is the balance in your list? Cara herself noted that there were various reasons for what happened, but the main one was that she had never worked anywhere that had anything less than a vibrant professional culture. She had made assumptions about behaviours which proved to be wrong. She felt that she needed to become someone with coaching skills, and made this a professional priority (among other issues that came from this scenario). Cara had been socialised into a particular way of understanding school leadership, a framework that proved unhelpful in her new position. It gradually became clear to her that the staff were not unwilling, as she at first supposed, but rather unsure of how to proceed in this new climate. She had also discovered, as Armstrong (2011: 4) puts very clearly, that 'crossing the boundary between teaching and administration precipitates a challenging cognitive, emotional and social journey across uncharted personal, professional and organizational territory'. Armstrong utilises a person-centric approach to the study of transitions as does this book. These transitions and the issues around them are the focus of the next section.

Working with transitions in leadership

In the first chapter of the book, I suggested that addressing the personal side of leadership is difficult, as it is concerned not only with a clearer understanding of self, but also an understanding of the changes that occur to an individual as more responsibility is assumed over their careers. In education, often this transition is most marked when formal leadership roles in schools are taken up. Transitions also occur when teachers move contexts and in between different facets of their career. Such changes can be viewed in different ways theoretically, often dependent on whether these differences are most influenced by the internal, psychological states, or by external organisational changes. Armstrong (2011) has discussed how individuals navigate the transition to more administrative (leadership) roles. Noting that most transitions are seen through the lens of organisational sociology, she argues for an interactive framework that allows for a much more 'person-centric' approach. This fits well with the standpoint of this book, as it allows readers to ask questions based on their own socio-emotional experiences of change. Armstrong argues that such an approach with her interviewees, assistant principals, 'provides a deeper understanding of the internal and external evolutionary processes that newcomers experience' (p. 25). Armstrong frames the leadership of assistant principals as existing 'in the relationships and processes between individuals and groups' (p. 27). Such a perspective also offers a way of looking at other formal transition points for leaders in education, not just the particular change of moving to assistant principal in Canada. Armstrong's work on transitions is a useful tool for personal leadership development because it also brings to the fore the differences in perspective that leaders have depending on whether they hold positional power or have personal power of influence. One of her key arguments is that exploring leaders' stories, their lived experience, allows a clear focus on the social and emotional factors associated with transitions. This is also true of other narrative approaches to studying leaders in England, Scotland and Australia (Cowie, 2011; Ribbins, 1995; Wildy and Clarke, 2008a, 2008b). These sorts of writings help illuminate the issues for the developing leader. It may be that you can find such work which has direct relevance to your country, as well as exploring some of the above. Keeping in mind the idea of transition means that your professional learning can be informed by the stories of other transitions within your particular context.

Structures

The way any organisation is structured influences personal learning. In particular, power dynamics will be examined more closely in Section 2 of the book. It is important for any leader to understand how the social structure of an organisation frames the relationships and processes between individuals and groups. As was noted in the last chapter, it is too simple to see 'leadership' as a magic wand that transforms organisations. Kilduff and Balkundi (2011) illustrate this by discussing how important the skill of being able to 'accurately perceive the network relations that connect people, and to actively manage these network relations' (p.118) is to a leader. It is from these network relations, they suggest, that informal leaders (those without formal positions of power) can use their own social influence with the group to move forward their own agendas. This can be counterproductive to those in the formal leadership positions or part of the organisation's positive development. Elsewhere (Crawford, 2009) I have focused on the role of emotion in understanding this social influence and will return to this when key capabilities for the evolving leader are discussed later in the book. I would argue that it is important to recognise that emotion plays a much more important part in the informal structuring of a school or college than many recognise, and so part of one's personal leadership learning is concerned with understanding social structures such as networks. For example, Kilduff and Balkundi (2011: 122) focus their theoretic attention on the role of network cognition or developing accurate perceptions of social networks. They note that a network approach 'emphasizes the extent to which individuals' thoughts and actions are embedded in their perceptions of networks [...] Leaders [...] generate and use social capital through the acuity with which they perceive social structures and the actions they take to build connections' (p. 131). Developing network cognition is not easy, as it is concerned with understanding the ties between people both in and outside the organisation, and from there understanding the role of people's perceptions in the leadership and management processes. For educational leaders, they may just have begun to have a better understanding of networks in one organisation when promotion moves them to a completely different set of relationships. So, in terms of personal professional learning, this is a complex area to master, but is foundational to understanding leadership strategies in organisations. From there, many developing leaders go on to pursue training in a more formal way, particularly when they are considering large transitions, such as to the principalship/ headship of an educational organisation.

Knowing what to do next

There are differences in how different countries perceive readiness for leadership, especially for formal roles such as the principalship. There are also distinctions in whether specific training is required and what this should consist of. This chapter is called 'working with what you have', which gives some idea of where I believe the focus should lie even if the process of working with what you have is helped by an official training course. Each person's leadership is unique and can be helped or hindered by the context that they find themselves in. Ways can be developed in which leaders can be tasked to draw on their strengths and build teams that spread leadership throughout the organisation.

In looking at areas for development, the easiest – and the hardest – way is to start with yourself: easy because everything you need is close to hand; difficult because people vary in their self-awareness and their abilities to see their flaws and strengths. I would argue that highly effective leaders must be able to see their own particular skills and talents clearly, in the same way that they would also encourage skills and talents in the teams they work with. They also need to manage themselves effectively over time. A key area for development for one leader may be of no importance to another leader, but there are several strategies that it could be argued are foundational for all leaders. Cranwell-Ward (1987) wrote about strategies for overcoming stress in the job. Looking at the list now, I would suggest that most of the items are strategic for any leader at any time because they deal with some of the issues above. They include:

- developing your self-management skills;
- improving emotional management;
- regularly reviewing your relationship with the job;
- developing physical stamina;
- finding outside help when necessary.

This could easily be a quick checklist for the evolving leader. The following activity is based on a real case in which I would suggest that the person involved was skilled in at least three of the above issues.

Activity 11

Rob was a highly successful secondary head teacher in Wales. His success was marked for his colleagues by his good relationships with staff, parents and the local community, the school's excellent exam results and the involvement of students in local environmental issues. When I interviewed him he told me that his key skill was understanding what he really could not do and which it wasn't worth training him on – timetabling and special educational needs were two examples he gave. His way of dealing with this was to recruit people who were good in these areas and to respect their judgement. I suspect he knew a great deal about these two areas but respected the fact that others knew more, were more interested in those areas and so should lead in them.

- Do the markers of the school's success chime with those in your country? If not, what are the differences?
- How do you respond to Rob's view of people?
- What are the dangers in such an approach?

If we relate Rob's story to the checklist above, I would suggest that his good relationships with staff, parents and the local community, the school's excellent exam results and the involvement of students in local environmental issues were informed by his key strengths in emotional management, using outside help when necessary and in particular an ability to self-reflect and review. On first reading, it could be assumed that Rob's natural persona was trusting and clear-cut. However, elsewhere in the interview it became clear that he had worked on this approach in his deputy headship, where he followed the example of his own head teacher, which he saw worked in that context. Not all potential head teachers will have such good role models. Principal training, based often, but not solely, in universities has been the pragmatic solution to help all principals to become clearer about their roles and responsibilities.

Readiness for formal roles in leadership

This chapter has focused on professional learning and the ways that leaders can think about their own development. Particular skills training is often the main function of leadership development for senior staff, sometimes with an academic qualification attached. Such training makes assumptions about what certain groups of leaders will find helpful and how they can refine this expert knowledge as they come to terms with a transition to a new stage of their careers. Many countries around the world have focused their work in this area on pre-appointment or post-appointment training to specific leadership roles, with varying degrees of success (Bush, 2008). Principal training opportunities are most often pre-appointment. These are frequently based on specific standards, e.g. the USA has the Interstate School Leaders Licensure Consortium standards (ISLLC). Some countries have tried introducing a mandatory principal qualification, e.g. England and Scotland, only to retreat from this position over time. What seems to be a constant is that such approaches are continuously under review and revision. This could be because there is no best route to the preparation of course. Research in different countries for the International Study of Principal Preparation (ISPP) (Clarke and Wildy, 2010; Crawford and Cowie, 2012; Nelson et al., 2008; Onguko et al., 2012) set out to ask the question 'How useful are principal preparation programmes to novice principals?' One of the key findings in many countries was that the preparation was often rated highly at the time of being involved in the course, but this was balanced by the realities of the principal's workload in their early years. Principals were more likely to find their preparation useful at the time of the preparation and then several years later as they assimilated their on the job knowledge into what they had learnt beforehand.

Cynics might argue that these positions on whether such training should be mandatory are only relevant when there is an oversupply of people for these posts. Others might argue that a focus on qualifications is not as important as helping leaders develop their new professional self-concept. The ISPP work reinforces this as participants talked about this development in their own minds of 'becoming a headteacher' (Crawford and Cowie, 2012).

Browne-Ferrigno and Muth (2004: 470–1) give a very useful overview for school leaders about what is involved in school leadership preparation, and in particular they stress the role of mentors. As noted earlier, socialisation is involved in becoming a leader; in formal leadership positions it is particularly acute. Browne-Ferrigno and Muth reflect that such socialisation is often unsystematic and

> does not occur simply because an individual participates in a formal preparation programme. Rather, role socialisation for aspiring principals is an intricate process of learning and reflection that requires working closely with leadership mentors in authentic field-based experiences, developing confidence through engaging in leadership activities and administrative tasks, and assuming a new professional self-concept grounded in confidence about leading schools.

This intricate process is linked by them to professional development which is ongoing for leaders at *all* stages in their careers and offers the 'construction of professional-practice expectations through mentoring, peer sharing and critique, and systematic induction. Carefully constructed and implemented mentoring experiences serve as effective professional development not only for aspiring and novice principals but also for veteran principals.' Browne-Ferrigno and Muth relate leadership development to the idea both of capacity building and of a community of practice (Lave and Wenger, 1991) 'in which steadily improving role performance is the ultimate goal' (p. 471). Stoll et al. (2006) undertook a very helpful review of learning communities in which they underscored the fact that teachers' professional learning takes place within a community of learners. Leadership development, similarly, can take place most effectively if a leadership community is formed. A key finding from the ISPP study was how much principals value being part of a community and their preparation had helped them form ongoing relationships with people in the same position as themselves. Being perceived as an ongoing member of a community of practice is something that many of the heads in the study seemed to value, more than some of the content-rich preparation that they had covered in terms of finance and budgeting, etc. This combination of making sense of their preparation through on the job knowledge and the strength of a community of fellow professionals learning about being a leader is part of professional learning being contextual.

> **Activity 12**
>
> Professional learning is contextual and develops through specific events at work. Write down at least three incidents (involving a person, a situation or a viewpoint in school) which have made you think differently about your own skills. Was it a skill that you already had enhanced? How? Did you develop a new skill? What skills might have helped to enrich the experience for future, similar events?

You may have had difficulty identifying your skill. It can be difficult to write down an internal reason why, for example, you looked at something differently. Support in the form of a critical friend can help (Swaffield, 2004). Swaffield notes that trust is a vital component of such work as is the ability to question, critique and provide feedback (p. 276), all of which can be developed through specific training. These sorts of critiques can easily be lost to school leaders if they are not able to keep their own focus on professional learning for leaders. This could be through some formal or semi-formal way within the organisation, or external to it, that helps the new leader focus on learning and developing in a specific way.

Not just the young?

In terms of professional leadership learning, as Browne-Ferrigno and Muth (2004) noted, veterans often get missed out, perhaps being seen as not able to take advantage of new ideas or not worth the time and investment of resources. A critical friend would be able to help them look at the opportunities for learning that are most pertinent to them at their particular career stage. I would argue that their experience and skills are also wasted if there are not opportunities in a system to develop their own skill set as critical friends, able to share and critique personal experiences which have their basis in practical wisdom. Some countries, for example England, have developed the role of National Leader of Education, whose function at first sight might be seen to be similar to that of critical friend. These roles, many might argue, are too linked to government policy on school improvement to be truly critical friends, because their work is often called upon when schools are seen to need help in terms of a national agenda on standards. They could be viewed more as coaches. Other countries have formal school advisory roles. It might be useful for you to note down if you have experienced any such relationships in your leadership development and whether they were helpful or otherwise.

What sort of knowledge?

At the start of the chapter, attention was drawn to teachers' professional learning. The last section focused both on skills training and developing oneself as a leader. This suggests that there are many ways to look at 'working with what you have'. To finish this chapter the evolving leader may like to take note of some conceptual distinctions that may be helpful to them in making sense of their leadership learning or which may cause you to revisit some of the assumptions in this chapter! Simkins (2005: 20–1) quotes Cochran-Smith and Lytle's (1999) work about teacher learning. Cochran-Smith and Lytle identify different types of knowledge, which Simkins applies to leadership learning:

- knowledge-for-practice;
- knowledge-in-practice;
- knowledge-of-practice.

Knowledge-for-practice is taken from research and applied to practice. Those who practise use the knowledge base of research to work out what works best and in what context. *Knowledge-in-practice* is an art form 'embodied in people rather than in abstract prescriptions, it can, perhaps, be coached and facilitated, but it cannot be formally taught' (p. 20). *Knowledge-of-practice* can be viewed as the process where practitioners begin to theorise about their own work and challenge the ideas and values that they may have held for some time. For example, Masters courses in educational leadership will typically utilise this approach with the community of students. Simkins warns that these ways of thinking about knowledge are inter-reliant in many cases, with much depending how they are being used and particular aspects of their use.

Activity 13

Turn back to mentoring or critical friendship as looked at in the last section – what kind of knowledge is being advocated?

Simkins suggests that all of the three types of knowledge mentioned above can help personal leadership development, as long as potential leaders are able to clearly understand the limitations of each and what theoretical thinking might lie behind each. In terms of the activity, he argues that coaching might be conceived as:

- instilling knowledge about 'best practice' (knowledge-for practice);
- encouraging reflection on a leader's own practice, perhaps through discussions with an 'effective' leader (knowledge-in-practice);
- challenging the underlying bases on which practice is founded, in relation, for example, to the assumptions about power and influence on which it is based (knowledge-of-practice). (p. 21)

In summary, thinking about professional learning is more demanding than it at first appears. You may want to try applying these types of knowledge to some of the information you have come across in professional learning or to how they are being used as you work through this book. The book returns to issues of developing capabilities in a later chapter which you may wish to read before going on.

Developing a career in leadership

Many leadership careers evolve in ways that were not foreseen by the person when they started teaching. This can be true even in countries such as Cyprus which have a defined path towards the most senior leadership positions which teachers are expected to follow. This often leads to principals being in the later stages of their career when they are appointed. This chapter has aimed to highlight the role of personal professional leadership development and its importance in helping individual leaders evolve through the different transitions that take place as their careers develop. At the same time, it has suggested that the way that knowledge is conceived by the learner may also have an impact on their development. The role of personal agency in leadership is often undervalued and this chapter's role in the book is to stress that a clearer understanding of both the cognitive and emotional sides of professional learning need to be made explicit as part of a leadership journey. Close and Rayner (2010: 213) state this clearly when they note: 'Leadership development is a symbiotic journey between the personal and the organisational.' Internal experiences frame leaders' actions, but the external organisational context where they grow and develop is also crucial if a complete picture of leadership development is to be painted. The next chapter turns to the organisation and its role in the leader's evolution.

5

Organisations and leadership

> In this chapter, I will:
>
> - argue that a basic knowledge of organisational theory is crucial for educational leaders;
> - invite the reader to examine their own leadership in the light of their current organisational context;
> - reflect on the various ways in which an organisation can be understood.

Chapter 3 debated several ways of viewing leadership and the part played by the leader. Bolman and Deal's (2003) seminal book on leadership and organisations puts it very well when they say that leadership is always situated in a context and a relationship (p. 336). This chapter aims to help you bring into clear focus your own understanding of how educational organisations work, and why and how that knowledge is important for leaders.

This chapter begins a discussion of context, which is continued in Section 2. I do this by looking at why the idea of the organisation is important for school leaders to think about more carefully. In some countries of the world, it is notable that leadership has replaced management as a key term, and in a similar way real knowledge of how organisations work seems to have disappeared in the ensuing debate. By real knowledge, I mean the huge amount of literature from both business and educational research about the study of organisations more generally, not just looking upon organisations as tangentially relevant to leadership and management. The study of educational organisations should not be seen as separate from the literature on leadership and management as there are many common influences. Westoby (1988) was the person who introduced me to the study of educational organisations. His view was a democratic one in that he felt that thinking systematically about organisations 'to penetrate their opacities and to understand their functioning and eccentricities better' (p. ix) was one way to make both the formalities and realities of life in them more visible to those who live and work in them.

Organisational studies have taken a back seat in the educational leadership field, as have what Westoby called the 'significant peculiarities' of educational organisations, often characterised by autonomous working in classrooms, and sub-units such as years, departments and so on which are organisations as well. These make up a particular social habitat, which shapes and guides those involved in the educational organisation's many activities. Westoby suggested that educational organisations heighten the tensions inherent around the educational interests of those involved. This makes it important that leaders develop some conceptual tools to examine the organisation culture in ways that take account both of the formal, visible order of the membership and also what is 'ephemeral and covert'.

It might seem that the school or college as an organisation has a common purpose – to educate young people. Surrounding this simple statement are the complexities of individual educational organisations and their particular social and personal contexts. Indeed, some might argue that there is no such thing as 'an' organisation, as any organisation can be broken down into smaller ones. In terms of education, this chapter keeps the personal development focus and looks at some of the key theoretical ideas that are particularly relevant to a developing school leader. It could be argued that they are a vital part of developing as an educational leader and manager and are often missed as people move through the promotion structures. As Bolman and Deal (2003: 338) put it very succinctly in their book: when we discuss educational organisations there is now a 'focus too much on the actors and too little on the stage on which they play their parts'. This chapter aims to help the leader to partly redress that focus.

As you read this chapter, bear in mind that my own theoretical standpoint is heavily influenced by Ogawa and Bossert (1997), who have suggested that leadership is a quality of organisations; in other words it is 'a systemic characteristic', not an individual one (p. 9). This does not mean that the organisation controls the leader but rather that effective organisations have leadership flowing through them in many different ways. Given that as a working assumption, it then becomes clear that finding ways of understanding their own educational organisation is one of the ways that leaders can use to progress strategic aims.

Of organisations

In 2006, Glatter called for a refocus within the field of leadership studies to pay much more attention to the organisation. Once organisations become the focus of attention, he noted that people pay much more attention to difficult, but powerful issues such as 'power, context, and complexity' (p. 74). Section 2 of this book goes into this discussion in much more detail. This chapter outlines some of the varying ways in which organisations have been conceptualised and suggests what this might mean to the nascent or experienced leader and manager. It will reflect the overall link of the book to personal development. Hopefully, it will also act as a jump off point for readers who wish to look more deeply into the whole field of organisational studies.

With any discussion of organisations, one of the dilemmas is where to begin. Organisational structure is often where leaders begin, perhaps because it is a relatively easy (it seems) management task to carry out, or because such structures represent symbolically as well as practically how the organisation wishes to be viewed by both insiders and outsiders. Structures also indicate to individuals how they should behave, and how in turn this behaviour might influence the goals of the organisation. A person's position in the organisation will also frame how he or she views the structure and its effectiveness. There is also a very close relationship between structure of the organisation and culture, which will be examined in more detail in Section 2 of the book. However, if a leader has a specific focus on structure, it could be that he or she is adopting a particularly rational approach to leading the organisation. In other words this viewpoint or model that a leader uses to frame their organisation can influence their style of leadership, but at the same time their style of leadership may influence the model used.

Analysising the organisation

As Simkins argues (2005: 10), 'in the leadership world, 'making sense of things' is at least as important as 'seeking what works'. Analysing the organisation and thinking about what makes 'sense' in terms of a particular organisation can give the developing leader insights into their own and others' stages on the leadership journey. This seemingly simple idea is behind much, but by no means all, writing about organisations in the educational leadership field. Typologies of organisations abound in the educational leadership literature when it comes to trying to make sense of organisations. Bolman and Deal (2003) and Morgan (1998), are both extremely helpful books to look at in terms of making sense of the organisation and will be referred to as the chapter progresses. Simkins (1999: 270) makes an essential point about typologies, which is important when looking at almost anything in the educational leadership literature. He notes how they might be used when he distinguishes between descriptive and normative uses of organisational models (my italics): 'The former are those which attempt to *describe* the nature of organizations and how they work and, sometimes, to *explain* why they are as they are. The latter, in contrast, attempt to *prescribe* how organizations should or might be managed to achieve particular outcomes more effectively.' This chapter aims to concentrate on the former use. At the same time, the typologies outlined below are ones which I have found particularly useful in practice, so there may be some unresolved normative overtones! The only way to reduce analysing the organisation to a meaningful part of this book is to be unreservedly biased in what is selected and described. The developing leader needs to understand that models of leadership and management are affected by the approach taken by their writers towards the organisation, and that bias is not always apparent on first reading. In a similar way, your own approach to leadership and management will be whether consciously or unconsciously influenced by the way you perceive an organisation. The same is true of the writing in this chapter.

Bush (2011) has developed a very useful text to consult for an overview of models of educational leadership and management and how these relate to conceptualising the school as an organisation. You may wish to read about them in more detail as only a brief outline will be given here.

Bush proposed that the main theories can be classified into six models:

- formal
- collegial
- political
- subjective
- ambiguity
- cultural.

Each of these six models has four elements which Bush suggests are useful to use when seeking to tell the models apart. These are to do with what the model says about goals and agreements about them, the emphasis the model gives to people and/or structure, the relationship between the organisation and the external environment and the strategies which the model protagonists suggest are best for leading an educational institution (Bush, 2011: 34–5). The book itself should be consulted for a more in-depth approach to the strengths and weaknesses of each model as an approach to leadership and management. These six models are outlined briefly below, with my focus specifically on the organisation.

- *Formal models* are so called because of their key emphasis on structures, such as timetables of meetings, formal titles – in fact Bush says that they 'present organisational structure as an objective fact' (2011: 56).

The focus of formal models is to make it clear that the organisation is a system with a hierarchy and an official structure, in which leaders have power and authority because of their official roles in that organisation. Many schools might be viewed in this way, as they would, at first glance, appear to have many of the characteristics of formal models, especially in the emphasis on the formal construction of the pattern of the relationships that exist within any organisation. Bush notes that such a hierarchical approach can be seen in the management of schools where there are key external demands on the managers of schools, such as in England and New Zealand (2011: 66).

- *Collegial models* tend to prescribe the best way to carry out the task of management. In other words, they are normative in their approach. These models assume consensus can be reached through a discussion of goals and values and by seeking to influence approaches in various ways. Members of the organisation thus end up with a shared viewpoint on the goals of the organisation. Distributed leadership would seem to be a model that is predicated on a collegial style, as it may or may not have formal roles attached to its working out in the organisation. Such a view treats the organisation as a place where consensus can be reached and strife mitigated.

- *Political models* presume that organisations are political arenas where agreement is reached through discussion, negotiation and the use of bargaining positions. A political view of the school organisation would see that different groups will have different agendas. For example, in a small rural primary school of two to three staff, a collegial model might be assumed by a new principal. Each of the members of staff may have their own interests which they are intent on pressing on the new incumbent, which could require some skilled political negotiation. A principal who viewed all schools as collegial would be ill prepared for such a scenario. Similarly a leader in a large school could find themselves leading a department which has gained power and influence in the school through what Bolman and Deal would call the political frame. The political frame emphasises the role of power over scarce resources. If the previous head of department managed to win in negotiations over equipment, for example, this will be expected of the new leader. A related concept in the literature is that of micropolitics (Hoyle, 1988).

- *Subjective models* in some ways could be seen as the underlying rationale of this book. Bush states that a central feature of subjective models is that they 'assume that organisations are the creations of the people within them. Participants are thought to interpret situations in different ways' (2011: 126). This sense of social construction of reality is a thread that the discerning reader will already have noticed. Later in the chapter, these will be drawn upon in more detail.

Bush also highlights the links of such models to emotion and leadership but suggests that subjective models do not offer a clear analytic framework, rather they are about belief. The second part of this chapter takes up that argument.

- *Ambiguity models* tend to cover most of the theories that look at uncertainty as the largest problem that the organisation has to grapple with. People in such organisations can opt in or out of decision-making and ways forward are often unclear. Cohen et al. (1972) in their famous article talked about the garbage can model of organisations, in which organisations can be described as anarchic. This is not because there is no structure but because they have to wrestle with their own organisation's characteristics and the pressures from the external environment. Cohen et al. suggested that organisational activity could be seen as unclear in terms of goals and with fluid membership. Accountability pressures in countries such as the US and England would be good examples of outside pressure, which could create such conditions, but are actually setting out to create the opposite – clear goals and formal pathways to improvement. One aspect of organisational anarchy that is still present as Cohen et al. described it is that of fluid membership with pupils and teachers changing on a regular basis.

- *Cultural models* of the organisation assume that the informal parts of the organisation are at least as important as the formal structure. Bush stresses (2011: 174–5) that the beliefs and values of the members of the organisation are very important, because creating a shared culture may be the aim of the leader of the organisation. Large organisations may also have subcultures in departments or groups of workers. Shared meaning is created by the leader of such groups, which is often expressed by particular school rituals such as Founder's Day, Book Week, etc.; by particular language used in that organisation, e.g. the school motto, aims, etc. ('Innovation, Excellence, Respect' is an example from a school in England); or by visual signs such as a uniform and also religious symbolism if the school has a faith aspect. Bush suggests that cultural models 'provide a focus for organisational action' (2011: 188). This would seem particular helpful to a developing leader, although in some ways I think you could argue that all organisations have a culture and so this model is not as helpful as the others. You might like to debate this if you go to the original source.

All these models, albeit briefly described here, give a hint of the richness of different perspectives on the organisation. As Bush remarks, 'Each has elements that provide a shock of recognition' (2011: 193). For the rest of this chapter, however, the direction of travel will be slightly different, as the discussion moves away from the many ways of looking at organisations. The next part of this chapter explores and expands the subjective

frame for organisations as a way of helping the leader understand some
of the complexities of social interaction in organisations.

Subjectivity and more

Viewing organisations as Bolman and Deal do as 'complicated, ambigu-
ous and unpredictable' (2003: xviii) might seem like a frightening place
for a manager to start thinking about the fit between the ideas of leadership and management and organisational theory. The opposite viewpoint is the one taken in this chapter: coming to terms with complexity
and the unknown are significant intellectually to anyone who would be
a leader of educational organisations. In whatever country or policy context you find yourself, one thing that never alters is that people view the
same situation in very different ways. As the saying goes, 'Perception is
reality', and cultivating an understanding of people and organisations
can help make a more subjective perspective useful for analysing situations. One of the ways of mitigating some of this complexity, and perhaps reducing leader anxiety, is to utilise various typologies of organisations, as Bolman and Deal do themselves. Before considering some of
these typologies and why they relate to leadership, one further point is
needed to aid understanding: that is the subjective and hidden side of
organisations. The subjective dimensions of any organisation are often
those aspects which resist rational plans. In other words, like Greenfield
(1988, 1991), I find it impossible not to put values at the heart of any
organisational analysis. His analysis is one which is clear about the role
of people in organisations. Greenfield (1988) noted that there is no point
in studying organisations as if they had a particular reality or were in
some way neutral – 'they are an invented social reality of human creation' (p. 132). His point is that people are the drivers of organisations, or
as he put it, 'people do not exist in organisations. Organisations exist in
and through individuals' (p. 133). Immediately a connection to the
developing leader can be made, as it is through leadership that social
order can be created or imposed. Conflict, Greenfield also noted, is
prevalent in all organisations, because people will hold different values,
and often those in charge may have to ask them to take up tasks that they
don't see as valuable.

Greenfield's view is a particular one, which you may wish to explore
further in some of his extensive writings on the subject. But how do
educational leaders grasp this very complex area and analyse what is
happening? A grasp of the various ways of looking at organisations
through a subjective frame can be helpful in aiding understanding and
provoking discussion about the role of leadership in organisations. There
seems to be a need in much of the leadership literature to make organisations rational place, and reduce uncertainty, despite all the caveats from

writers such as Greenfield. The reader's role is to take hold of that knowledge and critically examine it in a similar process to that described in Activity 13, and then to go on to consider in later chapters their own role in building and maintaining that social reality.

Schools, as educational organisations, also exist within a wider context which will influence the goals and priorities of the organisation. This could be local or national and may be concerned with policy issues that touch schools or with neighbourhood and community needs. Making sense of the swirling reality of educational life can be difficult, but there are models which help leaders understand the difficulties of sense-making, and understanding something about this theoretical background, it will be argued, can help leaders understand some of the reasons behind actions and the positions taken. Section 2 then goes onto expand this by looking particularly at issues of culture, structure and power in organisations.

Sense-making

The idea of 'sense-making' comes from the writing of Karl Weick (1979, 1995, 2001), and is an idea which is particular useful in educational organisations because of that swirling reality discussed above. Weick's ideas are briefly introduced and discussed in the hope that the keen reader will go away and read the original in much more depth than space allows here. Weick's writing has a great deal to offer for the educational leader, in terms of the depth of thinking that the effective leader will require and the way he draws upon organisational and leadership studies in order to discuss making sense of the organisation. His work also has a focus on the ways that people's beliefs lead inevitably to the actions that they take, which readers will have noted by now is something that this author finds a useful idea. He is concerned with the way that people need to make sense of what is going on, and the implications that might have for what they do next. As Weick put it (2001: 5): 'I view organisations as collections of people trying to make sense of what is happening around them.' He used the idea of map-making to illustrate his point. Cartographers can represent the land before them in varying ways, as there is no right or wrong way to make a map. One map may be useful to climbers, another to botanists. The role of a sense-maker is not to find the map, but to make sense of all the competing claims of experience within an organisation, which, he argued, means that the activity of sense-making is primarily social (2001: 9). Organisational map-making is made even more difficult because, unlike a map, the ground in front of the sense-making is not stable and can be looked at in varying ways. This is an aspect that will be returned to in the vignette below. The organisation ebbs and flows with the people and the situations that occur over time, as it commits to other people or particular projects, revising their views on what is happening over time and often after the event. This is why it is often very interesting to go back over the history of schools in terms of achievement and see the ebb and flow of events over time and what might have influenced them. Weick put it like this: 'Reality is an ongoing accomplishment: sensemaking is about flows, a continually changing past, and variations in choice, irrevocability, and visibility that change the intensity of behavioural commitments' (2001: 11). Commitment is a central precept in sense-making because, the argument goes, when a person commits to something or someone, they are likely to view anything that happens later in a way that confirms that they made the right decision in the first place. So, commitment itself restricts the meanings that people impose on the 'terrain' of the organisation. The leader's role then becomes more about helping people find their particular commitment within an organisation. This is a helpful way to begin to make sense of why followers commit to certain leaders and yet how difficult it is to manage this in a complex organisation.

Bolman and Deal (2003) suggest that it is the frames that leaders use to understand complexity that can illuminate such situations and that reframing organisations can help the leader understand more clearly the dynamics of any given situation. As they suggest (p. 5) frames are not wrong or right ways of looking at organisations, they are just incomplete. In other words, the evolving leader needs to use a variety of frames. Subjective views of reality are important for leadership because they acknowledge the difficulties of really knowing what is happening at any one time. As Bolman and Deal put it, 'Effectiveness deteriorates when managers and leaders cannot reframe' (ibid.). Their frames are described briefly now, and would repay further study in order to understand the details. Bolman and Deal suggested that the four frames can be used to diagnose what is happening and give ideas for action. It is important to note as you read on that pulling all of them together for effective action is as important as knowing what they are.

Activity 14

As you read the next section, note the similarities and differences with Bush's models.

Each of the four frames shows someone's reality and has different consequences both for the leader and the organisation. The whole idea of reframing is about leading and interpreting or, as Bolman and Deal suggest, it encourages 'a more expressive, artistic conception that encourages flexibility, creativity and interpretation [. . .] the leader as artist relies on images as well as memos, poetry as well as policy, reflection as well as command and reframing as well as refitting ' (2003: 17). These frames are as follows:

- *Structural frame*. This draws on the way the organisation divides up its work and helps avoid putting resources and energy into the wrong parts of the organisation. The structural frame asks whether the current structures are suitable to the external environment and if not why not. It allows leaders to understand more clearly how to bring about structure that works 'for, rather than against, both people and the purposes of organisations' (2003: 58).

- *Human resource frame*. This book draws a good deal on the human resource frame. The HR frame draws on the fact that organisations exist for people's needs, not the other way around. The 'fit' between the person and the organisation is very important because when this is managed well both the person and the organisation are satisfied with the outcome; there is no misuse of those scarce resources, people, and the organisation has what it needs to succeed. Both ways are important. As Bolman and Deal articulate, 'both individual satisfaction and organisational effectiveness depend heavily on the quality of interpersonal interactions' (2003: 158). Some of these interpersonal interactions will be looked at in more detail in Chapter 12.

- *Political frame*. This frame asks the leader to pick up some of the issues in Section 2 of this book – power in particular. It suggests that in every organisation, there are differences of opinion and differences in access to scarce resources. This means that in any organisation there are groupings around political dynamics. The frame assumes that differences in organisations are long-term, and leaders have to be able to make things happen despite this. In particular the political frame suggests that goals are not 'top down' or 'bottom up' in an organisation. Rather, 'they are set through an ongoing process of negotiation and interaction among the key players' (2003: 165). The political frame sees political behaviour not as an individual characteristic but rather as an inevitability, because of scarce resources, power relations and organisational interdependence. As Bolman and Deal phrase it, 'from this perspective, every significant organisational process is inherently political' (2003: 211).

- *Symbolic frame*. Schools in particular frame things symbolically. From uniform in England to pledging allegiance to the flag in the USA, schools use symbols of all kinds to reinforce what the organisations stands for. This frame goes further than that, as Bolman and Deal explain: 'Meaning, belief and faith are central to a symbolic perspective' (2003: 216). They see this frame as bringing together theories from a wide range of fields from sociology to the psychoanalytic. As an idea, it has a great deal in common with the subjectivity of meaning-making described above. Symbols are used by leaders to provide direction and show that the organisation will remain stable in troubled times, for example. Everything that happens in a school can be woven together symbolically into a tapestry of the organisation, and rituals, ceremonies and stories make up the frame of meaning for the school and its leaders. Metaphor can be used to bring together ideas and move them forward, and the culture of the organisation will be shaped by them and through them. The next section of the book looks at this in more detail. The symbolic perspective notes that 'the essence of high performance is spirit' (2011: 262).

As you read the following vignette, bear these frames in mind.

Vignette

Carlos Sanchez had worked in his elementary school in Chicago for most of his educational career. At the age of 45, he was now the principal and had been for two years. He had a deep commitment to working in challenging urban areas that directly reflected his own background of growing up in New York of Mexican parents. He was unhappy about some of the implications of national policy towards 'his' school and was justifiably proud of some of the achievements of the pupils, not only in literacy and numeracy but also in art and state drama competitions. A newly appointed teacher, Sara, was becoming a problem to him, and he was sitting in his office trying to work out the nature of the problem and what he and his senior staff should do about it, if anything. Sara had come from Teach for America, an organisation that puts high-flying graduates into challenging urban schools, and she was an excellent teacher in many respects. His problem, he decided as he doodled on his pad, was the influence that she was having on the other staff in her team in the lower part of the school. She was holding what he called 'revivalist' meetings where she showed staff pictures of other schools where teachers where practising different methods and her passion, he felt, made him feel old and tired. He was sure, however, that some of her practices were not helpful to pupils and there had been a steady, if small, stream of complaints from parents. His deputy principal told him to ignore her, and that 'she would soon tire of all this once she has been in teaching a year or so'. Carlos was not so sure.

Analyse the situation from the viewpoint of Carlos but using the four frames. What aspects come to the surface which might provide him with a plan for action?

This vignette highlights the practical difficulties for leaders in schools and you may have come up with other ideas through reframing. Carlos has a dilemma in terms of making sense of this new teacher and the way she appears to want to map the terrain of his school. Nothing that had happened to him before in his teaching or leadership career had prepared him for this particular teacher. He needed to view his school as 'collections of people trying to make sense of what is happening around them', and reframing the situation did help him move forward. He realised that the current structures of the school neither enabled his new teacher to share good practice nor were tight enough to stop difficult situations occurring. Looking at the situation from a human resource frame, he noted that the 'fit' was not a good one and he needed to attend to ways to make it work better. He decided to open up the discussion with the staff in a way that did not lead to an open clash with the new teacher and further difficulties. He did not want all the parties scrabbling to rearrange their own ways of looking at the map, but he knew that he did have many sources of power in the organisation because of his position and his experience in teaching. Finally, he realised that the school, like him, had become tired. In response therefore he strove to bring his passion for teaching back to life through symbolically reframing the school as a drama and utilising his role as the principal to hold several powerful team-building sessions with the whole staff that drew on the history of the organisation and his own experiences in the community.

Understanding the stage and the drama

At the start of this chapter, it was suggested that too often in writing for leaders there was a concentration on them as players and not enough about the stage they played on or the drama they were in. The ideas in this chapter are just ways to begin to think about these important aspects of organisations in a richer and more meaningful way. One of those symbolic reframes is that of a stage and players. Before you go onto the next section, you may want to briefly work on the following activity and relate it to the stage on which you act at the moment. Metaphor is often used when thinking about organisations, even when people are not consciously reframing anything! Bolman and Deal suggest that metaphors (and humour) are particularly useful when there are complex, difficult and perhaps personally threatening issues to deal with in an organisation. Before moving on to Section 2, look at where you work now from a slightly different perspective. Certainly in one school that I worked in, a suitable metaphor I would have used would have been the Twilight Zone – dark, dangerous and difficult for both pupils and teachers. The head teacher who moved the school on often used the phrase 'Let's clear a path through the jungle'!

Activity 15

Use a metaphor to describe your current organisation. Note down in your journal why it is apt and what it tells you about your own viewpoint just now. You may like to ask a close colleague to do the same and then compare and contrast your metaphors.

Section 2 now takes the journey on a closer focus into the particular aspects of context that may be most useful or most troublesome to those who lead. It may not be a path through the jungle, but reading it should help you bring your organisational issues as a leader into sharper focus.

Further Reading for Section 1

- Bush, T. (2011) *Theories of Educational Leadership and Management* (4th edn). London: Sage.
  Excellent overview of models of educational leadership and management which applies leadership theory and concepts to a range of educational settings. Case studies from across the UK and internationally make clear connections between theory and practice.

- Earley, P. (2013) *Exploring the School Leadership Landscape*. London: Bloomsbury.
  A very useful overview of recent changes in the English landscape, with reference to developing new models of leadership for teaching and learning.

- Glover, D. and Coleman, C. (2010) *Educational Leadership and Management: Developing Skills and Insights*. Buckingham: Open University Press.
  Full of case studies and reflections on key leadership insights in education such as values, diversity and taking an ethical stance.

- Halam, S. A., Reicher, S. D. and Platow, M. (2011) *The New Psychology of Leadership: Identity, Influence and Power*. London: Psychological Press.
  A book which looks at the breadth of arguments in the area of psychology of leadership.

Section 2

Leaders and the context

Power in context

This chapter aims to:

- open up the different meanings of 'context' and their implications for leadership;
- extend the discussion on organisations to explicitly look at issues of power;
- discuss the leader's role in influencing the direction of the organisation;
- stress the interconnectedness of power, leadership and the organisational context.

The first section of this book reintroduced the personal into leadership by looking at some of the areas that new, developing and experienced leaders might have to consider as they build, shape and redefine their own leadership over time. This second section builds on this focus by examining the contexts in which such leadership skills develop and posing questions to further develop leadership thinking over time. The idea of context will be a thread that brings together these next four chapters.

Context is a seemingly simple word. In educational leadership, it has come to mean several different concepts. As discussed in the last chapter of Section 1, the context for many leaders is the organisation within which they work. This context can be as challenging as any outside context. Secondly, many leaders also have to wrestle with the neighbourhood or state context and the national policy context. The third part of context which many aspiring leaders forget about is the personal context. Life's ebbs and flows touch both those who have formal positions of leadership and those who work with them. All three of these contexts have one thing in common: the fact that they will be forever changing, and one of the key skills of a leader will be adaptability to change while at the same time maintaining their own core values and those of the institution in which they work. These three contexts will be looked at in turn in this chapter while Chapter 7 will return to them and examine what this means specifically for leadership skills.

Organisational context

The organisational context is obviously a key issue for leaders, and Chapter 5 grappled with ways of examining the organisational landscape so that the view was clear. The organisational context is closely tied to issues concerning culture and structure, and sometimes it can prove difficult to unravel the two. At the same time, the previous discussion suggested that people's perceptions of context were subjective and subject to differing interpretations. This sounds, on the face of it, as if the task of those in formal and informal leadership positions might be intrinsically hopeless. However, this is the very area where leadership and management become essential. Fineman's argument (2000: 10) that management is about order is useful to consider. Order could suggest issues of structure, viewing the organisation through a structural frame so, as Bolman and Deal (2003) suggested, the focus is on the designated leadership positions, such as principals/head teachers, and 'designing a pattern of roles and relationships that will accomplish collective goals as well as accommodate individual differences' (p. 40). So, new head teachers may view restructuring as a way to order and manage their new context. The structural frame here is used as a way to 'design' how relationships within an organisation can be used to best effect, as teachers may well employ a structurally focused seating plan in order to maximise student interaction or minimise poor behaviour. The difficulty for a new leader is that the structure he or she designs may not be effective, even if it has worked previously in another organisation. Designing job roles on paper may give the illusion of helpfulness, but probably not if the fit of the people for those roles is not actively considered at the start. Fineman sees ordering as something which can be carried out by using emotional preferences and emotionalising people's understandings of situations. Thus the structural role may reflect both the aims of the organisation, and current emotional concerns. In a previous book (Crawford, 2009), concerned with emotion and educational leadership, I argued that it was very tempting for leaders to pay attention to purely rational approaches to organisational context and attempt to restore rationality by managing our own feelings and those of others in a 'rational' way. This is partially the view of those that advocate a competency view of emotional intelligence (Goleman, 1995). Context matters because of the uniqueness of each educational organisation and the adults and young people who work within it. Fineman (2000) proposes that this focus on people and emotion helps redefine what is meant by rationality. He defined rationality as the presentation of emotionalised processes so that they are acceptable to others. Because we want to think and believe that what we are doing is rational, we create social discourses in education that define how we ought to feel and display emotion. This can mean that it is difficult for either a new leader or an experienced leader in a new context to understand the emotional states that are behind, for example, people's resistance to change. Justifying how one behaves emotionally in a social situation in school could be termed 'professional behaviour', for example. It can also mean that part of the process of change may include looking at difficult issues early on and building trust. This returns to making sense of the terrain in front of you and understanding the meanings that are attached to people, rituals and symbols – in other words understanding the cultural frame.

Before looking at culture specifically, read this vignette about an experienced leader in a new context.

Vignette

Mark was a very successful depute head of a primary school in a challenging urban environment in Scotland. He had been there since becoming a teacher ten years previously, and had been actively looking for new leadership opportunities for two years. Eventually, he was interviewed for a head's position in a similar school in terms of size, catchment area and pupil profile. He noticed two things while looking around that were different to his school – the exam results seemed to be very erratic and the students seemed far less engaged than at his school. He reckoned his experience and skills set could address this. After the interviews, he was invited to relax in the staff room that afternoon, which was full of the remains of the takeaway from the day before left by the staff after parents' evening. Mark said later that if he had understood the significance of the Chinese takeaway, he would not have taken the position, which he left after two years.

What did the meal signify to him and to the staff?

Mark found himself in charge of a group of people whose organisational goals were far removed from the ones that he wished to pursue. He had come from a lively school where the staff were focused on ambitions for the school, themselves and the neighbourhood, and had a tremendous work ethic with mutual support in times of difficulty. The new staff seemed to him to have no real long-term interest in the school, the children or the area. In his mind, they viewed organisational life as social but had no tangible interest in improvement as long as they could get by. He viewed the fact that they had collectively left the smelly remains of a meal to moulder in the staff room for a day as symptomatic of a staff where no one was willing to take a leadership stance and had no pride in the school. As you read on, you may want to consider any actions Mark could have taken early on in his leadership there to progress change. It may have helped him to make connections and applied them to the new context earlier. Mark also wished he had paid more attention to the local context before he became the leader, as he now considers it vital for any successful head.

Local context

The local context matters in many ways, some of which will be taken further in Chapter 11. Elsewhere (Crawford, 2012: 157) I have noted that the relationship between the school, the parent body and the local community is vital to school progress, and that leaders not only need to understand but be active in managing the relationship. In many countries this is still a foundation stone of how leaders work, especially in small schools in rural localities worldwide (Wildy and Clarke, 2008a). In other countries, such as England, the connection with the local is more tenuous, as schools become parts of chains of schools and local accountabilities decline. Local contexts themselves can be quite diverse. A head teacher in a large metropolitan area could find themselves dealing with a group of very diverse parents; this could be economically and socially, as well as different ethnic and religious backgrounds. In spite of these differences in the local context, schools engaging with their communities and identifying ways to do this can promote community cohesion and build social capital, an idea drawn from Bourdieu. Bourdieu's (1986, 1991) analysis concerning different forms of capital is helpful. His insights concern social fields. He argues that people and institutions work within a social field seeking to maintain or enhance their position in that field in relation to others by using the resources that they have. This means that different stakeholders will have different resources to use to enhance their position. These resources can be seen as different forms of capital. He identified economic, social, cultural and symbolic capital, all of which could be part of the local context when a leader analyses the situation. Social capital is the closest linked to the personal side of leadership and concerns the gains that occur through social networks and positive social settings.

Leadership in some community contexts can be viewed as flowing through and around the organisation with leaders from the community taking a major role in what happens in schools. The contexts are infinite and vary hugely. As your leadership skills develop, you will bring together your own experiences and view of what constitutes a community. These views are very important, as this will influence the way that any particular context might be viewed in the future.

National context

There are several ways of conceiving the national context, some of which are directly relevant to the discussion of culture in the next section. The discussion of national contexts is pulled together by a sense of place. The national context can be viewed as being more about identity and your own sense of place in the world (Riley, 2013). As Riley eloquently phrases it, 'Place is a physical entity, a building, a location that is important to us. It's also an emotional response to the world around us; connected to our sense of self, identity, worth' (Preface). Everyone who reads this book has their own sense of place which might drive their leadership to areas which are specific to that place, such as girls' under-achievement in school in Malawi, or ways of looking at Native American Leadership in Saskatchewan. Values are again at the heart of this kind of leadership. Context may also open up a different type of leadership. Bryant (2003) researched leadership in the Native American context and found that their values meant that leadership was decentralised, where every person in the tribe has a role to play, and each person had a contribution that was vital to the whole way forward. The book will return to this idea when I look at the leader and teams.

   Whatever your sense of place might be, every educationalist works within a policy framework that reflects the national context. As a component of the process of globalisation, for example, there is much education 'policy borrowing' across the globe, where East looks West and vice versa (Dimmock and Walker, 2005). Even more concerning is what Dimmock and Walker call 'the ethnocentricity underlying theory development, empirical research and prescriptive argument' (p. 145). This book adopts a critical stance towards leadership and it is hoped that you will ask whether some of the personal leadership approaches described in it would work as well in a different national culture. Dimmock and Walker used a focus on 'culture as an analytical concept' that draws on the work of Hofstede (1991) who looked at the workings of a multinational company in various localities around the world. Although he found commonalities in values in different sites, there were different cultural practices in various countries. He drew on these different cultural practices to construct a six-dimensional framework. Rather than go into the details here, I suggest that you examine those yourself in your own time. (A quick overview can be found at http://geert-hofstede.com.) One of the dimensions which ties in with Dimmock and Walker's work to note in particular is that of power distance. This dimension shows the degree to which less powerful members of society take for granted that power is distributed unequally. Hofstede suggested that people in societies, such as many Asian countries, which display a large degree of power distance, are more likely to accept a hierarchical order in organisations. Hofstede's work can illuminate how national culture can affect educational practices, and often in unexpected ways. Later, I will look at a Japanese example of working with parents that might be seen as an attempt to decrease the power distance in that society.

For most people, national context will first bring to mind the national *policy* context. Educational policy frameworks vary hugely from country to country, but what many have in common is change. Many countries find that they are subjected to what appears to be ongoing policy change in their own national context. The word 'subjected' in the last sentence suggests a depth of feeling that has directly arisen from my own work with head teachers in England particularly, but the twins of autonomy and accountability are something with which many leaders grapple. If the country's policy for schools is based on numerical accountability measures, what is the role of the leader? To lead in order to get the best results for the school, and acknowledge that some pupils will inevitably fail to get the desired grades? Or is it to provide opportunities for all inside that framework? If your building is falling down and your community living at subsistence level, what are the things that matter? The values of educators again are important in understanding how the national policy context can cause dilemmas for leaders and in extreme cases lead to disillusionment and even ill health.

One of the reasons for such dilemmas is the power of policy-makers in many educational jurisdictions. The next section discusses power on an individual and group level. While reading it, keep your national policy context in view, and try to apply some of the theoretical aspects of power to policy-making.

Power – an overview

Power, authority and influence are often used interchangeably when writing about leadership. The language used to discuss power in the literature also talks about authority as well as influence. As discussed in Chapter 3, this often means that discussions return to the idea of the charismatic leader, with great resources of personal power. All the ideas discussed in this chapter and the preceding ones return eventually to the issue of power and the leader. Power was a significant aspect of the political frame, but it also has implications for all aspects of the developing leader's thinking. People's organisational lives can be overtly political as they try to use their power and influence to change or adapt organisational goals over time. This is especially true when change is in the air. The leader has to be able to influence in order that organisational goals are met (Haslam et al., 2011), and that can mean understanding the things that matter to the group, not just considering power as something to do with authority, being authoritarian or wielding a 'big stick'. Power is a fascinating concept to look at in detail. After reading the next section, there will be an activity to help you develop your thinking.

In these areas, clearer definitions do help you in your leadership journey to understand more of the nuances of power and its relationship to the related concepts of influence and authority. The charismatic leader referred to above might be viewed as having influence, but that influence is dependent on a relationship with their followers. The relationship that they have is an important part of the dynamic. Personal influence might be used when you are trying to persuade someone to back you on a specific initiative, for example, and the power comes from past trust on issues, your colleague's estimation of your overall values and respect. In power dynamics, relationships go both ways. Mutual influencing will go on even during the discussion in the previous example, especially as the characteristics of trust and respect may lead you to change your mind in some way about your plan. Power is dynamic. Everyone has some power, but some have more specific sources of power than others.

If the leader is able to affect what a person or a group does in their daily work, or even how they think about issues of importance to the organisation, then s/he is using influence. How are they able to influence? Understanding power as the potential of an individual or a group to influence others highlights the link. Authority then could be viewed as one specific type of power which comes from formal roles within an organisation, or from a secure knowledge of the organisation over time – an example might be: 'Ask Mr Groves, he will be able to take you through those issues as everyone respects his views – he's been here 24 years!' The role itself does not guarantee authority because of power dynamics. Power depends on several key elements, one of which is context. Mr Groves may well be able to lead on neighbourhood issues, but he would have no source of power if what was needed was swimming instruction as he is a poor swimmer! Power draws on differences – the differences in the values that people hold and their access to resources in an organisation. Power is also about what people believe. People believed Mr Groves knew the neighbourhood and its issues, and his power derived from this knowledge and access to community resources. Crucially it is not about the actual power that Mr Groves has locally (his information may, for example, be out of date) but on what the staff at the college believed about his community influence. Even in this example, power and influence are very closely interlinked.

Theoretical viewpoints

Within any context, there will be within it sources of power both for individuals and groups. The question of how the leader uses these sources can be looked at differently depending on the context and the leadership skills of those in such positions. French and Raven (1959) developed a classic taxonomy of power that sets out six ways that leaders have power over others. Each power base draws upon the leader being the gatekeeper in an organisation either to physical or psychological resources. The leader is able to use these resources in whatever they consider is the best way, which in itself can be a leadership dilemma. They are:

- *Reward*. The leader is able to give out financial rewards for taking a certain course, or might help them to gain something they view as rewarding (new position, title).
- *Coercion*. Leaders can use the opposite of the rewards mentioned above by making it difficult for such goals to be achieved or in some way making life more difficult for them (being given a difficult task to do). At one end of the spectrum it can lead to bullying and harassment.
- *Expertise*. Expert power is what Mr Groves had in the example above. He was someone who had an overview of a particular situation, developed over time, and, importantly, was able to balance his own expert knowledge and the goals of the college.
- *Information*. Mr Groves might also have informational power, where he could argue a case for a certain action based on his expertise in the community. A working party in a school could also have informational power which would help when they presented the findings to the staff.
- *Legitimacy*. A school principal has legitimate power given to them by another authority: the school board or the governing body. Legitimate power gives the principal the authority to oversee certain tasks and functions that make school life run smoothly. They may also have referent power, based on respect from previous work or in the community at large.
- *Respect*. Referent power is perhaps what the colleague in the example of trying to persuade someone to back them on a specific initiative had – the trust and respect of that colleague.

Haslam et al. (2011), quoting Turner (2005), note the importance of the difference between 'power *over* and power *through* [… leadership] is not about coercion and brute force but about influence and inspiration' (2011: 35). They note that this two-way process does not depend on someone asking, 'What's in it for me?' but in asking 'What's in it for us?' (p. 37). This takes on a particular meaning when attached to the management of change which will be looked at in Chapter 10. Social connectivity is very important in a leader's harnessing of sources of power.

Activity 16

Look back on a recent situation when you had to influence a group of people, either in an educational context or outside. You felt that you had the knowledge to move something forward. Drawing on your understanding of power as the potential of an individual or a group to influence others, ask:

- What sources of power did you draw upon?
- If you drew upon expert power, was it recognised by the group?
- What else could you have drawn upon to influence the outcome?
- What did you learn about the group and yourself?

You will probably have noted that you drew upon several sources of power to influence the group, and that they are all in a dynamic relationship with each other. Personal characteristics will also play a part.

The way forward

So far, we have discussed how context matters in terms of your leadership role and the way power operates dynamically and, I would argue, it is, like leadership, all about perception and subjectivity. Law and Glover noted (2000: 32) that people operate at several levels in an organisation; as individuals with their own personal agendas, hopes and fears; as team members with a role in contributing to the views of a collective; and as leaders who have to read the messages that are coming from the other levels. This all contributes to the micropolitics of the school (Ball, 1987; Hoyle, 1988), or what Hoyle describes as the darker side of organisational life where individuals seek to use power and resources to further their own interests. It was in Ball's book that I first became aware of how educational organisations work at a time when my own leadership life was proving tricky. The ways that power operates in any educational context will be subtly different, and you may like to ask yourself how much of what goes on in your school is actually within the control of the leader(s) inside the organisation. What are the power sources in the local or national context? Any educational organisation needs in some way to order its activities, and many debates over the future of schooling can be viewed in relation to the organisation resisting or adapting to external influences. Context and power remain important issues tightly bound up with leadership. The next chapter asks how leaders in their specific context can develop the necessary skills to ensure the effective running of the organisation and clear outcomes for the students. At the same time, it asks whether the influence of context on outcomes is much more complex than that previous sentence suggests.

Crafting the context

This chapter will:

- discuss what 'crafting the context' means in practice;
- look at the skills needed by a leader to craft the context;
- examine the challenges and concerns that leaders may have.

Crafting the context might seem like a strange title but it will hopefully make sense by the end of the chapter. Matching leadership style to context is a key part of many leadership preparation programmes, which makes it all sound very easy to move between styles. Just as the last chapter focused on the idea of contexts and how an understanding of power can help an overall understanding of the organisation, in this chapter we will discuss what 'crafting the context' means in practice, look at the skills needed by a leader to craft the context and examine the challenges and concerns that leaders may have.

I am assuming that the leader in any organisation, at whatever level, wishes to shape the context in which s/he finds themselves – to 'set the mood music' as one leader put it to me at a workshop – in other words to create a culture where everybody can flourish – staff, students, parents and visitors. This may be an idealistic aim, but it is such an important facet of leadership that it is worth focusing on in some detail. This chapter builds on some of the early chapters, so you may want to remind yourself of the notes you have made in your journal for previous activities on leadership and the context, or re-read some specific sections.

Culture: mood music or martial beat?

There are many ideas that a leader might want to utilise when finding that they are leading in a new context. They may be an experienced leader in that context, or a newly promoted head of department, perhaps moving from considering him/herself as a teacher leader to a more formal leadership role within the organisation. Whatever the context, there will be a need to make sense of the organisation, and to understand how the people in it make sense of some of the issues that are going on. Huczynski and Buchanan (2001) have an attractive definition of an organisation as the 'social arrangements for achieving controlled performance in pursuit of collective goals'. Some of these social issues were discussed in Chapter 5 and elsewhere in the book, and you will already understand that creating meaning involves understanding the organisation through various frames and taking action to move the organisation towards a vision for the future. All of this is inextricably bound up in the school's culture. In a way, culture is the mood music of the organisation, providing a continuous background melody to the social interactions that go on from day to day.

Many educational leadership writers have dealt with culture and schooling. Given that this book's centre is on the personal and social side of leadership, one of the writers that focused on this particular aspect was Sergiovanni. In his article on the lifeworld of leadership (2003) he suggested that culture provided the norms for daily interaction and a framework for making sense of what is happening. In order to be successful leaders of a school culture, he argued that a leader needs to pay particular thought to the 'informal, subtle and symbolic aspects of school life' (2003: 14). Shorthand for this that is often used on leadership programmes is 'the way we do things around here'. Yet, the longer you are within a culture, the less able you are to stand back and look at what is going on, unless something in the context becomes turbulent – a change of some kind is the classic example. This could be new leadership or a change in the policy context or many other types of change. New leaders can encounter resistance to change for many reasons, but often it is because they have not understood the culture of the organisation and what lies behind seemingly mundane interactions or within the environment more generally. It is valuable to return to Bolman and Deal's symbolic frame, where it is not so much what something is or what actually happened in some event but what it means to the people in the organisation. They carefully define culture as both a product and a process (2003: 217) because it is, at one and the same time, bringing the wisdom of the past to the present (product), and yet it is fluid and changing as new people and new events create a new wisdom. In particular, they note that cultural symbols are part of the definition of 'who we are' as a group. The following vignette gives an example, drawn from a real situation.

Vignette

Amanda was a newly promoted senior teacher in a new context. The school was in a deprived urban area, and part of the new head teacher's plan for moving the school forward was to make the school and its environment more pleasant to work in. She threw herself into this new role, and, after having been there six weeks, decided that the ugly statue of a owl perched on a tree, which stood near the school gate, should probably be moved and even got rid of. It was worn, not very well carved and had not been painted for years. The head teacher agreed with Amanda. She rang a local company to ask them to come and take the statue away. The next thing Amanda and her head teacher knew, they were all over the local news, generating headlines such as 'Save our Owl', 'New head removes local landmark' and similar. Unknown to the new management team, the owl had been the centre of a community project in the 1990s, was well loved and, for some, it symbolised the school and the way it had worked with the local community in the past. Amanda found out more about the previous project and, instead of jettison-ing the statue, made it the centre of a new parent/student project, resulting in better relationships with the community and a much nicer artefact for the school entrance. When it came to redesigning the school logo as part of the 'rebranding', Amanda suggested that the owl symbol should be a feature of the new school identity.

Culture is about meaning and is important for several reasons. Amanda had initially completely failed to understand the meaning of the statue to the community as a symbol of how they had worked with the school in the past and how changing this familiar landmark could cause so much upset locally. She was able to turn her new knowledge to her advantage eventually, but it could have been a very difficult situation. Sergiovanni advocates that school leaders need to pay more attention to these informal cultural symbols, because shared meaning is one of ways that communities can find shared purpose. Leaders are then more able to provide a map to work from. Finding out what's important to the school's purpose and by asking themselves key questions about the things that come together to bring meaning to an educational commu-nity is a significant part of the task of leadership, Sergiovanni suggested. Shared meaning creation as part of the task of leadership means that the imposition of values or moral guidance could be seen as part of the school's role. Putting aside for a moment some of what is problematic about this statement, we can still see leaders as promoters and protec-tors of values which is the way that Sergiovanni framed their role. Amanda found herself more able to promote the newer values of her school once she had understood something about the past. The new culture that she was seeking to embed drew on the positives found in the old culture. To use the musical adage, she was creating new mood music that set the scene for culture change, but she was also using some of the beat pattern from the old score. To return to Sergiovanni, in his work he drew together the ideas of culture, meaning and significance to create what he called 'the lifeworld of the school' (2003: 16) which coexists with the systems world of the school. Bolman and Deal call bringing together the lifeworld and the processes of an organisation the development of a 'cultural tapestry'. The lifeworld and their role in creating the tapestry can be the part that many new leaders find difficult to understand, as Amanda did, and have to learn that it is this part of the institution that impels the systems to be their most useful. Bringing these two aspects of the organisation together is a key leadership demand, because when this is done well both aspects increase each other's effectiveness. Sergiovanni uses a distinction drawn from Habermas, that the lifeworld has three dimensions: culture, community and person, and as you work through this book, you may notice that there is a great deal of emphasis on these three. After all, this book is about the personal side of leadership and one's own identity as a leader over time, which changes as the leader evolves and develops through relationships in various kinds of communities. It is important not to assume that leadership skills will only develop when a formal leader is mixing with other formal leaders. Community in educational organisations can be the internal teams or the interface with the local community, and may involve many different types of people in those various communities. One secondary head teacher I spoke to recently said that he had learned a great deal about teamwork from the support staff and the way they worked together so well.

Skills for crafting the context

This section looks at leadership and the context, and discusses some of the skills that leaders might need to utilise. The next chapter goes on to suggest ways that these might be developed, adapted and honed in the context of team-working.

Leadership is never static. Boydell's work (1985) may be some while ago, but his idea of managerial competence on three levels is still a useful one. Level One is the manager as technician who aims to do all the standard management routines correctly. Level Two is the manager as professional, who is self-aware, creative and builds up systems in his or her personal style. Level Three is the manager as artist who is able to weave all their knowledge skilfully together to move the work of the organisation forward. It can be very easy to stay on Level One where everything is safe and secure (most of the time). The manager/leader as artist is the one who will be most able to craft the context to provide a cultural tapestry where others can also become more effective leaders, teachers and culture builders. Artistry is a demanding concept. It involves change and development on many personal levels. The factors that will constrain your work at significant moments in your leadership career are multifarious. Some of these have been mentioned already, as you have focused in on your personal development as a leader. They can be concerned with:

- *who you are* – personal characteristics, life circumstances, motivation, how you present yourself to others;
- *who you want to become* – self-development, skills training, career aspirations;
- *where you are* – length of career so far, current context, personal relationships.

Use the following activity to reflect on some of these aspects, as well as looking back on any notes you might have made in your journal.

Activity 17

Imagine you have arrived in a new leadership context. What would be the differing approaches you might take at the different levels discussed above? What would enable you to have confidence in your ability as an artist, ready to craft the culture? Use the list of factors above to help you think about your current position and map out some areas that you need to take action about for the future.

Skills for crafting the context are rarely possessed by just one person. Even if, for some remarkable reason, they were, that person would be unwise to rely totally upon themselves for several reasons. Before building teams to move the organisational culture, it is useful to have a good understanding of your own strengths and weaknesses. In fact being clear about *who you are* when you present yourself in a new context is one of the ways in which you signal your personal values to the people you work with. Everyone has context crafting skills, but some are more suitable for particular contexts than others. If you have worked the first few years of your career in a dynamic environment with pleasant colleagues and good exam results, it can be difficult to translate the skills you have into a very different context (as Amanda found above). It is often by being conscious of your own skills and weaknesses that can help to make such transitions more seamless and less personally painful. You may wish to keep some of your more unhelpful characteristics hidden, for example, or make light of them, but your own development rests on understanding any personal limitations you may have and taking actions to mitigate them. This relates to *who you want to become*. Are there particular skills that you could actually manage if you had a session of training? If you want to be a principal, do you really have to be able to carry out all the skills needed in a school yourself? One principal suggested to me that, because he knew he would never have any skill at timetabling, he avoided it. However, he did know what a good timetable should do for students and awareness of his lack of skill in this area made him make sure that he appointed someone who excelled at timetabling in his Senior Team. Finally, *where you are* is often an aspect of self-development that is not taken very seriously. If you are a new leader in a certain context early in your career, you may have some of the skills needed naturally which may work in the right context. Someone coming to the end of their career would bring different skills to that same context which might include the accumulated wisdom of their entire career. Both of these scenarios would also be very different if something happened in the personal lives outside work of those two examples. Such emotional events outside work, such as family trauma or ill health, can rapidly wear away at a person's sense of who they are and result in loss of confidence in abilities, uncharacteristic outbursts or lack of focus at work.

The following vignette gives an example, taken from research, of a leader unable to draw upon personal reserves because the context and their personal circumstances are too toxic.

Vignette

Tessa was an experienced head teacher of a medium-sized (200 pupils) Church of England junior school in a market town in England. The school was her third headship in the church section of education and she had been in post for just over 18 months. I knew her from a training course that I had led, where she had been vocal in her opinions about staff shortages in primary schools. I interviewed her at a time of great local and personal tension when it had become obvious that her school was to close in a local merger with the infant school to become an all-through primary school. She had decided to apply for the new headship but expressed the view that she would not be the favoured candidate as the infant head was 'better liked' by the governors and would get the post. Whether the infant head was 'better liked' or not, Tessa's bitterness shone through, and this in fact turned out to be the case. Tessa later took early retirement. Staff and children with queries constantly interrupted us. Tessa seemed unwilling or unable to stop this happening, despite requests from myself. There was tension in the school that day because one of the younger pupils had been the victim of an attempted abduction by a non-custodial parent the day before. However, Tessa was very forthcoming about why she had gone into headship – it seemed to be the expected thing in teaching to do that. She enjoyed being a head because she valued 'seeing plans come to fruition with children' but found that tasks such as having to deal with staff redundancies alongside the merger 'ripped me apart'. The word she used to describe life in the school seemed to reflect the difficult situation she found herself in: 'tense, angry, overwhelmed, astonished' were the words that came to her mind when I asked about the previous year. She told me of the situation regarding the merger and the governors meeting that dealt with how staff would have to be made redundant and that she would have to apply for the merger headship. She felt that it had been made very clear that her job was to 'clear up' the staff before the merger but that there would be no place for her afterwards. The language she used to describe her feelings as she came out of this meeting was very evocative: 'I was wearing a beige jacket, and when I came out my skin was the same colour as the jacket!' Coupled with all this, her husband was also under threat of job loss. The picture that was presented to me was of a head teacher being rapidly deskilled by the new context in which she found herself. Others might argue that she was just ineffective (though her past career pattern did not suggest this). What's your view?

In many ways this vignette is depressing, but it is included to reinforce the interplay between context, who you are, who you want to become and where you are. For Tessa, stressors in all of these areas played a part in making her feel powerless and unable to create any context for the merger when, it could be argued, it was very important for her to do so.

Specific skills

Activity 18

Before looking at specific skills for crafting the context, jot down your thoughts on these questions. Then find a trusted colleague who is able to give you truthful feedback and discuss them with him/her:

- What evidence do I have that I am effective in my current context?
- What additional skills can I draw on?
- What is the one important leadership lesson I have learnt in my current role?

From this exercise, you may begin to get an inkling of where your skills lie. Crafting the context means working with other people towards an agreed goal or vision of where you want to be. In other words, a great deal of the skill is about understanding human behaviour and appreciating the points of views of others, even those that you don't agree with. You are not a neutral observer in this process, even if you were very honest in answering those questions because, as Bolman and Deal's work reinforces, leaders view behaviour through the lens of their own understandings of social norms and behaviours.

The leader who wants to begin to weave together the competing agendas in any new social situation needs to be skilful at understanding behaviour, realising that people may not share their values or be as dedicated to the school goals as they are, that emotions are as important as rational facts and arguments, and that when people's behaviour does not make sense to you, you need to have the skill to find out what is behind the presenting behaviour. At this point you may want to remind yourself of some of the key points about values covered in Chapter 2. Conflicts inevitably arise, sometimes based around those values and at other times because individual agendas clash with the organisational goals that leaders are trying to achieve. The skills a leader needs are concerned with being clear about what the issues are, where the organisation is going and tackling them in the most constructive way for both the person or persons involved and the team/organisation as a whole. It is often an area that many leaders, as they move up the formal hierarchy, can find difficulty in tackling. The set of skills needed are those which can be improved with coaching and feedback.

Rationality and emotion go hand in hand in organisations, although there is a tendency for leaders to try to portray, often in retrospect, the actions that they have carried out as being purely rational. Leadership is about understanding how those different meanings of situations are influenced by emotion. Fineman (2003) writes that leadership is 'imbued with emotion and central to the organising process' (p. 76), so that that leaders and followers are bound together by emotion 'in a complex emotional web' (p. 90). Understanding that emotions play a part in a person's understanding of situations enables leaders not to be swayed by emotionality, but to come to a much more complete understanding both of the person and of the situation. This may well help in any decisions that need to be made, and enable the creation of a culture where the leader's skill in decision-making is informed by their understanding of the different meanings that people hold of situations.

When crafting a culture means that large changes to ways of working or routines need to be made, leadership skills can help in understanding when you don't understand behaviours. Not all leaders are equally skilled in understanding behaviour, but most leaders realise when another person's behaviour in a particular context makes no sense at all. The skill is being able to understand what this means in that context. It could be that you are missing some important personal or organisational fact about the person, or it may mean that, especially as a new leader in a new context, their behaviour is a challenge to a new rule or convention that has been put in place. In either case, the skill is recognising that this merits some investigation.

Although people skills are not the only skills needed for leadership, they are particularly important when understanding and leading in a new organisation or making changes in an existing organisation. Other skills will be looked at in Section 3.

Challenges

Hopefully the last section will make you think about your skills with people and your knowledge of your own potential. Here is a story told by John Nolan, an aide of the American politician Robert Kennedy. It concerns Kennedy's leadership skills: 'What he did was not really that mystical. All it requires is someone who knows himself, and has some courage.' Some of the issues discussed in the last section will involve courage and most of those people skills mentioned can be coached to a higher level and refreshed at various times in your career. Leadership coaching that concentrates on the particular fit between you and the context can draw attention to the specific skills that need working on, which can give any leader the courage to take action in a particular context. Before reading on, write three positive skills that you already have in your journal. As you go on to read about teams, consider whether you need more of these skills in your team or whether there is a leadership skill that you know you lack. Are you able to develop it, or should you develop your team selection skills instead? Most leaders in formal roles will work in and with teams of people, and the next chapter will turn to the idea of leadership development in teams.

Leadership development in teams

In this chapter I will:

- ask you to think about the concept of a team and its processes;
- discuss and define the role of the team leader;
- suggest that there are specific processes that the leader can manage for the better through teamwork.

Earlier in the book different forms of leadership were discussed and debated. Whatever your view about distributed leadership – and there are many different viewpoints – on one thing most educationalists concur: successful leadership of an educational organisation involves more than one charismatic person at the top of a hierarchical organisation. That person does have an important role, however, in setting up, developing and moving forward in teams. Silins and Mulford (2009) argue, for example, that being successful as a principal involves many people and is a mutual, dynamic and evolving process involving many players interacting at all times and being changed by the context in which leadership occurs.

Even the most dynamic of leaders needs good team players. The charismatic John .F Kennedy, president of the USA in the early 1960s, said of his brother and Attorney General, Robert Kennedy (mentioned in the last chapter): 'If I want something done and done immediately I rely on the Attorney General. He is very much the doer in this administration, and has an organizational gift I have rarely if ever seen surpassed.' This, for me, sums up the benefit of working in a really good team. There is space in an effective team to allow people's own special skills to shine, and in the interactive dynamics of teamwork, to learn more skills as an individual which in turn enhance the team.

Working well in teams is challenging, partly because, while working together can be very effective, most readers of this book will have examples of instances when working in a team had a nightmarish quality. This chapter focuses on your role as the leader in a team, partly due to limitations of space, but primarily because developing your team leadership potential is crucial to the dynamics of any team you work with.

The team as a concept

In education, it is common practice for any functioning group to be labelled a team, but examine these teams closely and you may find they are just a group of people meeting in the same room. Teamworking is often based on the premise that a group of people can draw together their collective knowledge and experience and apply it to the workplace. This means that they will be able to make better decisions and support each other in the carrying out of those decisions. Teams, as opposed to groups, share common goals within the organisation, but there are many thorny questions for leaders to ask about team membership. O'Neill (2003) talks of the double-edged sword of teamworking, for while it may seem good practice to get as many people involved as possible, team leaders need to pay attention to many factors when they draw together teams. Equity issues such as differences in status, rates of pay, time allocated to teams and many other factors may mean that some potential team members have less power than others or less real opportunity to take part in a meaningful way. Team membership can also be difficult, stressful and time rich, especially if it involves meetings. For some so-called teams, the only defining characteristic that they have is that they are involved in regular meetings. Leadership of teams is crucial to make the experience of the team one that enhances the organisation's goals, rather than being a source of time wasting. In order for this to happen, one of the tasks of leadership is to manage group processes so that team membership is a positive part of work life. I like Everard and Morris's (1996) emphasis on a team being able to bring together the best contributions of each of the members: through the team, people are able to excel because the team both draws out and is supportive of their input. You will find that there are many definitions of team in the literature both in business and in education, but most concur that it is the focus on the common task and the opportunity for more effective work than people could have attained by themselves or in an unstructured group.

The leader of the team has many roles to play, one of which is realising that s/he cannot do everything, so they need to focus on the processes which enable all the team members to give of their best. They can do this by helping the team focus on goals, making sure that the procedures of the team are agreed and allowing safe ways to allow conflict to enhance rather than de-rail the team's goal. Clear communication between the members of the team is vital, and the leader's own skills in communication can make sure that clarity is at the heart of the team's work. Apart from the formal leader's skills, other members of the team can take up leadership when it is needed, especially if they have a specific skill that comes to be needed as part of the task in hand.

Cultural differences should also be taken into account when thinking about team leadership. Hofstede's work on the different dimensions of power in national culture could be worth revisiting as you think about team leadership.

Vignette

Heidi was assigned to be the team leader of her year group at school which consisted of five classes. She had been a teacher for three years and thought that it would be relatively easy to bring her colleagues together to discuss some of the really interesting ideas about teaching that she was reading about and progress some of the work with the challenging children in the year group. Heidi's principal gave her a list of what must be covered at each meeting and asked for minutes to be given to him after the meeting. He made it clear that the agenda for the meeting was tied into the overall school strategic plan and that deviation from it was not an option. The first meeting she held with the formal agenda dragged; one teacher left early and she caught herself and several others yawning as they had to redraw part of the strategic plan for the school. They were a very pleasant group, so fortunately Heidi did not have a direct rebellion on her hands, but she felt that if the team continued like this, she would eventually! She felt it was a waste of both her time (and ideas) and the other staff's time and experience.
  What would you do in her situation?

The team's purpose had been decided by someone in a more powerful position which had led to a lack of commitment to any discussions. The options open to her all had potential difficult consequences: directly tackling the principal or openly changing the focus of meetings. In the end, she decided to pay lip service to the formal agenda for the first part of the meeting and then use the experience of her colleagues for a more informal second part. This conclusion was reached because she was confident of the personalities and characteristics of the team members, who she was sure would make an successful team if allowed to work in a more effective way.

This last example shows that a good team leader will concentrate on building teamwork while still maintaining the core tasks of the team.

Activity 19

Think of a team you have taken part in recently which seems to work relatively well. Why is that? What are the leadership skills you can observe in the formal leader or in others? If you have an opportunity in your current team, try to observe effective behaviour which either moves the team forward or helps maintain its work. Note these in your journal.

Some of the skills you may have noted are concerned with building good, professional working relationships and how team members encourage and support each other, freeing members of the team to use their specific skill sets to maximum effect. All of these good outcomes for teams are facilitated by the leader, although there may be times when the non-formal leader of the group takes a leadership role, perhaps when the team are tackling an area which requires that particular expertise. In order to share leadership around a team, trust is an essential component.

I think that trusting relationships are among the most important cornerstones of effective teamwork. The leadership literature constantly notes this as important (Bennis and Nanus, 1985; Bottery, 2002; Fink, 2013). Trust can only be built up over time and should be something that the team leader understands as an important focus of the work the team does. Fink notes that trust seems to have three basic components – honesty, reliability and caring (2013: 3) – and when relational trust is built up in any organisation, it enables people to work with confidence. When I was asked to be on the group that was going to set up a new school, I knew that the 15 strangers who assembled in that room on a winter's evening were a group of people who knew nothing about each other, a prerequisite for trust. It soon became apparent that most of them had no experience of education. How then did this group of people go on to create an outstanding school? For me, trust was incredibly important, as I was elected chair because the group saw I had the most education experience. They put their trust in me, and I, in turn, endeavoured to put in place group processes that would enable us to become a team over time by:

- encouraging them to ask when they didn't know what was happening;
- allowing people to listen to each other's opinions before taking decisions;
- discussing our values as people and how that might apply to the school;

- celebrating success on the way to the new school and when it opened;
- giving everyone a voice in decision-making, even those members who appeared initially to be 'difficult'.

There was, of course, more than that. We made mistakes and learnt from them for one! The key thing that made us into a team from very near the start was that we had a key purpose – to set up a new school. I trusted that even difficult members had this in mind and that I could learn from them. The difficult member of the team is often the one that is least like you, and whose motives you find difficult to fathom. If you can focus on their skills, rather than their behaviours, then you may be able to find the job that is best for them in the team. Our team member who was always asking questions about detail could hold up meetings, but was a star turn when we needed someone to get details out of non-responsive builders. As the formal leader of the group, I also had to decide when such behaviour was blocking the team purpose and take action to make a decision that not all agreed with or made me unpopular with some of the team. Trust was a fundamental component of the success of that team, and an awareness that we were not all the same but had different personalities and skills which would mean that there would be different roles that suited some better than others. Bolam et al. (1993: 96) put it well when they wrote: 'We are now comfortable enough to disagree with each other and it is very productive.'

Roles in a team

There are many theoretical viewpoints about teams and their leadership, and it is an area where there is still great debate and discussion about what is the most important aspect to focus on (Adair, 1998; Duignan and Macpherson, 1992; Frost, 2008; Goddard, 1998; Katzenbach and Smith, 2003). In the personal example I have given above, I realised that I had no choice in the membership of the team, so would need to work with what I had. This is a similar situation for most 'formal' leaders of teams in schools, as they usually inherit a team, which may have effective practices, but the dynamics will change as the membership alters.

One of the most influential, well-known pieces of work on teams is that of Meredith Belbin (1981). Although there have been challenges to the work he did in industry with teams of managers, there are still some useful lessons that leaders can draw from his work. He suggested that teams worked best when the members understood that their formal role in the team may not be the most useful for the team at the time, and that part of their role in the team is affected by their personal characteristics and the way the team members interact with others. This requires team members to understand what their preferred role would be. Belbin drew together a typology of nine roles from his research, which can be found at http:// www.belbin.com/. You may find it helpful to look at the roles he identified and see which one appears to match your personal characteristics best. It is a useful way of examining how you behave in teams and can make you think about what your team might be missing in terms of how it works. One of the ideas I like particularly about Belbin's team roles is that each of the roles has what he calls an 'allowable weakness'. So, if we return to the governing body that I was on, my role as the chair, or coordinator in Belbin's scheme, would have an allowable weakness of perhaps not being very creative or inspirational because they are so focused on the task in hand. If you had that weakness as a chair, you might want to look for others in the team who were able to fill that gap. Crucially, I find that teams in schools find Belbin useful as a thinking point for where they are with their teams. The same is true of the work of Tuckman (1965) and Tuckman and Jensen (1977). Tuckman looked at the stages through which teams move: *forming*, where people get to know each other, and *storming*, where members test out ways of working, are the first two stages. There may be conflict around these stages and the underlying values. The suggestion would be that teams should move on to the next two stages of *norming*, where skills are revealed and leadership patterns emerge, and *performing* as a mature team, able to tackle the team objectives effectively. Again, if I look back to my governing team, it is obvious that, although we did move through these stages, they were not linear, and often we had to storm to perform. A later stage that was added was *mourning* where events mean that either they team breaks up or reforms in a different way. Mourning is an important stage, to acknowledge both what the old team has completed and the feelings that may have occurred during the team's time together. Mourning may also be important when the team continues but there is a significant change in team leadership. The following vignette is an example of real-life mourning that also applied to teamworking.

Vignette

Simon had just gained his first headship of an English 7–11 primary school. The previous head, who had been in post for 15 years, had died after a long illness. This head had been a mainstay of village life and popular with parents, staff and children. Simon realised at once that he could not make his mark as the new leader either with the team in school or the community by not acknowledging and celebrating the life and work of his predecessor. He began his work in the school by finding out informally about the previous

(Continued)

(Continued)

head and encouraging the staff to consider what would be a good way to remember all the things that he had done. In all of this he was sensitive not to impose his own ideas but to offer the staff time to reflect and share. The idea of a new garden in the school grounds with a sundial dedicated to the previous head was the finished idea. This was then made into a project for the whole school community and was opened at the end of Simon's first year. It enabled him to have a part in the past, but also meant that the staff were able to mourn yet look forward with good memories of the past.

Most team's mourning will not be of this type, but Simon's approach could be used effectively to move a team on by acknowledging the past, while signalling to the future. This would be particularly true of a very long-serving team.

Team leader skills

The work of Belbin and others might suggest that there are some team leadership skills that are innate. There are also some personal team leadership skills that can be learnt and developed over time, even if you may never be quite as good at them as those team members that just seem to have whatever the skill is innately. The team leader needs the wisdom to know whether to augment their own skill level, rely on someone with the skill already highly developed or suggest another team member makes that a priority for them. Take, for example, the skill of time management. There are countless books, quizzes, etc. on how to improve your time management, and I am sure you can find one of these if you know this is a skill you need to work on. Time management is a very personal skill, but if you are a team leader you do need to be honest with yourself if there seems to be not enough time in the day. Is it because you know that no one else can do this task better than you? Or perhaps you secretly like being on the go all the time as it deflects from other problems in your life? It could of course be nothing to do with you but with the team task. Is the objective doable in the time given? Ronald Reagan, the US president, apparently was once told that there was a specific task that needed doing. His reply was: 'Do you want it good, or do you want it Friday?' neatly summing up the leader's dilemma between the perfect solution or the one that they can realistically offer in the time allocated for it.

A linked skill for leadership to time management is that of delegation in teams. Again, trust is a major component of effective delegation. Once a task has been delegated to a team member, the leader has to trust that person by giving them the authority to make decisions as they go along and to be accountable to the team if there are mistakes. From the leader's point of view, this can seem like a risky enterprise as it may all go wrong. Team members will never be able to take on more responsibility if they are not given a chance and the leadership skill is to match the task to the person best able to do it and learn from it.

Anyone who has held a formal leadership role will realise that meetings are usually a large part of that role, but are they used well?

Vignette

One university leader in the UK on taking up a new post felt that all the meetings that happened were mostly not helping the university move forward. He took the decision to remove the chairs in all the meeting rooms, telling staff that this would facilitate only meetings that were really necessary. This grand leadership gesture had two functions. It showed that he was serious about reforming the faculty's culture but also that he knew that the current meetings culture was not serving the needs of the faculty. The chairs were eventually returned, but meetings never returned to the length that they were before he arrived. People had learnt to ask whether they really needed a meeting.

There are times when only a meeting will serve the purpose of the team. This is usually when the objectives are concerned with aspects that are best dealt with face to face. If that is the case, then it is important that anyone who is not able to come to the meeting is offered the option of virtual attendance or to be filled in afterwards. When meetings are seen as important to an organisation's functioning, they are usually well attended. These kinds of meetings are useful because they:

- can facilitate understanding between the team members, both of their roles and also their characteristics as people;
- allow everyone to hear ideas at first hand and ask questions;
- help foster joint responsibility for decisions.

This will only happen if the meeting is well run and that may depend on the actual purpose of the meeting. Some are for information (but sometimes this can be done better outside a meeting) while others are for problem-solving and/or decision-making. A smoothly run meeting leaves the attendees thinking and feeling that it was well spent in terms of their time and that the result will be acted upon by the team leader (if that is the function of that meeting).

Activity 20

Take time to examine the next meeting you are in. Was it necessary? If it was necessary, why was it needed? If not, why not? Was there a tangible outcome or benefit to the team, the organisation or just one individual? Write down one specific skill that you saw exercised for the benefit of the team and the progression of the meeting.

The role of the leader probably came into your answer. Their skills at keeping the meeting on track and involving the maximum number of people are crucial. Tone of voice, skill at summarising and managing the allotted time are also vital. The room itself probably came into your summary, as it can be set out to ensure maximum participation. Finally, the notes or minutes taken at the meeting need to be fit for the purpose of the meeting and accurately reflect the views expressed. Length of meeting is also a crucial factor. My rule of thumb is that any meeting longer than two hours is ineffective. Do you agree?

The ideal team

This brief chapter has set out to show that there is no ideal team but that the formal or informal leaders of teams can make a great deal of difference to whether it is useful to have teams in an organisation and not just groups that meet occasionally. What makes one team effective in a situation will be down to many of the items this chapter has covered, but it will again be contingent on the context. Leadership development in teams is all about having the skills to lead the team through the various scenarios that will occur, from making a decision to framing a new way of working for the school. The ideal team probably does not exist without the context that makes it work so well. As we have seen over these last two chapters, the leader is vitally important in crafting that context to enable progress to be made on whatever issue it is that the team was formed to tackle. There are many challenges to this ideal along the way and many mistakes to be made. Leadership challenges are part of the intrinsically social nature of leadership, and are in some ways the fire in which the leader's skills will be forged. The next chapter looks at some of these challenges in detail, and how leader's own skill development is fundamentally bound up with the task of learning from challenge.

Personal leadership challenges

In this chapter I will:

- examine challenges from inside and outside the organisation you work in and your ability to directly or indirectly influence them;
- discuss the positive and negative parts of leadership challenges and their effect on the personal;
- ask you to use your journal to define your own key challenges at the moment;
- why you define them as such and what action you might take.

This chapter looks at what makes a challenge for all kinds of leaders as they develop. My view is that *personal* challenges are important, and will vary for you as you develop as a leader in different types of organisation. As this book focuses on the personal, that is the thread that runs through the chapter which seeks to remind you that leadership is a process as well as an individual characteristic, and through several vignettes asks you to look at what constitutes a challenge for you and what the key components are that can make a situation difficult or challenging. It is a truism that someone's challenge is another person's opportunity, but in many instances this can be the case. I will ask you to think about what has happened in your past leadership experiences to make you embrace some challenges and yet avoid others.

The chapter helps you begin to analyse the skills necessary to make those good judgements that move situations forward and refine your own skills and knowledge. The effective team described in the last chapter might be able to help a team member rise to the challenge or alternatively use it as an opportunity if they have particular skills in that area.

There will be reminders about the role of teams in challenges but much of the focus here will return again to the personal, while overall the chapter aims to help you focus on your current personal challenges and how you handle them in order to develop your ability to make sound judgements around challenges in the future.

What is a challenge?

A challenge is one of those words that can be used to mean several things. At its most basic, a challenge is a test of some kind – of your own abilities or the resources you have available in your organisation. Any task needs to have a level of challenge in it to make it interesting. In this chapter, the word is used to specifically mean something that comes along that you find difficult initially and eventually leads you to change your personal perception in some way. In the leadership literature and often when I am talking to educational leaders, challenge often seems like an optimistic way of describing a difficult problem involving people. Downs and Adrian (2004) make a powerful point when they suggest that people have a tendency to define problems in the light of the solutions that are already available. Your reaction to a challenge may mean that you rise to the occasion magnificently, or just the opposite. A challenge which really should be easy causes you concern. This may well come from your past and the personal narrative you have been building up in your career. Earlier, I discussed how organisations use narratives to manage meaning, to communicate core values and to negotiate social order and identity (stories, legends, myths), and how your own personal narrative or personal interpretative framework (Kelchtermans et al., 2011) helps you understand your own leadership development. Narratives help leaders express their emotions, help them to understand their organisational reality and at the same time assist them in constructing new realities. Each new challenge will be woven into your narrative for use in the future. One of the aspects of leadership which was mentioned earlier was that leadership is about creating a framework of meaning for followers (Fineman, 2000) and that we are all capable of holding and resolving different social-emotional narratives about who we are, who we were and who we wish to be (Armstrong, 2011). This holds particularly true when we face a personal challenge, but is also important for other types of challenges where your judgement of the 'people, task, and situation' may be crucial.

Types of challenge

There are of course other challenges that leaders face, from ones that can mean dealing with old buildings, planning and maintaining finances to what it means to be a leader in international schools. These will still involve working with others to a lesser or greater extent. While the former is practical, the latter is more concerned with values. As a developing leader, these sorts of situations are ones in which you will have to judge what your resources are, when to deploy them and perhaps who best to deploy. The answer may not be you. There may be someone else who could take on that particular challenge – part of the bank of skills that effective leaders build up among their team members. Recognising that most leadership challenges are part of the leadership throughout the organisation is important too. The way that formal leadership roles are constructed is essential, as is the informal or hybrid (Gronn, 2011) forms of leadership that are part of the leadership context. The experienced leader knows when they need to step in and when to trust others. The exercising of judgement, and growing wisdom, built up from your personal narrative is an important thread that runs through most challenging situations. As Einstein once said, 'A clever person solves a problem. A wise person avoids it.'

There are also many conceptual challenges that developing leaders face; where values are challenged; global changes provoke challenge or professionalism seems to be compromised. These kinds of challenges are beyond the remit of this chapter, but are worth extra exploration (Bottery, 2004). Bottery notes (p. 143) that although individuals are progressively more identified by global forces, there are still opportunities for personal freedom and agency in building their own professional identity over time. It would be unwise for a developing leader not to understand these opportunities.

Emotion and personal challenges

My own view is that emotion plays an often unacknowledged but powerful role in the way a challenge is viewed in the context of both the person and the organisation. Emotional rules (Hochschild, 1979) govern who can feel what and when in organisations. What is acceptable socially in one situation is not in others. Fineman (2008) reminds organisations that more general societal discourses seep into the construction, meaning and politics of emotion. He calls this societal valuation an *emotionology* – society's take on how certain emotions are directed and expressed, which is embedded in and shaped by organisational routine. I have already noted in Chapter 7 that the emotional society of the school is an important strategic resource in crafting the context. Within any challenge, there will be an emotional element, but these emotional components will differ in intensity as emotional practices are saturated with values and group interests. Fineman calls these practices the products of the cultural emotionologies to which we are all exposed and which is a source of power in organisations though often unacknowledged. In other words, leaders may be able to face a personal challenge with all their planning and strategic skills in place, but if they fail to take notice of the emotional component of social settings, they will be missing one of the most influential aspects. This is also true of the personal side of any challenge: how emotion affects the inner life of the leader and their own sense of what might be emotionally important in any situation. When you look back on the challenge as part of your leadership narrative, you will absorb the learning you had from the challenge, and its abiding characteristics are the ones that you will most often weave into the story of how it all happened. This does not mean that all challenges will have a positive outcome. In some way your narrative will change, the meaning of the event will alter and perhaps even aspects of your professional identity will adjust to what you have discovered about yourself.

Activity 21

What aspect of leadership practice do you hate/avoid/do badly? How do you know this to be true of you? Note down in your journal at least two instances of this practice recently where you know that you either avoided a challenge or handled it ineffectively.

If you were to compare this activity with a trusted friend, you would be likely to discover that the scale of the challenge differs and, even if it was the same or a similar challenge, the way you resolved it will be different. The useful thing to remember is that practice in certain areas that you find challenging will overcome those difficulties. When a personal situation arises that is extremely challenging, all of the previous similar events will coalesce to either help or hinder the outcome. Another aspect of personal challenge that is often forgotten is to do with experience of similar challenges in the past and how you have dealt with them. Context and experience are particularly important when starting a new organisation. While writing this book a head teacher of a new school in London who had had no teaching qualifications and little experience in running a school resigned after being in the post for only six months. Using your own experience of challenge, your reading so far and your journal notes, you may want to consider what aspects of the leadership challenge might be most difficult for someone in this situation. I would just note that challenge will also have a personal component, where the individual has to decide whether they have the knowledge, skills and experience to deal with the unique circumstances that face them. The next section looks at how personal challenge is framed by whether it is from within or from outside the organisation you are working in.

Inside and outside

As you develop as a leader, your 'bank' of skills and experiences should grow and change at the same time. Other chapters in the book have discussed how you might build particular people skills within your educational community. Bottery (2004) makes the point that individuals are not part of just one community anymore, but may work within different 'communities' where they can develop their leadership identities by choosing the challenges that they face. These challenges will be easier to overcome if that community is both supportive and yet questioning of their leadership. The community that forms an effective governing board highlights this mixture of challenge and support as leadership decisions are carried out. Helping the school leader to make sense of ordinary events as well as particular challenges is the governors' role in the school community in countries such as England. Many leaders will find their community support in their teams or from organisations such as unions and professional associations. The local social community will be as varied in its characteristics as the people within the organisation, from negative to supportive, from connected to disconnected to their local school. The ideal would be to face any challenge (inside or outside) fully equipped with the skills, advice and resources (physical and emotional) to complete that challenge successfully. For the leader, one of the big 'people-focused' challenges is to be able to communicate both inside and outside the organisation clearly about its values, its progress and the subtle interconnections between parents, school and students. When there is a different challenge to the status quo such as financial problems, communication becomes even more important.

Communication

Clear effective communication is a challenge for organisations but also for the individual leader. Communication is one area where many leaders seem not to understand the nature of the challenge. As George Bernard Shaw, the Irish playwright once said rather pithily: 'The biggest single problem in communication is the illusion that it has taken place.' Communication is part of the way new leaders can define their identity as a leader in any given situation; their aim is to express what the leader is thinking or doing in a certain situation. Through the way that leaders communicate, effectively or otherwise, people in the organisation are given the evidence with which to evaluate the leader's thoughts and actions and decide how they may react in response. This is not just relevant to official communications such as emails or newsletters because communication is an essential social component of organisations, and one of the essential components is talk. Emotions can be described and emphasised through talk, providing the frame within which people relate to each other. Oatley and Jenkins (2003) give a compelling suggestion for the power of talk in social relationships. They suggest that it is through talk that people define and redefine both their relationships and their own sense of self. By presenting experiences to others through talk, they argue, people build both positive emotional bonds and deep aversions to specific people. For the leader, then, talk can be a way of building social networks and connections, and also a way of redefining situations when discussing them with others. Even the most mundane everyday conversation is structured by rules and power dynamics.

Vignette

This vignette is based on an conversation overheard while waiting in a school reception area. Inside a very small area there are three people and myself. The school receptionist, behind a desk in the corner directly next to the door, has asked all three of us to take a seat while waiting for the appropriate member of staff. Other people go in and out through the front door, in front of reception and the visitors during the conversation that follows:

Parent:	*Will Mrs Brown be long?*
Receptionist:	*I have called her. She is in a meeting.*
Red-eyed adolescent:	*I don't want to be here.*
Mother:	*Stop crying.*
Adolescent:	*I can't* (sobs)

(The crying gradually gets louder and is ignored by both mother and receptionist.)

(Mrs Brown, the Year Head, enters from the school side of reception.)

Mrs Brown:	*Good morning Mrs Jeffries, come with me and we will discuss where we go from here. The situation is getting to be extremely difficult for all the staff you know.*

(All three go into school, adolescent still crying.)

This is a small snapshot in time but illustrates some of the complications of communication. The first thing that struck me at the time is that the young person is virtually ignored as part of the communication. There are communication conventions such as greetings being attended to, but Mrs Brown's attitude and body language suggested to me as a disinterested observer that the student's views or emotions were not important to any solution to whatever 'the situation' was. The receptionist did her very best to ignore all three of us. Apart from what it says about communication in general, it also reminds us that *place* is also important in conversations, and the cramped reception area was not inviting and very public. It also is very telling about the power dynamics in that school.

Communication aids clarity. There are many important issues, which you may want to follow up in more detail in a specifically communication-focused work (Hargie, 2006). Actively thinking about what, how and why you are communicating is a key skill. There are so many ways to communicate 'the message', from social media to paper to talk. The context, as was shown above, really does shape the meaning of the message as it is received by the listener. There are often subtexts to the original message that the speaker does not identify but the listener hears. The challenge for a leader is to remember at all times that communication is a two-way process, not just dependent on what is said but on underlying cultural issues, where leaders sometimes draw unwittingly on what they assume are a shared cultural background and beliefs. Effective communication relies on everyone recognising those shared values. This is true when looking at the school context, but is particularly important in international contexts, where verbal or non-verbal clues might be misinterpreted by a new leader from outside that context. Context and identity are again closely linked. The identity of one group can be based on shared experience, shared language (often including jargon) and reflect dissimilar views about 'the way we do things around here'. Leaders who take on a merger of any kind will be particularly aware of this, as that context highlights all the dangers of poor communication. Hargie (2006) emphasised the importance of a good communication climate in an organisation when he pointed out that what staff value most is face-to-face communication, good communication with senior staff, ready access to information and good upwards communication. The challenge for you as a leader is working out how to make this happen in your organisation. Another communication challenge is working with those people in your organisation who do not seem to share your beliefs and values about the nature of work or appear to be getting in the way of progress.

Difficult people

The challenge of the 'difficult' person is one that features in many discussions in organisations. It is salutary to remember that there are many types of difficult person; one person's difficult person is often another's valued colleague; sometimes people become 'difficult' for a whole variety of reasons. There will be instances where the difficult person seems not to have good relationships with anyone in the organisation, but these are rare. Even the latter instance is workable if the job they do does not involve much people-focused work but is unlikely in such a person-focused environment as education. The difficult person is usually the one who you view as getting in the way of the strategic focus of the organisation or causing the climate in work to be unpleasant. The challenge is how to tackle this problem, for as there are many kinds of challenges, there are many kinds of difficult people and diverse levels problems to face.

What is certain is that if the difficulty is left unchallenged it will grow and possibly become a crisis. You may want to note down now in your journal one difficult person for you, and what you have done to make sure that they don't block the real challenges that the organisation is facing. There are many books that suggest ways of coping with difficult people. It is important that communication should be fact based avoiding emotional language, especially if you know you have a weak point where you could become upset. Planning difficult encounters in advance can be one way of making sure that you do not push any 'buttons' that will make the conversation even more tricky and allow you to perfect what is often called the 'broken record' technique where you stick to your key focus for the discussion. Hargie (2006) noted that you can only draw on how people behave to deal with them, as in a sense that is all you can really 'know' about them. One lesson that many leaders learn early on is that you cannot change the person but you can change how you interact with them. They may change over time, but it is unwise to make this a foundation stone of your work with them. It is also salutary to remember that there have almost certainly been occasions when you were that difficult person!

Difficult people are part of working in social groups, as are people with personal difficulties. Despite the personal power often exercised by the difficult person, most leaders will find that it is more likely that day to day they will be dealing with the personal side of people who are affected by situations beyond the control of the school. The person with problems, often from outside the organisation, may attempt to manage them in many ways from finding work a refuge to not being able to concentrate on the tasks in hand. Leaders who know the people they work with well and some of their background are often able to understand when a previously effective teacher becomes unable to cope and look for solutions. In many cases, this can stop a difficulty becoming a crisis with people on long-term sick leave.

Vignette

A head teacher I knew told me that knowing staff well was an important part of how he made judgements. He illustrated this by telling me about a member of staff who came to school very upset and he was asked to see her. It turned out that her cat was very ill. As she lived on her own, the head felt that the cat was as important to her as an ill baby or spouse so should be her first priority. He sent her home and said to me: 'Staff remember the little gestures. You can have all the vision and values you want, but it is the support at moments of personal crisis that people remember.'

The importance of judgement here is again crucial. Leadership in education has many personal challenges. It is all too easy to get caught up in the difficult and the challenging and think that by putting in more hours, working around the difficult person or trying harder to convince someone that the difficulties will cease. Your own 'outside work' life will only suffer as a result and the challenge of a formal leadership role can destroy your health and relationships. Much of the writing in this area concentrates on stress and leadership.

Stress in leadership positions is part of the emotional side of leadership. Many leaders are aware of the concept of emotional intelligence, developed by Salovey and Mayer (1990), often called the architects of emotional intelligence. They define this as 'the ability to monitor one's own and others' feelings and emotions, to discriminate among them, and to use this information to guide one's thinking and actions' (p. 189), and two of its the key components are managing your own emotion and that of others (Goleman, 1995; Salovey et al., 2001). Tuning into emotions can help leaders read the warning signs in themselves and others. Hess and Kirouac (2000) talk about how emotional displays are able to provide information not just about the feelings of the one displaying the emotion, but also about their relationships with those around them. Hess and Kirouac underline the difficulty of knowing what emotional displays actually mean when you view them in others – is the angry colleague using anger to dominate a discussion? However, when your own emotional regulation goes awry, this is a sure sign that something in your work or home life is out of kilter. The leadership challenge is to your own view of how a leader can or should behave.

There are also many positive things that can lift some of the emotional stresses that both individuals and social groups can suffer from. Foot and McCreaddie (2006) examined the uses of humour as a social skill, as a means of communication in an organisation, because it is 'an essentially shared experience' (p. 298). One of the social roles of humour is its role in managing stress and anxiety. Foot and McCreaddie suggested that humour is a coping mechanism that can help you save face in a difficult situation, help you cope with embarrassing moments and be a safety valve in difficult and anxious times. It appears to be a very effective way of reducing stress and building up social bonds. Although there has been very little research work on humour and leadership, you might like to consider your own sense of humour and how you deploy it (or not) as a leadership skill.

Activity 22

This activity is in four parts.

1. Think of a point in your leadership career where you struggled with either a difficult person or a person with difficulties. Note in your journal the actions you took.
2. What would you do differently if a similar situation occurred?
3. Write down three important personal challenges at the moment. They should be challenges that relate to you personally in terms of knowledge, relationships, time or something that you may not display on the surface as you continue to portray the unflappable leader.
4. What actions might you take now to avoid your life getting out of balance?

If you have a critical friend as part of your leadership development plan, you may wish to share aspects of this with them and ask them for feedback. For example, you might not know how you display stress. It may not be the way you suspect. A colleague of mine has a hugely untidy office but she can always find important bits of paper. However, she cannot find paperwork when she is stressed, and would find it impossible to admit to most colleagues. You may think your wonderful sense of humour helps you sail through challenges but a critical friend may have another view. These social interactions are part of that facet of emotional intelligence that speaks to understanding your own and others feelings and responding in the most appropriate way in that particular context.

Summary

This chapter has taken an unusual approach to the idea of challenges by concentrating on the personal dimension. It has begun to explore the ways in which your personal challenges can be viewed and suggested that the personal side of leadership skills is very important. In particular, clarity of communication is central in most challenging leadership situations, whether they be in one-to-one situations or in groups where influencing is difficult because of the context. I have sought to emphasise that contextual factors may heighten or diminish personal challenges but that social relationships are a cornerstone of effective communication at all times. This chapter does not mean to suggest that the personal side of managing challenges is more or less important than some of the other leadership skills that this book discusses. Leaders need to develop the skills to judge the most effective ways of building and maintaining relationships in social groups. I find Hargie's (2006) idea of communication as skilled performance or Goffman's (1959) presentation of self in everyday life very useful in terms of thinking through challenging situations and would be works that you might want to read to expand your knowledge of this area. Hargie said that skilled performers realise the importance of the interpersonal and are able to blend together all aspects of their knowledge about human behaviour in order to respond to others in the most appropriate way for that context. As you become more attuned to your own personal challenges so your leadership skills in this area will develop.

Further Reading for Section 2

- Bolman, L. G. and Deal, T. E. (2003) *Reframing Organizations: Artistry, Choice, and Leadership.* San Francisco: Jossey-Bass.
  Broader text looking at different organisations through 'frames'. Covers useful issues such as power and conflict which can be applied to an educational setting.

- Jones, J. (2005) *Management Skills in Schools.* London: Sage.
  A very practical book which looks at the skills that leaders need to manage effectively, covering coaching, team development, coaching and performance management.

- Preedy, M., Bennett, N. and Wise, C. (eds) (2012) *Educational Leadership: Context, Strategy and Collaboration.* London: Sage.
  Edited book with excellent chapters on collaboration, partnerships and external and internal contexts.

- Riley, K. (2013) *Leadership of Place.* London: Bloomsbury.
  A book which brings together many educational voices, especially those of young people and the contexts in which they live.

Section 3

Leading across boundaries

10

Boundaries and change

This chapter will look at:

- the concept of boundary spanning and its relationship to leadership;
- change and educational leadership;
- personal leadership skills and change;
- the emotional and cultural components of change.

This section's title requires an explanation before moving on to approaches to change, though they are linked. The concept of boundaries in this section is used to focus in on both your personal boundaries in terms of skill and expertise and the boundaries that are created by people, consciously or unconsciously, so that they can be comfortable with the limits of their expertise. Leaders need to be able to *boundary span* in their leadership and move from managing and protecting boundaries (although this will still be necessary at times) to the capability to create direction and commitment across boundaries as the educational leadership environment becomes ever more complex in many countries. In other words, the aim of this section is to make you think about the way boundaries are used, both by yourself and those you work with, as a way of managing strategic goals and the changes that may become necessary in order to reach those goals.

The emphasis on boundaries will continue throughout the section, as you consider how the landscape in which your leadership is based is never static and the implications for leadership within that context. It may also be useful to add a reminder that leadership is not for the titular leader or leaders alone, but is part of the social relationships within the organisation as a whole and the way people relate to each other in groups. Particularly when change is being considered, the way that followers confer leadership qualities (Haslam et al., 2011) on a particular leader is crucial. Leadership then is concerned with engaging the followers with the change in hand.

Boundaries

Earlier in the book boundaries were discussed when looking at transitions. In this chapter, boundaries are viewed as permeable and shifting in a globalised world. It is no longer feasible for solo leaders to lead and manage effectively in isolation, because without the ability to span boundaries, leadership and management can be insular, unproductive and static. Ineffective boundary spanning can lead the organisation and its leadership into difficulties not only because they fail to take account of some of the richness that can be found in collaborations, but also because they may miss something crucial that is happening either inside or outside the organisation.

Yip et al. (2011: 15) have a helpful categorisation when thinking about boundaries and boundary spanning. They see boundary spanning in five dimensions:

- vertical – across levels in the organisation;
- horizontal – across different functions and skills;
- stakeholder – working with external partners;
- demographic – working with diverse groups;
- geographic – working across regions and localities.

In their research, they identified horizontal boundary spanning as being one of the most often needed within an organisation, but with all the others growing and developing in a globalised world. Although this work was done outside education, it has relevance because it is a reminder to educational leaders not only of the importance of dynamics within the organisation but also of the changing nature of relationships within education. In education, boundary spanning will be concerned with reaching across internal and external boundaries in order to develop partnerships and collaborations, to sustain key relationships and to build alliances/networks and other forms of collaboration across organisational boundaries. This can involve very complex patterns of interaction at both local and national levels. It also involves developing a heightened awareness of what is going on in both the internal and external environments. Some of these myself and colleagues have discussed elsewhere (Coldron et al., 2014). Although that article is primarily about England, other leaders may find the ideas expressed useful in their own contexts. We suggest that the response of an individual head teacher will be understandable only when, by thinking of heads as people who make decisions, we realise that their actions may be judged in many different ways by differing groups of people. So, individuals will be participating simultaneously in many different fields in plural forms of identity and agency; formal leaders tend to pay attention to their position and identity in fields and areas of life other than that for which they are explicitly held accountable as head teacher. Similarly, developing leaders in organisations will also consider their position and identity within and across boundaries. Although this seems to be increasingly complex in many settings, an awareness of that complexity is vital when an organisation is thinking strategically about the future. Complexity management needs leaders to confront the ways in which their own and colleagues' personal leadership skills can be exercised and developed.

Yip et al. (2011: 20) draw on the idea of a nexus – a place where 'organizational leadership is more than the sum of its parts [...] it is the nexus of groups working collaboratively across boundaries that produces direction, alignment, and commitment.' This has echoes of hybrid leadership strategies that were examined in Chapter 4.

Activity 23

Identify the ways that you currently work across boundaries, and write them in your journal. What are the skills that you use and what are the particular contexts in which they have been most successful. Is there anything crucial you need to develop or change for the future?

Having thought carefully about your personal experiences of boundaries, boundary spanning and the idea of a nexus where people, groups and ideas meet, you may think that this is idealistic, given some of the challenges that you may meet. Finances and external accountabilities are some you may think of. However, the leader who is able to boundary span strategically may be more able to meet the challenges of the changing context because they are more able to utilise people and resources effectively.

Educational change

When I first came into education, change was something that happened in a very slow planned way. As my teaching career and then my academic career progressed, change began to be regarded as inevitable, and often thoughtless of consequences. Leadership and management are inevitably about change, because effective change is about development and achieving potential. Difficulties arise when the changes demanded externally challenge organisational or personal values, and often current ways of working which may have appeared to work well in the past. Productive change, Michael Fullan argued in the early 1990s, is 'too important to leave to the experts' (Fullan, 1993: 39). Many of the skills needed to manage change are the personal ones that this book has discussed in some detail. For leaders, change can mean a focus on being clear about what it is important to hold onto when boundaries are shifting and new alignments are being made. Change may involve innovation, where people are given the opportunity to take hold of a change with their own ideas. Very often, however, when there have been years of initiatives, the very idea of change can be viewed as something difficult that frustrates plans and alienates people. This can be for many reasons, including the short-term nature of much educational change, and the lack of long-term commitment to any one particular change. This leaves the educational leader at all levels with a dilemma, because they realise that the idea of change can be as destabilising as the change itself. Fullan's work on educational change has influenced greatly how change can be regarded in education. In particular, he argued that leaders need to know who actually benefits from the suggested changes and what the real educational purpose of the changes is. Looked at in this way, it is not difficult to see why educational leaders can become extremely frustrated by imposed models of change from regional and government levels, where the impact on the ground is either not effective or goes against the experience and values of the leaders who are asked to implement them.

Each context will view change differently. Examining the theories which you can draw upon in terms of change may be a useful way for leaders in whatever circumstance to understand something more about what is actually happening in the process of change. Change may be gradual, sudden or incremental. Leader's roles will themselves change and adapt during the process of change. Complexity is so much a part of change that it seems obvious, but leaders are often unaware of the processes they can utilise to manage at least some of the complexities.

Looking at change

There are many different ways of conceptualising change generally, not just the specifics in education. One of the most well known writers on change, Bennis (1969; Bennis and Nanus, 1985), suggested that internal change strategies are deeply embedded in organisational culture and the assumptions leaders make about that culture. The *empirical-rational model* assumes that most people are responsive to clear explanations about why change is necessary and will put the necessary structures in place. The *normative-re-educative* model presupposes that effective change needs values, attitudes and behaviours to alter, and activities are designed with this in mind. The *power-coercive* model is used when leaders have access to different sources of power – political, financial, personal – and many national changes to education can be viewed as being conceived in a power-coercive mode, which is then replicated within individual institutions. You may want to think whether these models work across different countries and contexts, and whether there are particular instances where one sort is more applicable than another.

The organisational context is again crucial.

Vignette

Dana had taught all her career in state schools in England. She applied for, and got, the headship of an international school in Spain, with an international staff and local and ex pat students. As a new head teacher, she wanted to make some changes in the way that the school was run and build up better relationships with both the parent body and the local community than had been the case before her arrival. The ongoing challenges that she had never faced before, and for which she had to both develop new skills and utilise her team, were concerned with the tensions of a more mono-cultural student body then she expected partly because the school was a private fee-paying organisation. The values she placed on the affective side of schooling had to be balanced by parental pressures related to academic tests and achievement. One of her key personal skills was working with people effectively, as well as being multi-lingual. These skills gave her a good basis on which to learn more about the new context and what boundary spanning activities she needed to put in place.

International schooling provided a very different context for Dana's growing skill set. The changes she faced there were internal, and would be viewed very differently by different parties in the organisation. Both internal and external changes can be related back to the subjective view of organisations and what people think is actually happening. Change can not only create, but can increase the already multiple realities that people have of their work challenges. Coupled with this, external policy change usually suggests that compliance with a greater homogeneity of officially sanctioned 'effective' practice can be completed rationally without reference to the subjective life of the school. Dealing with these subjective realities requires both intellectual and emotional mapping and sensing the areas of transition that are going to be most difficult for certain people. Leadership at a time of intense change is very unlikely to be the solo endeavour so beloved of policy-makers. Instead, leading in teams is more likely to both uncover some of those subjective realities and develop ways in which people can work towards new initiatives by helping them discuss and debate those areas which require particular commitments from them. The leadership dynamics already present in an organisational culture are thrown into sharp relief by any change process, and leadership may need to change too in order to facilitate the implementation of any alteration. Fullan also notes (1991: 49) that 'change is a process, not an event', and this is an aspect of change where personal leadership skills become vital.

Personal leadership skill and change

Resistance to change is natural, and many models of change initiation and management stress this point. Where the change originates can be the reason for resistance, as can tiredness or inertia after a plethora of change initiatives. Whatever the initial reason for resistance, the personal skills of those in formal or informal leadership positions can help develop an approach that acknowledges this natural tendency to stay where we are, especially if what we have done in the past has been effective and even commended by our partners.

Communication skills are such an important part of change. Many leadership writers recommend audits of how your organisation communicates before initiating important changes that touch on every aspect of the organisation, especially those that involve building a new vision for a new situation. The responsibility of those in leadership and management positions, who are either tasked to change something or see the necessity for change, is both to think about strategic implementation and to communicate the vision for change as carefully as possible. Planning, structuring and monitoring change initiatives also rely on communication skills. Communication skills in a time of change require clear knowledge of the essentials of leadership: 'know the people, know the task and know the organisation'. The culture of the organisation may be positive or negative with regard to change, and leadership communication may be concerned both with subtle communications of meaning through symbols and words on signs and notepaper and larger meaning-making activities such as development days. Ways of communicating change and the range of leadership strategies available at any one time are also closely linked to the established power bases in the organisation. Personal skills can involve leaders being able to manage the ambiguities inherent both in the dynamics of change and in the eventual outcome, by being flexible enough to make considered choices of differing pathways of action at different points in the implantation of a major change.

Fullan suggested (2001) that staff require leadership during change both to maintain the core values and stability of the organisation and also instigate new ideas for moving forward. Earlier, I noted that the ideas of Weick have a real resonance for educational leaders because of his focus on the ways that people's beliefs lead inevitably to the actions that they take, that people need to make sense of what is going on and the implications that might have for what they do next. The concept of sense-making is particularly useful when leading organisational change. Another of Wieck's ideas – that of 'loosely coupled systems' (Weick, 1976) – is also relevant. Drawing on March and Olsen, he argued that rather than viewing educational organisations as somehow consisting of tightly knit components, the idea that they were only loosely connected was much more useful. He argues that many things that happened in such organisations can 'prove intractable to analysis through rational assumptions' (p. 1). When thinking of Weick's ideas in terms of personal skills, I find it useful to remember that he describes concepts such as loosely coupled systems as *sensitising devices* that make you notice and question assumptions you may have taken for granted before. Also, viewing educational organisations as loosely coupled systems enables leaders to see how the 'identity, uniqueness, and separateness of elements is preserved' (p. 7), even when a great deal of change is afoot. As Wieck put it, 'the system potentially can retain a greater number of mutations and novel solutions than would be the case with a tightly coupled system' (ibid.). Many of the modern change dilemmas for educational organisations could be viewed as arenas where the boundaries of tightly coupled accountability systems meet those loosely coupled systems locally.

In education, there is a tension between the need for balancing the requirements of the organisation, the demands of the system and personal issues around work/life balance. I have mentioned earlier that writers such as Gronn (2003b) have characterised leadership as 'greedy work' eating up huge parts of leaders' time, but seemingly never ending as the personal stresses of misunderstanding and ambiguity leave little room for strategic overviews. More of an emphasis on the emotional components of change may help leaders make sense of what is happening outside the rational planning process.

The emotional and cultural components of change

Leadership and management are often conceptualised as rational processes, whereas much of my own writing has argued for the value of emotional insights as well. Henry Mintzberg (1979) argued that the work of leaders, including decision-making, sometimes involves the application of rationality – which he calls the 'cerebral' aspects of leadership, and sometimes rests on the development of vision and the encouragement of others – which Mintzberg refers to as the 'insightful' aspect. The cerebral approach stresses calculation and tends to see the world as if it were the components of a portfolio, using the language (words and numbers) of rationality. The insightful aspect stresses commitment and sees the world as an integrated whole, using a language that emphasises the personal values of the individual. Competing strands of an organisation's life cannot be ordered and controlled as rationally as some change management manuals would suggest. Such cultural understandings gained from trying to make sense of events emotionally are something I have argued in detail elsewhere (Crawford, 2011). In that research I agreed with Oatley and Jenkins (2003: 82), that emotions arise in our daily lives largely in terms of problems to be solved. The power of emotion is usually within a specific social context. Leaders often find themselves at the centre of much of this creation of emotional meaning. Understanding the importance of emotions in any change scenario is very important. Emotional understanding can allow both formal processes to develop and people to see progress. Most emotion is about something that is happening (Gordon, 1974; Oatley and Jenkins, 2003; Parkinson, 1995), simply because most emotions can be said to be 'about' something. To understand what change is 'about' leaders may think that one of the key competences of emotional intelligence (EI), self-awareness, is crucial. Also any circumstances where emotion is heightened are likely to result in behaviours that are not always desirable in terms of moving the organisation forward. These difficult and more elusive aspects of emotion for leaders are a feature of the work of Ackerman and Maslin-Ostrowski (2004). Their writing acknowledges that there are leadership events that leave 'wounds', and many organisations facing change have to deal carefully with emotional fallout. They argue for that leaders need to pay more attention to the affective realm and in particular the inner emotional experiences of leadership (p. 312). Any shift towards the affective in leadership does not mean a total dismissal of all cerebral, cognitive, rational insights, but it does suggest that leaders need to rid themselves of the view that to act rationally is to be in control. As looked at earlier, leaders also help define the emotional context of an organisation. It is within that context that people's definitions of emotional meaning take place, and part of the leader's role is also to help define those meanings. This can bring a great deal of pressure onto 'a leader', and is not good for long-term personal or organisational well-being.

Summary

Change can mean many things, from forced change to innovative new practices. Whenever change happens, the culture of the organisation and its boundaries move and regroup. Sometimes, the culture change can be huge, with consequences at all levels of the organisation, and other times small amounts of change may cause unlooked for resistance because they challenge the culture as it has been. What Pollitt (2007) calls 're-disorganisation' is not always the answer to the difficulties an organisation faces. Bolman and Deal (2003) noted that leaders need to justify why large-scale change is necessary, because change is costly emotionally for the people involved and for those who lead it, and can cost more than is expected financially. The sensitivity and adaptability of leadership strategies are essential to any thought-through approach that takes people with you and creates a climate where change is viewed positively. The next chapter looks at how a strategic approach, coupled with personal skills, is essential both to change and to leadership and management.

11

Strategic leadership, change and communities

This chapter highlights:

- change and strategic thinking;
- changes in education and schooling;
- managing engagement and partnerships;
- the importance of strategy leadership skills.

The context within which most leaders are working is usually evolving quicker than they are. Strategic leadership is a key part of change management and also a vital component of leadership.

Although this book's main focus is on the personal side of developing as an educational leader and manager, it is very important to stress that the ability to utilise your personal skills to manage boundaries will more than likely be ineffective if you ignore the importance of strategic thinking. The reason that strategic leadership has been left to later in the book is because strategic thinking grows out of your own personal development. Your own development needs to be thought about strategically. Personal strategic ability is part of developing as a good strategic leader. Growing and developing strategically is easier if you have developed some of the necessary skills in yourself and your teams. The strategic relationship between the school and the local community is also vital and can vary hugely depending on context. Leadership is concerned with actively influencing boundaries in order to really engage with communities, and identifying effective ways to do this (Crawford, 2012).

Where the boundaries lie in these areas is a concern that will run through this chapter. Leaders' understanding of boundaries remains crucial to understanding some of the strategic issues. At the heart of strategy is the ability to develop and maintain a sense of direction for your organisation over a period of time, and through changes of policy and personnel. This book was described in the introduction as a personal journey. It will hopefully enable you to plan your development as a leader more actively. So it is with strategy, or route maps as Gill (2011) called the process of strategic planning: 'ways of pursuing the vision and purpose of the organisation, identifying and exploiting opportunities, and anticipating and responding to threats' (p. 203). This apparently simple process, Gill emphasised, highlights for people the tensions inherent in 'what we are' and 'where we want to be' (p. 206). The context is again crucial.

Strategy and internal change

The last chapter discussed how organisations continue to change, sometimes slowly, sometimes as a necessity due to new issues. The focus there was on the personal side of change management, and how your own attitude to change and your personal skill set influences the approach you take to change. The context of the change is also important as some change initiatives have a higher potential to generate disagreements and the chances of making larger strategic errors. All change is also subject to the law of unintended consequences, where you have assumed the change is a 'good' thing, but others react in an unexpected manner. Strategic thinking may produce what is grandly called 'the bigger picture' but unless it is enacted carefully, paying attention to the cognitive and the emotional, the bigger picture may turn out in a rather unexpected way. The vignette below, based on a true story, illustrates this point.

Vignette

Ralph was a new head teacher of a small secondary school in an affluent area of England, where parents had the choice of several very good schools. He was much concerned with the thought of an impending inspection by the Office for Standards in Education (Ofsted). He knew an inspection was due within the next year, and he was concerned that the Maths department was not performing as well as it might. The three senior members of the department had been at the school a long time. Ralph had a meeting with them, where he discussed the school's exams scores in Maths which, though not bad, were not as good as the national averages suggested they should be for their particular group of

(Continued)

(Continued)

students. The maths teachers appeared to give him a good hearing. He then embarked on a period of lesson observation and feedback which he felt would help the staff become even better. He was therefore very surprised when all three resigned at the end of term to take up posts at nearby schools. As one of them said to him, 'There's a shortage of Maths teachers around here – we don't need all this hassle as we are good teachers.' The change that Ralph had initiated to improve his Maths department had led to him being three Maths teachers short for the next school year.

There are many points one could draw from such a scenario. If you work in a country where principals don't or aren't allowed within their contracts to observe teachers, you may wish you had the ability to influence in this way and are sure you would be more skilful at it than Ralph was. On the other hand, you may argue that the external pressures he was under caused him to overlook the personal in his quite reasonable plan to improve the Maths department further. As a new head, he had an enthusiasm for change which was not reflected in the personalities of his Maths teachers who were more cautious and were generally sceptical about the benefits of his approach. It may be useful for you to think about what he could have done differently. He had completely missed the local opportunities and how his actions threatened a well established group in his overall strategy to do well in the next inspection.

The vignette showed how a personal response to change can be as important as the need for clearer strategic thinking before embarking on changes.

Activity 24

Your own experiences of change will be varied. Try to think of an example of an instance where large changes were suggested in your workplace. Use these prompts to note down in your journal both your own view of the change and the strategic issues that were in play at the time. Ideas to consider are: your own role in the change and whether it was something you agreed with initially; your strategic ability to influence the change; the clarity of the strategies employed; the result with any unintended consequences. What were the personal implications for you? What were the strategic implications for the organisation?

Strategic leadership of change involves huge amounts of personal resources. Leaders need to think through their available resources and potential difficulties before they embark on change. A good basic premise is to emphasise clarity. Strategically, leaders need to be persuaded that the need for the change outweighs the difficulties of managing the change. As with all leadership issues, clear communication from the start is important, because persuasion (O'Keefe, 2006) as an influencing mechanism requires the ability to hone messages for different audiences. O'Keefe noted that skilled persuaders are able to see what is causing resistance and can construct messages which have the strategic aim of either reducing or getting rid of altogether those difficulties. They are also very good at following up their initial persuasive efforts as the changes begin to take effect and people's views alter.

Internal change has some advantages for anyone in a leadership role as in many cases they are the people who suggested or see the need for the change. Many leaders in schools are more often faced with the strategic implications of enforced externally mandated change. Ralph, for example, might not have approached his Maths department had he not been under very high accountability pressures himself.

Strategy and external change

This section could require a book on its own as schools all over the world face up to different external changes within a globalised environment. From high accountability to heavily unionised cultures, leaders' strategies will be very much influenced by their own context and personal educational values. Strategic leadership may involve engaging with previous socially excluded communities or actively attempting to mitigate the effects of such dynamics in schools. Other leaders may view the latter approach as imposing the values of one dominant group on another less influential group. In many cases, leaders are involved in new roles at the boundaries of schools (Edwards et al., 2012) which test their own personal beliefs about the role and meaning of education in any given society. Edwards et al. noted the development of the concept globally, through the Organisation for Economic Cooperation and Development (OECD), of a child who is at risk of failing at school and risking his or her future work prospects. Inter-professional working has been seen, in countries like England, as a way of schools being involved in all the local systems where the aim is to work together for the well-being of the child more generally than just schooling. Edwards et al. draw on the concept of *relational agency* where 'practitioners are not only able to recognise and draw on the expertise that is distributed across local systems, but also to contribute to it' (p. 250). This is particularly demanding in countries such as England where local accountability mechanisms, through the role of the local authority, are rapidly changing and losing power. This leaves the leadership of local schools to develop their own strategic responses to local issues partly determined by the positioning of their institutions (Coldron et al., 2014). Gill (2011) proposed that effective leaders are able to bring together and then communicate their strategies to their followers and other audiences in the community. Crucially, he noted that strategic leadership requires a sharing of values and an ability to continue having 'strategic conversations' (p. 200) as the organisation grows and changes over time. Strategic leadership is clearly cognitive, but at the same time it is a social and emotional process. Community-orientated leadership roles throw up new challenges (Riley, 2012). Riley identified layers of leadership 'of and with the local community, and of and with the broader locality' (p. 216), which raises not only personal demands on leaders, but means they have to wrestle with dilemmas such as the limits of the school sphere of influence and the different nature of leadership in particular contexts. For example, the social sphere of influence will be very different for First Nations school leaders in Canada (Carr-Stewart and Steeves, 2009), South Africa (Riley, 2012) and Scandinavian countries such as Norway and Finland. Urban and rural contexts will also play a part in the distinctive nature of your strategic approaches.

Activity 25

Try to answer the following questions about your own strategic approaches in your journal:

1. What are the most important *external* strategic dilemmas for you at the moment?
2. How far do your dilemmas cross boundaries both internally and externally?
3. Can you identify any strategic conversations that you have had so far, or ones that, with hindsight, might have been helpful?

Strategic skills are one means of maintaining momentum and moving the whole school community forward. All leadership is about influencing, to a greater or lesser extent, and the motivations of individuals, organisations and even communities are an important part of strategic leadership skills.

Managing engagement

The idea of engagement has a great deal in common with the idea of leadership. Gill suggests that both of these are subject to many and varied definitions, but he defines engagement as being about the commitment people bring to the workplace that is informed by their intellect and their emotions (p. 257), and means that they will bring to the organisation their best efforts, often beyond what is required of them in job descriptions. For a leader who is engaging strategically with the idea of where the organisation's future lies, the commitment required may be perfectly clear to him or her. Crucial to the carrying out of strategic plans is not only the positive attitude and clear motivation of a leader, but his or her ability to engage everyone else in the plans. People are motivated by a range of needs and desires, and at a very basic level leadership strategies need to understand the link between a person and they way they feel about their work. One person in your school may feel different levels of motivation depending on how their work is organised; another person may be motivated by personal financial necessity; another by love for a particular aspect of work. These varying scenarios are what makes motivation a huge and involved topic of which we can only scratch the surface. I have been surprised, over my years of working with individual educational leaders, how often they assume that what motivates them will motivate others. Many times, it may well be better to assume the opposite, as the vignette below suggests. Although the vignette is situated in the UK, the context is not as important in this case as focusing on the individual and their motivation for being at work.

Vignette

Christina was in her late forties and had worked at a primary school for the majority of her career as a teacher. She was known to community, staff and pupils as a firm but fair teacher, who seemed to get the best out of certain types of student. In the small (five staff) school she was also known for her ability to have a good reason why any plan was not going to work with 'these children', 'at this moment when there are so many other changes' and 'because you haven't taught as long as I have'. She never discussed her home life, although it was known she lived alone, and never volunteered to take on any extra work outside her contractual duties. Several younger staff felt she was a bit of an old misery. The newish head teacher Steve had great plans for the school but saw Christina as a bit of a blockage to his vision as nothing he said or did seemed to alter her 'this is what I do, and it's fine for me and the students' attitude. He classed her as a difficult person. It was only when a new teacher Paul arrived to run the expanded nursery that Christina became more involved in school life and the strategic journey the head wanted to take it on. Paul immediately identified her as a lonely individual, and he went out of his way to get to know her and to understand the role a private tragedy had played in her seeking to control her work life. He also discovered one thing that she was really good at, and encouraged her not only to share it with the staff, but among local schools. A much happier Christina began to engage with school life outside the classroom.

This is an interesting vignette for several reasons. It would be too easy to draw from it that the most important idea is that people should be happy at work. This is a difficult concept because, like leadership, there are many ways to conceptualise 'happiness'. What seems to be clear from much of the literature is that the relationship people have between their work and their emotional state are important (Hosie et al., 2007), and that the linkage between the two, although complex, means that people who are feeling involved and engaged with work may just feel more satisfied and therefore appear happier. This could be used as an analysis of the vignette. The alternative view would be that the reason happiness, engagement and related concepts are so hard to pin down is that there are great individual differences in people's own perception of them. Returning to work on emotion, I might argue that for Christina, affective emotional commitment was brought about by another's understanding of what it was she did well, not what she did competently. If you are interested in motivation and engagement, there are many avenues for you to explore to gain more insight. In terms of strategic engagement, your skills will be drawn upon in a variety of ways and fresh abilities may need to be created, whether personally or in teams, in order to meet new challenges.

The importance of strategic leadership skills

In some senses strategic leadership skills are neither more nor less important than many of the other skills this book has focused on. Some skills, like those concerned with communication, are a prerequisite for influencing outcomes more generally. One of the theoretic insights that I have found extremely useful in thinking about what is happening when change is planned or just when strategic ideas are being discussed is that of the psychological contract. Those of you who have read the book straight through to arrive at this point may be totally unsurprised by this as my book is heavily influenced by psychological constructs around emotion. Put simply, the idea of a contract between leaders and followers suggests that there are expectations on both sides of what needs to take place to fulfil the contract. These expectations can be physical and concerned with rewards or workplace provisions of offices, or relational to do with ideas such as respect, trust and commitment. Many of these expectations may be written down in job descriptions but others will be more multi-faceted and difficult to tie down. The idea of a psychological contract is useful in many ways to leaders who are contemplating a new direction or some strategic idea which may unwittingly change the nature of the contract. People come to expect certain dynamics in the workplace by custom and practice and by observing how people relate to each other. When change alters the dynamics of relationships, leaders can find it difficult to understand why people are still working on 'how we used to do it around here' instead of moving forward. Although strategy may be focused on the outcomes which will hopefully ensue if plans are implemented, people may be more concerned with the clarity and equity of the strategic processes that are put in place. What I think really matters about the idea of a psychological contract, and which you may want to explore further by reading more about it, is that the idea really stresses the intricacies of people management. As a leader what you promise to people is crucial, as is managing their expectations of what can be achieved, by whom and when. Although earlier in the book caution was urged around the idea of the charismatic leader, the concept of *transformational leadership* (Bass, 1985; Bass and Avolio, 1993, 1994) is particularly applicable to strategy and change management. Bass and Avolio suggested that a transformational leader was someone who was able to inspire followers by providing meaning and the right level of challenge in their work. This is rarely a solo task, and personal charisma is not a necessary personal characteristic to be an effective strategic leader. Accomplishing the strategic task may be eased by charisma, but it can also be achieved by the working together of many people in an organisation to achieve something they value ethically, and within the human and financial resources available.

To finish this chapter, you may like to try the following activity in your journal.

Activity 26

Returning the focus to the personal, note down your strengths when it comes to any issues to do with strategy – focus, vision, plans. What are your emotional reactions when the strategic plans that you have made come into contact with colleagues' worries about the future or distrust of the motivations behind what is planned? Note down three specific skills that you have already which help manage the uncertainty of others and yet maintain morale.

I hope thinking about these aspects will help you not only identify skills but also view leadership even more clearly as a process which is essentially relational.

12

Managing stakeholders and partnership boundaries

This chapter will:

- discuss the varying expectations that groupings or communities can have of leadership and of leaders personally;
- examine the various accountabilities of leaders – to whom are they accountable and for what?
- scrutinise the idea of boundary management.

Leadership in education is complex in ways that business leadership is not. The complexities of leadership and management are amplified by the variety of people who might be seen to be stakeholders, partners or even 'clients' in the educational endeavours of schools and other educational organisations. Glatter (2006: 9) put this clearly when he suggested that leadership in education is more akin to the not-for-profit sector. Schools and other educational organisations should be viewed as 'human service organizations whose core task is transforming humans'.

Those engaged in educational leadership have a focus on changing people in all sorts of contexts which is not often replicated elsewhere as a leader. I would also argue that this places a moral obligation on leaders to bear in mind the human cost of managing expectations and dealing with accountability mechanisms.

Educational organisations are often literally at the heart of a community. Leaders have to work hard to understand different community cultures and different professional cultures. They may reflect the values of the community they work with or stand for different values. Depending on your context as a leader, you may also need to be aware of governance and understand how leadership and management can be enhanced by good practice in this area. In some countries, school governance arrangements draw heavily upon the community. Although my own experience is context bound to governance in England, working with people in and from different contexts is the lifeblood of leadership in almost any context you might find yourself in.

Expectations

Different groups of people will have different expectations of what school stands for and how it should interact with the local community. Stakeholders can be defined as those groups who affect or are affected by an organisation (Hannah and Freeman, 1984). Education has a wider variety of stakeholders from students to employers, which adds to some of the intricacies of working across the various boundaries. You may find it instructive to look at who appear to be the main stakeholders in your country. Governmental policy may be full of rhetoric around parental and community involvement and the needs of the national economy, or it may stress the importance of the individual school. Individual communities will also have specific stakeholders in terms of education.

In most countries, school leaders value the input of the local community and seek to be effective facilitators of community involvement, both in day-to-day transactions and in broader community issues. Identifying the boundaries of the school's relationship with the community can be a tricky task because, as with all boundaries, the relationship will be flexible, porous and multi-faceted (Crawford, 2012). MacBeath and Kirwan (2008) have talked about 'a quality of leadership able to share a vision and sustain moral energy in the long term' (p. 37). Vision and moral energy are qualities often aimed first at parents, before being shared more widely with the community. Many school leaders' experiences as they develop their leadership skills are first with parents, and some communities will have a more homogenous set of parents than others, which adds to the skills needed to make boundaries flexible yet adhere to the core task of schooling.

Parents

I would suggest that power dynamics play a large part in all boundary relationships, but particularly with the parental body (remembering that this may not be one cohesive group). An individual parent entering a school may not feel an equal partner if their own school experiences were less than satisfactory. Alternatively, an individual parent may feel more powerful in any discussions that take place, drawing on their own workplace and viewing themselves as a client. As well as this some groups of parents may have more power than others, presenting you with an equity issue. This could be based on their socio-economic grouping, where one group has much more access to influence in the local community and their interface with the wider world.

A question you might like to ask yourself as you think about these issues is: how far is democratic participation of parties outside the school boundary really possible in strong accountability cultures, such as the USA and the UK? The role of head teacher (Bauch and Goldring, 1995; Goldring, 1986) appears to be central as to whether the parent/community relationship works and how well they are able to balance competing demands. They need to both support their own staff's authority and respond to the needs and interests of parents. Contextual factors for leaders to take into account include the geographical area, socio-economic factors and ethnic, spiritual and other dimensions which makes each school's context unique. Working with parents is an area where head teachers and senior leaders have built up experience from their time as classroom teachers, but a more facilitatory or other role may be required of them as senior staff.

Thinking of the boundaries throws up many different terms for working with parents, which can equally be applied to the wider external community. Some terms include parental involvement, parental engagement and parental partnership. Some schools have a history of working closely with parents and the community; others have deliberately kept the boundaries relatively impermeable.

Activity 27

How would you sum up the current state of boundaries at your school? Engagement, involvement, partnership, or none of these? What are the actions that have been taken that have either benefited the school/community relationships or damaged them?

Your answers may be more difficult to sum up than you thought. All of these concepts are worth exploring but the idea that they have in common is they all involve the wider social domain of the school. These social transactions exist across boundaries, and your own values as a leader influence the decisions that you will take over time and could depend on how worthwhile to the school's greater accountabilities such time-consuming boundary spanning is.

All schools sit within a wider national policy context and many leaders face a relentless focus on accountability and the standards agenda from central government. Gordon and Seashore Louis have argued (2009: 9) that this unremitting focus may mean that some schools create the kinds of involvement that privilege some groups of parents over others. I have noted elsewhere that a major premise on which schools function (Crawford 2012), within the social norms of the society, is that which constrains students to conform and obey authority. This premise could also be applied to leaders and the community more generally. This hypothesis does not always apply in different educational environments. Misunderstandings can occur due to many issues: differing values, the weakening of social bonds in society generally and less respect given to positional authority in some cultures. Your school's educational environment (another key part of its context) may be characterised by one of these issues or another more relevant one. The environment may also be one of stability or constant readjustment to external changes, and all of these will colour leadership issues and responses to issues.

As well as the formal leadership in school, many countries have governing bodies/councils/boards of trustees which are made up of varying groups depending on the setting. The accountability of the governing body will also vary. In England, there have been many high-profile cases since 2010 where the governing body has resigned or been asked to resign and has been replaced by an interim governing body chosen by the Secretary of State for Education. This highlights both the power of central government and the accountability of the governing body for standards in that school. A question that arises from this centralised policy concerns the role of parents and the local community in the life of schools. Many governing bodies will only have a small parental representation and many have no community advocate at all. The boundary has been drawn clearly here, with the governing body now sitting firmly inside the school boundary with clear responsibilities. Where the boundaries are drawn is dependent on many factors, including the willingness of all parties involved in education to work together.

Many school leaders can end up feeling overwhelmed as they strive to manage not only the educational outcomes but also aspects of community cohesion. At the same time, the idea of who or what represents the local community is changing, as in some countries changes to policy mean that the concept of the traditional neighbourhood school is disappearing. A good example of this is the free school policy in England as parental views about choice are given impetus by central government, and certain groups can then have access to funds to set up their own school after a designation process.

Boundaries can be flexible but in different ways. This is particularly the case in countries where the role of the community and parents is seen as particularly important. The vignette below gives a brief example of another context.

Vignette

In Japan there are 1,570 schools which run the School Management Council system. Their role is that of a critical friend and partner. In community schools, the School Management Council is established and appointed by the Board of Education. Appointees can include parents and, local residents. The principal has to report on school activities and school management policies need to be approved by the Council. In Mitaka City, Tokyo, there are councils in all the elementary and junior high schools in the city. The Council actively supports regional goals to meet the needs of the school. In Kasuga City, Fukuoka, all elementary and junior high schools have a Council too, with the school and community cooperating to support each other. The Council is actively involved in local events and festivals in the local community, and encourages students to become involved too. The outcome of this partnership is that problem behaviour among students has decreased. In Kyoto, they have established councils under the principle that children should be supported by all local people.

This vignette suggests a different kind of partnership and boundary drawing to the English system. One particular aspect that most school leaders will want to know is how far their own autonomy in any given situation will stretch. In many or all of these boundary relationships, school leaders are caught in the nexus of accountability and autonomy.

Accountability and autonomy

Accountability and autonomy are tied together in a symbiotic relationship in many educational contexts. On the one hand, leaders are urged to use the advantages of autonomy over their finances and perhaps the curriculum to develop new ideas for schooling, while on the other hand, systemic accountability mechanisms are put in place with the purpose of improving quality and achieving equity. In such accountability-driven systems, there is only so much autonomy allowed. This results in a paradoxical relationship, where leaders have to strive to make sense of how much autonomy they have within a particular policy context. Paradoxes arise every way you look in education. Hargreaves' (1997) notion of five paradoxes, framed by the social and educational changes in the Western world in the 1990s, is still a useful way of considering this because some of the paradoxes he identified have strengthened their hold in the intervening years. He suggested that growing decentralisation in systems was coupled with more centralisation, that the parental role seemed to be about giving up on parental responsibility for children's actions while expecting schools to take this on, that globalism creates more tribalism, and that calls for diversity in education are matched by an emphasis on core standards.

The very concept of accountability is in itself multi-faceted. It takes different forms in different countries and is bound up in the local context. Burke (2005: 2) stressed that accountability raises several deceptively simple but devilishly difficult questions such as 'Who is accountable to *whom*, for *what* purposes, for *whose* benefit, and with *what* consequences?' Holding individual schools accountable can be positively encouraged by government policy. Outcomes-based educational accountability relies on some form of compulsory assessment of student achievement. From this student achievement, governments decide whether educational standards for that country are reaching some nationally or internationally defined level. High-stakes accountability is a term that is often used when federal or national governments bring in sanctions of varying kinds when schools fail to perform to the decided acceptable level. Often in these scenarios parents and/or children are viewed as customers able to choose and change schools to find the best options. Critics argue that this means that instead of the system working to improve local schools, choice gives an illusion of control to parents which, in reality, cannot be satisfied. For educational leaders, the twin concepts of accountability and autonomy can be incredibly difficult to manage at a personal as well as an institutional level and contribute to some of the stress levels mentioned earlier in the book. Those in formal leadership positions can often pass the stress they feel onto the rest of the staff. Usually this is unwitting, but it is a danger that all leaders need to be aware of. Equally school self-evaluation, while suggesting accountability in which more people can be involved, has the potential to feed into both high-stakes accountability measures and stress levels.

Managing personal boundaries

In educational rhetoric, accountability is often presented as a strategy devised to improve educational outcomes and ensure equity. Performance measures of various kinds are introduced as a way of letting parents and the community make judgements on schools. This is predicated on the assumption that such measures are fair and equitable, and that hard data can be treated as reliable and valid as a predictor of quality for individual children. The tension is between individual progress and indicators of school progress in the wider system. The short vignette below illustrates part of this tension.

Vignette

Ben went to his local school in England. While he was there, the school received a judgement from the inspection system (Ofsted) that it required improvement. Despite this, Ben did very well in his exams, as did several of his friends. While he was studying for his university entrance exams, the school was re-inspected and found to be good. Ben applied for, and received, a scholarship to study at a prestigious American university. He valued his time at school, and did well. The school was proud of his achievements.

Why did Ben succeed? Ben may have been an exception in this school which could have been failing many others. On the other hand, Ben might have come from a background where education was highly valued and he had good parental support. Alternatively, many writers would argue that the inspection system itself is flawed and only examines a very narrow range of success indicators. The vignette does not tell us enough detail to make a judgement but it can already be seen that this is a complex area. What it brings out is that there is an inherent tension between the individual and the schooling system. Changes in policy make it more difficult for head teachers to use their professional judgement with young people such as Ben, as accountability measures, such as inspection in England, mean that they are always conscious that they may fall down on particular performance measures. Ryan and Feller (2012) have noted that performance measurement, particularly when it relies on quantitative data, has three problems. First, the setting of criteria for any kind of performance measurement is complex and implies agreement about the purposes of education. They noted 'selection of criteria of measure may implicitly determine educational values or priorities'. Second, because of the high stakes used with these measurements of performance, this has led in several countries to 'gaming the measures or opportunistic behaviour' ranging from teaching to the test to cheating. Finally they suggested that the link between budgets and performance has remained surprisingly 'relatively loose and limited'. This may well be changing as policy-makers realise the power of budgetary mechanisms.

As more and more educational contexts become decentralised and yet subject to hard accountability measures, individuals are asked both to take on more work and to progress work that may not align with their personal or professional values. Managing boundaries, literal or personal, becomes an ever more difficult task, because leaders can often no longer take for granted that their professional knowledge and leadership experience is the most important factor in a school's success. I am writing this from an English perspective, but you may like to think how much this is true of your context, and what the particular local features are that leaders need to bear in mind.

Ethical boundaries

The consequences of putting into practice various accountability and performance measurement constraints will vary in different national and local contexts.

Activity 28

Note down in the journal the key accountability mechanism that your policy context utilises. What are the consequences of this 'on the ground' for school systems and for your personal view of what education is for?

Begley (2012) has noted that leaders in many countries 'confront as a normal condition of their work a veritable quagmire of reform initiatives, curricular innovations and policy dictates' (p. 38). To succeed in this quagmire, leaders are often faced with ethical dilemmas, such as the allure of gaming, as mentioned above. Begley's suggestion is that leaders need to keep their own educational values and purposes at the top of the agenda when considering any of their leadership practices. This can lead to a multiplicity of ethical dilemmas for the principal dealing with parents, students and community as well as his or her policy context, because the ability to use professional discretion can be severely compromised. Begley's research found that the school principals in the study were often willing to try to sort out professional dilemmas on their own, seeing such dilemmas as not suitable for sharing with colleagues or a team – they were private dilemmas. This idea of a private dilemma runs counter to the idea of working across boundaries and in teams and would seem to burden the formal leader. Being able to share professional dilemmas with a team or be part of a professional learning community (Stoll et al. 2006) would seem to offer a way of steering your way among the complex and competing demands of the context.

The future: permeable or less permeable boundaries?

As a leader in education, you will come across many diverse stakeholders wanting not only your attention but a chance to work either with or against you in the local context. Your own knowledge and skills, closely linked to your professional ethical focus, may help you to navigate the boundaries with judgement, integrity and compassion for others. Trying to manage all of these boundaries on your own may come at unnecessary cost to your own health.

The following vignette is based on a research interview that I carried out into the challenges of headship.

Vignette

This head was relatively experienced and had once found himself in a situation where his life was out of balance because he was trying to do too much in the school, in the community and with national agencies. He had learnt from it.

> *Leadership can be a difficult job at times, but I remain convinced that the role can be both do-able and enjoyable if you have the confidence to set the right parameters. I have been to the brink and pulled back, and that's why I believe so strongly in home/work balance. Being a head teacher doesn't have to destroy your health or relationships.*

The last sentence of the vignette above is stark because it shows clearly that some of his colleagues had found leadership a destroyer of health and relationships. This bleak outlook may resonate with some readers. High-stakes accountability can be viewed as paying no respect to people's personal worth under the cover of improving the quality of learning for students. While formal leaders and potential leaders are viewed as disposable in what many call a 'culture of football management', the boundaries of the school may have to be less permeable in order to protect staff. On the other hand, the educational needs of young people are at the very heart of schooling, and educational leaders have a professional obligation to leading and learning. The ethical dilemmas for leaders are bound to grow even more complex, as the move to a more globalised education agenda continues.

13

Knowing your own boundaries – the capable leader

> This chapter will discuss:
>
> - whether there are key capabilities that leaders need to develop and enrich their professional practice;
> - how these relate to your own practice now;
> - how theory and practice interrelate for developing leaders;
> - assessing yourself.

This book's focus is very much on the individual and how they interact with their environment. Leadership draws on many capabilities, and a capable leader, in my view, is one who knows his or her own strengths and weaknesses.

On a personal level, the idea of being a capable leader draws on the whole leader – their personality, their life experiences and their leadership skills. Capabilities are closely related to your own personal leadership narrative and the capabilities of those individuals with whom you work. Some of the skills already discussed in this book have been concerned with those needed to manage change, communicate well, and understand and manage personal and professional boundaries, and this chapter will draw on these and other skills.

Many countries, including England and Scotland, have key standards for head teachers drawn up by professional groups and which may be linked to qualifications. These were looked at in Chapter 4. This chapter focuses on what you can do in order to explore the interplay between your own individual development and that of the organisation in which you work. By exploring your own capabilities, I hope that you will be able to draw upon your own sense of what Bolman and Deal (2003) call personal artistry. Personal artistry is about calling upon all your leadership and management capabilities to make sense of both everyday and challenging situations. As you read through this chapter, note in your journal if there are any particular areas of leadership that cause you tension, and how you might alleviate some of that by understanding what is behind the tension. Personal artistry is about enriching your professional practice in order to respond more effectively in the midst of change and ambiguities in education. It is about building up professional capital (Hargreaves and Fullan, 2012). Before looking at some of these ideas in more detail, I want to return to the difference between leadership and management, and if indeed it is a useful distinction.

Leadership and management

Almost everything that you do as a leader or manager is closely related to people both inside school and in the community. Being able to value and develop the work of others is something that is at the heart of all leadership and management work, because no matter how wonderful the systems you may devise as a leader, they are only as good as the people working with them in the organisation. For me this is where leadership and management meet (Crawford, 2003), as for me what is often called 'leadership' is about inventive management, and those who write just about leadership are looking for some sort of exceptionality that is rare. These terms, along with the one most often used in North America, administration, can be very confusing to the novice leader. Often leadership and management are used interchangeably in the educational literature, but occasionally management is used on its own to make specific points. Levicki (2001) argued that being able to understand the difference between leadership and management was a key differentiating tool of organisational analysis because management is about bringing order and consistency to key dimensions of an organisation, while leadership is most often about managing change. I see them as having a symbiotic relationship, where one feeds upon the other. Levicki put it well when he suggested that a manager has the ability to 'transform the complex and difficult into the simple and doable' (2001: 149), while a leader must be continuously strategic and have a vision of how the organisation can be at its very best. It is easy to see from that description that both functions can be carried out by one person or a team, and that effective leaders can also be inventive managers and vice versa. As leaders develop they may well be good managers, who learn more about how their organisation works through management of people, information and action. In that sense, I would argue that management and leadership are bound up together, and that there are times in an educational leader's career when one or other will come to the fore, depending on the context. If you can understand that the terms are complementary, it is easier to understand why so many different kinds of people can be effective in different contexts. They are also, I believe, the leaders and managers who are able to develop and enhance their own professional practice over time.

Developing and enhancing professional practice

In Chapters 3 and 4, various ways of developing as a leader were discussed and you may want to refresh yourself on those aspects before you read on. This chapter focuses in on becoming capable as leader, as people will vary in the leadership roles they take on, the boundaries they have and the contexts they work in. Most leaders in educational organisations started their work as a classroom teacher and will have taken part in various forms of professional development. Once you move into a leadership position, explicit focus on both the art and the science of leadership should become a recurring part of your professional practice. Making the most of the knowledge you develop over time can help you to build those professional qualities which make you even more capable at your work. However, a great deal of that knowledge may be context-bound or subjective. It may also be tacit, in that it may be difficult to verbalise or share at first. This is where sharing cognitive frames can be useful. Bolman and Deal's frames, as discussed earlier, are one way that can help individuals and groups share knowledge and learn from it within a particular structure. This may require feedback and support at different times. Becoming a capable leader requires you to ask yourself, and others, how you need to develop, and in what ways. It also requires you to encourage similar participation in learning of those you work with. Leading and managing people, developing their talents around the aims of the organisation and understanding our limitations are crucially important for professional development. One of the ways that has gained currency in recent years is that of key competences for leadership.

Competences

One way of looking at how capable people are has been mentioned above: the idea of standards or competences for leaders. Much of the work on competencies in education draws on the work of David

McClelland (1988) and Hay McBer, and Richard Boyatzis and colleagues (2002). They are all cognitive and social cognitive perspectives on motivation and capability.

McClelland's work on what motivates people is particularly insightful when thinking about what makes a capable leader and also an exceptional leader. McClelland's work is far-reaching and complex, and I would suggest following it up in detail if this brief overview engages you. He was very interested in what motivated people in the workplace, how thinking and motivation are linked. This led him to develop various assessment tools to help both employers and employees get the best out of their time at work. His research work was based around the idea that people have different motivational profiles; they therefore have different motivational needs. These motivational needs are found in differing balances in individual profiles, and McClelland felt that this mixture of motivational needs impacted on both leadership style and personal behaviour. When you are working effectively, he argued, it will be in jobs or positions where most of your motivational profile is met. Your own profile also influences how you work with others and the ways you most naturally use to motivate other people. These motivational profiles are based around three particular needs: the need for achievement, the need for power and the need for affiliation. When your profile has a large need for *achievement*, it means that you like jobs where you can progress individually, you like to set challenging but realistic goals, and you get good feedback from your manager often. The need for *power* revolves around both social and personal power. This profile fits what we commonly see as a leadership profile in that the need for power is all about wanting to influence. Some people want to achieve this through personal prestige and power; others, who may also have a need for affiliation, want to influence through the use of social power in groups. The need for *affiliation* is a motivator to work in groups and to achieve harmony. Its downside is the need to be liked, which can make difficult decisions in leadership even more taxing if you score highly on this need. McClelland's profiling tests are used by the Hay McBer company to look at what makes an outstanding leader, not just a capable one. Having worked with the profiles myself, I think they can also help leaders to understand more about themselves and the way that they portray themselves as leaders, which in turn makes them more capable leaders.

Boyatzis' work followed on from McClelland's, by looking at whether competencies could be seen to predict or cause outstanding leadership performance. He noted that effective leaders tended to have abilities in three particular clusters, which they were able to draw upon as the need demanded: *cognitive* abilities around such items as problem-solving and decision-making; *intrapersonal* skills such as flexibility and willingness to adapt your style to new situations; and *interpersonal* skills such as good communication and network building. These clusters are similar to the skills that we have already discussed as being part of the set needed by a leader. All of them may be qualities that are necessary to be a leader but will vary in their usefulness, depending on the situation. Essential competencies are drawn up for many jobs, and education is no exception. Apart from defining the basic skills that are needed, competencies are also used to assess and develop leaders, by putting together a personal leadership development plan.

Activity 29

Investigate, and then make a note in your journal of:

- the framework or frameworks that are used in your context;
- whether your institution has an ongoing, consistent development strategy for potential leaders;
- if not, what would you like to see involved in such a development plan.

Leadership development is a multi-faceted process, and it would not be surprising if your experience of it was both context-dependant and variable. Many of you will have noted down ways of assessment that include such aids as leadership questionnaires and 360 degree appraisals. So far, your development as a leader may have been informed by many items: the personal characteristics that you have brought to your context, the way that others in the organisation view your behaviour, and the realisation that your motivation needs to be sustained over time by the work you carry out and the social relationships that are created. This balance between personal agency and the context is important because it reminds any leader of the equilibrium that exists at all times between leadership and followership. If you are able to draw upon your own personal qualities, honed over time by effective feedback, support and challenge, then your own personal practice should become more capable. Not everyone can be an exceptional leader at all times and in all circumstances. Examining your own personal practice on a regular basis enables you to tackle any given situation very effectively, even exceptionally at times, but more usefully perhaps it can also develop your abilities to help you be a capable leader most of the time.

Your own practice

Having engaged with the book so far, you will have seen that one of my arguments is that the exceptional leader is usually found in the nexus between personal practice, the context and the people. Different leaders will fit better in some contexts than others. However, that doesn't mean that continually hunting for the perfect context is any more tenable than hunting for the perfect leader! Engaging with your own leadership practices, and how they relate to those you work with, should help you think about how you can improve your chances of success in any given situation.

Leadership judgements develop with experience, but it may be that those leaders who clearly recognise the peculiarities of their context by looking at their own practice over time will become more self-aware and more able to adapt to the changing situations in education. Flexibility may well be essential when you focus not only on your own personal competencies but also those of others. The experiences that you have will vary from working in different contexts with great leaders (or learning how not to lead from working with an awful leader) to completing state or national skills training programmes. All of these will interact to build your knowledge, make you more experienced generally and help you understand when you have become an expert at certain leadership dilemmas. Professional practice promotes both cognitive and emotional competences if it is carried out within a framework of continuous learning and development.

Vignette

A head teacher I once worked with on a training course was very experienced in one particular leadership area. He had been asked to close down a school with falling roles, which he found emotionally draining and difficult because of the anxiety of staff and pupils about their own futures. Having completed this experience, he was asked to repeat it at another school in a different area because their governors had heard of his success at managing a difficult situation. He was able to use some of the lessons he had learnt in the previous school, particularly about managing people, in order to manage the second project. He told me that he had found both positions hard, but that he had learnt from them in terms of his own resilience in difficult situations and had drawn from the experiences that he was able to manage in a dynamic and positive way in the face of forced change. He had learnt a great deal about his leadership behaviours, his own emotional makeup and his ability to remain calm at all times. He did tell me though that his next post would be a school that didn't face that particular challenge!

Reinterpreting challenges for future success draws on your willingness to try to understand your own abilities, particular talents, and skills more completely. Furnham (2006) has said that there are six kinds of learning experience that are formative for leaders in industry. They could also be applied to leaders in education, and some have already been mentioned when discussing your own leadership narrative – your early work experiences, formal leadership training and the influence for good or ill of those you work with. The other three are interesting to apply to education. One is the opportunities that you get for short-term projects where you are able both to have new experiences and learn from them. Does your educational institution build that sort of opportunity into developing future leaders? Perhaps you can remember some good examples of such opportunities that you have had or were provided for someone you knew. Furnham also talked about hardships, perhaps a crisis of some kind, which provide learning about oneself and how able you are to manage through difficulties.

Earlier in this section, Ackerman and Maslin-Ostrowski's work on the emotion of leadership was introduced. This work suggested that a leader is defined by difficult experiences so as to become what Ackerman and Maslin-Ostrowski (2004) call the 'wounded leader'. Their research looked at how leaders managed what they call 'the chronic conditions of leadership life: vulnerability, isolation, fear and power' (p. 311). If wounding is a defining characteristic of leaders, particularly in the way that it helps them learn more about themselves as leaders, then it would seem correct to argue that this experience is essential and cannot be rationalised out of the leader's experiences. Wounding may have a purpose in that it can help leaders learn more about themselves as leaders, but it will also be related to their inherent selves and those early experiences mentioned above. Finally Furnham noted that your first big promotion, where you have a great deal to lose if it all goes wrong, can be a powerful learning experience. This was certainly true for my own experience of early promotion to deputy headship. I learnt a great deal both about myself as a leader and about the interplay between the public and the personal side of leadership. I hope I have managed to build these defining experiences into my leadership narrative in a way that helps me shape future leadership projects.

Looking forward with others

These personal leadership experiences and the behaviours that you may have learnt from them are crucial for helping you become a more capable leader. Such experiences can help you to see not only what is stopping you becoming a more capable leader, but also how you can draw upon the capabilities of others in order to enhance leadership and management in your school. Stoll (2011), in her work on professional learning communities, noted that helping adults to have the capacity to learn continuously themselves is not at all clear-cut. Professional learning communities are, she suggested, a 'critical key' (p. 193) to institutional capacity building. This is because such a community could build collaborative work about developing teachers' work as professionals in order to improve outcomes for students. This may be in one institution or across several. Such communities, Stoll argued, are defined by trusting relationships, collaboration, collective responsibility and reflective dialogue in which group and individual learning can be promoted. These communities focus on building up deep knowledge in a systemic way that does not rely on one-off professional development opportunities either inside or outside of the organisation. Timperley has argued (2011: 128) that leaders must be prepared to overcome initial resistance and put in place the conditions that motivate people to take advantage of professional learning opportunities in communities and individually. She suggests that leaders should ask themselves whether they have the knowledge and skills to work with teachers' professional expectations and, if not, how they can begin to find the kinds of professional learning that both deepens and improves their own skills. Timperley stressed that leaders engaged in professional learning need to concentrate on those process issues that optimise learning conditions for staff and help everyone to learn and grow through developing practices that adapt to the ongoing needs of the organisation.

Your educational organisation may be a place where staff development is as important as student development because leadership at all levels sees them as going hand in hand. I would argue that leaders have a responsibility to develop such professional practices as part of their culture-building role. This may mean developing professional learning communities as well as drawing both on their own institution's strengths and also relevant expertise from outside that organisation. My view is that leaders should not only view such development as part of their own deeper professional learning and model behaviours that progress professional learning, but also view it as part of creating a sense of identity focused around such developments. Leadership as an organisational quality can be developed in this way rather than an over-reliance on individual leaders and their particular behaviours.

Whose meaning?

As discussed in Section 2 of the book, a great deal of leadership is about creating meaning and making sense of situations where there appears to be no sense or where the current way forward is not working well. Map-making is one idea that was discussed in an earlier part of the book. Whatever way you choose to look at it, the leader's own identity and the ways s/he goes about meaning-making will be viewed in differing ways by the people they work with. Individuals may be dependent on their own perceptions of what a leader should be, and how a leader should 'perform'. Haslam et al. (2011: 142) argue that any leader needs to proactively shape the social context by identifying the vision of who we can be and how we can get there, or as they call it 'a collective sense of us' (p.145). The leader's identity is further shaped by how successful they are at influencing people towards the new collective identity while building on the past identities that have served the institution well. The building blocks of a common identity have a great deal in common with the building blocks of professional learning communities which Stoll identified in terms of trust, collective responsibility and respect.

All groups that you will work with, either in formal or informal leadership roles, will already have a sense of their common social identity and where they belong in relation to each other. You may have been part of the group yourself, which may give you some insight into the key connections within in it, or you may arrive from another educational institution and have to find out what is important to the group identity. Whichever way your role has come about, your social identity in the group is important because it will affect the way people relate to you and vice versa. The group's 'collective sense of us' is important because, as Haslam et al. argued, for most people social groupings are a very important part of their work world and leaders need to be a part of that group identity as well as being able to stand apart. Any leader, they argue, has to be able to interpret the social world to the group effectively, and help them with the sense-making process, which in turn helps the group function better (pp. 145–6).

Haslam et al. are interesting because they suggest that leaders provide a function that is more than sense-making. They argue that leaders' work is all about creating and encouraging a particular version of identity, which they call being 'entrepreneurs of identity'. Entrepreneurship in the case of leaders, they contend, is all about making social identity credible for the group, but at the same time hiding all the effort that goes into the identity creation. The example they use is of Ronald Reagan who put a great deal of effort into presenting himself as homespun and folksy in his speeches in order to position himself as the leader of the American group identity, noting 'there is much complexity in being a simple man of the people' (p. 147). Their view is concerned with a leader being political with a small 'p' in order to help the group make sense of where they all are going and why. This sort of labour could be viewed as artificial or somehow unethical because there is an element of fakery in the presentation. However, a striving for authenticity as a leader may involve actions which strengthen the leader's identity *and* the group culture. Stories and speeches are one part of this. Notions of authenticity are contested in the psychological literature. I find Ashforth and Tomiuk (2000) helpful. They defined authenticity as the extent to which a person behaves according to what they consider to be their true and genuine self. Although such definitions are bound by deeper questions about what is the self and whether authenticity is contextual in itself, this definition struck me as particularly relevant to those who work in schools. In your own personal leadership narrative you can believe in the authenticity of your leadership and its values while at the same time promoting and sharing them in various ways with the group, depending on the context. Thus your own narrative of being a capable leader will harness your authentic skills and abilities, but also look for new ways to emphasise what is important and valuable for your group in that particular context. This is a version of McClelland's social power which was discussed earlier and in this view of leadership the power of the group is also seen as being vital. A capable leader realises that this is the case, I would argue, and works with the insights that come from understanding the power of identity and followers in order to create a scenario that people want to commit to.

Summary

This chapter has asked you to think about the issue of what makes a capable leader in terms of competences and skills, but has also suggested that you need to consider the boundaries which are personal to you. I have also looked at what it means to work with others in professional communities of various kinds and whether leader/follower relationships are partly at least bound up in identity formation and recreation. Your own sense of capability will be forged by significant learning experiences that you have during your work and personal life, and may fluctuate in times of difficulty. These temporary fluctuations should not be seen as a test of your basic capability as a leader and manager. Developing a sense of your identity as a capable leader will enable you to manage these difficulties much more easily, and also help you to know what help you may need to access to continue being capable.

This section of the book has looked at boundaries of varying kinds. In developing your own capabilities, you may find that there are boundaries you are either ill-prepared to or do not want to cross. These might be concerned with what motivates or inspires you personally. They might be difficult boundaries to cross because of the power dynamics of your current situation. The contexts you work in will be many and varied but you will know when your capabilities have been stretched to beyond what is physically and mentally possible for you.

Activity 30

Most people need what a good friend of mine calls a 'stroking file'. This contains examples of things you have done well or positive reports in evaluations, etc. Such a file has similarities to Sparrowe's view, outlined in Chapter 1, of 'the narrative construction of an esteemed self'. To conclude this chapter, finish this quote in your journal: 'People know I am a capable leader because ...' Put it across the front or back page and return to it when you need to give yourself some self-validation.

If having read that activity you feel that you don't ever need reminding of your capability then this is probably the wrong book for you to be reading at the moment.

This chapter has suggested that everyone can be capable and develop their capabilities as a leader in terms of cognitive, emotional and behavioural aspects. Being willing to be self-critical can enable you to move forward as a leader. Before I bring the themes of the book together in Chapters 17 and 18, the next section addresses another way of looking at developing as a leader and manager through research and further study. It can be read next or after reading the final two chapters.

Further Reading for Section 3

- Bottery, M. (2004) *The Challenges of Educational Leadership*. London: Sage.
  A very useful book if you want to look at the way leadership policy is driven by globalisation, and our conceptions of trust and identity.

- Dimmock, C. and Walker, A. (2005) *Educational Leadership: Culture and Diversity*. London: Sage.
  This book is a useful one to use to reflect both on boundaries and contexts.

- Hargreaves, A. and Fullan M. (2012) *Professional Capital: Transforming Teaching in Every School*. London: Routledge.
  A book in which Hargreaves and Fullan challenge readers to look at educational policies with new eyes.

Section 4

The educational leader as researcher

14

Becoming a leadership researcher

> This chapter will:
>
> - help you to consider your own role as a researcher in the area of leadership and other areas related to school effectiveness;
> - discuss the building blocks of researching practice;
> - look at examples and ideas for research.

The purpose of this chapter is to help you understand some basic ideas and fundamental principles about research, including, most importantly, that research must be ethically carried out so that not one is damaged in the process. I hope it will give you the desire to get started on a small piece of research or to read more research. There are many opportunities to engage in leadership research and one of the core underpinnings of this book is that research should be part of an aspiring leader's tool kit. Research could include:

- your own research;
- encouraging others to research;
- learning where to look for relevant research in books and journals.

In this chapter I am going to try and dispel some of the mystique around the idea of research, and in particular encourage you to research in your educational setting. This chapter is aimed at someone who wants to know more but doesn't know where to start. If you are thinking about or are already studying for a degree which includes aspects of research, this chapter may prove helpful as a starter too. It's very much an introduction to the area, and you may wish to continue to the next chapter if you are already involved in research. Research will be used as the overarching concept, although the terms 'investigation' or 'enquiry' could just as easily have been used. Indeed some might find these terms much less daunting. You may want to carry out some research into practice such as ..., or you may wish to investigate some of the more theoretical issues around education such as ... that excite your interest. However, the focus in this chapter will mainly be about research into practice within your work context, as this is a clear place to start as a new researcher.

As a leader, whatever form of research or investigation you undertake, the findings should be presented in ways that are clear and relevant to the target audience, whether that is teachers or even other researchers at the many national and international conferences that showcase research in education. This chapter will look at these issues. The overall aim of this chapter is to help you both to improve your knowledge of research methodology and methods, and also to make being a researcher part of your daily practice. As a leader or an aspiring leader, not only will a focus on research impact on your own personal practice and that of others, but it could also help you to look in a more informed and critical manner at policy issues and find out about research that is relevant to your own context.

In addition, an aim of this chapter is to make you feel more confident when discussing research more generally. My focus will be on leadership, but many of the points made are directly relevant to research in other areas of the educational landscape.

You as a researcher

As a leader, or aspiring leader, there are various arguments about why research should be part of the educational ethos. I will be asking you to be self-critical and systematic as you work on your research ideas, and, given that your time is precious, the ideas will be related to issues that are of relevance to, for example, teaching and learning issues within schools. This does not mean that research has to be purely focused on these, as I would suggest that research is also about developing the ability of both yourself and others to build up your professional judgement and expertise.

If you are new to this whole area, it is important to note that there are far too many ways to 'be a researcher' to be outlined in a brief chapter, so you will need to look for specific guidance so that you can follow up your own particular research topics. The idea of getting involved in research can often be just that, an idea. In the busy world of education, leaders of learning can find that ideas often crop up that they would like to follow up but are crowded out by the more urgent priorities of working with pupils, parents and staff on areas of life that seem more directly relevant to what is happening now. Research may take second place to these other activities or be nonexistent. As well as time, you may feel that you are not equipped with the right tools for research, or that the process is somehow mysterious and difficult, maybe even involving huge amounts of mathematical data. You might like to look at research that has already been done in an area that interests you. Even a brief search of the web, however, can be confusing and raises many questions. For example, is that research reliable, and will my own research be of interest to anyone else? A good way to begin is to read articles that have been written in your area of interest, are relevant to your context and are readable. Even finding these can often be a challenge when you start out because it is very difficult to know where to go and what to read. Many countries have subject or educational interest groups that run their own journals and this may be an excellent place to start out. For example the British Educational Leadership, Management and Administration Society (BELMAS: http://www.belmas.org.uk) has two journals for members. One is aimed at practitioners in schools and colleges and the other is more aimed at university lecturers and students. Publishers also run free trials of their journals, and often there are areas on their website where very popular articles are available free. This can be an opportunity to read and reflect on areas that interest you and be introduced to current topics of research.

Hopefully these next few chapters will increase your confidence in knowing how useful and relevant a piece of research is and allow you to begin to build up key questions that you would need to ask when you are reading published research for yourself.

Being reflective

First, however, I would suggest that you start with yourself as a researcher, and your own point of view from which you will try to build a claim for knowledge in a particular area.

Activity 31

Note down what the word 'research' means to you and any examples you have of research work.

In essence, research is approaching specific problems in a systematic way. The main points for you to think about are identifying a problem that you want to look at and finding a way of looking at it that is appropriate to the problem and one that you can manage in the time you have available. If you work in a large school or college, you may want to look at whether a new policy or activity is working well on the ground in the classroom. You could ask yourself whether the federal or national government have introduced something recently which your organisation is struggling to come to terms with. There are many ways that you could frame this work, but let us suppose that you want to get a quick response to see what is happening at the moment. You might wish to put together a questionnaire survey and aim to get a good response. There are many online survey instruments, e.g. Surveymonkey or similar, so that, once you have written the survey, you can send a link to the people you wish to fill it in. Survey response rates can be poor, as people may not see them as a priority like you do! Swift reminders may be necessary and it is very unlikely you will get a 100 per cent response rate. You also need to allow time to analyse your answers and present them carefully. So, if you wanted to run a survey, for example, that dealt mainly in numerical responses, you would need to know that you were able to analyse these carefully. The same is true for interviews which often generate huge amounts of data, even if you only speak to a few people. So, another way of finding out whether that policy was working well on the ground would be to interview four people who have been involved in the area. Interview questions need careful thought, and a try-out or pilot before you start. A pilot allows you to eliminate questions that are badly phrased or irrelevant to the core issues. There are many books that can help you with the interview schedule. Allowing time to analyse the results is again important. For example, a taped recorded interview of about 45 minutes will take at least four times that to transcribe! There are now many items of software that can help you with data management, but you must always be aware that you are still in charge of making sense of it all, no matter how advanced the software is. If you were able to frame a large piece of research on this imagined policy, you might like to do an initial survey, then a follow-up with interviews. This allows you to have both the bigger picture and some of the detail of why things are showing in the data as they are. Qualitative data can help you to fill out some of the areas that a survey might miss, such as how people are feeling about a particular approach or why something was particularly useful in their classroom.

Research in the social sciences involves a variety of approaches and methods. It involves thinking clearly about what you already know, what you want to know and deciding how you are going to get there. Social science research is not easy and requires you to be both reflective – looking at your own work and practice – and reflexive – going over that practice again to examine it for bias etc. (Hammersley, 1993). You need to be able not only to put together work that is ethically sound and that will provide you with reliable and valid information, but I believe it is very important to be able to position yourself within the investigation. When you engage in investigation of any kind, you need to be able to justify your own preconceptions and how you might be influenced by theories of education more generally. This relates back to your values as discussed in Chapter 2. It is certainly not an easy task as you need to develop the ability to reflect not only on your own behaviour and actions but those of colleagues in a different way than if you were engaged in, say, lesson observation for the purposes of inspection. This is because, in lesson observation, you do not have to think about your own practices and concerns. However, if you have been writing your reflective companion throughout the book so far, you are well on your way to this process already. There is a great deal of literature concerned with critical self-reflection and research in education (Robson, 2002; Delamont, 2002; Bassey, 1999), and I hope you will follow these up as you develop your professional expertise. Key readings are provided at the end of the chapter.

Broader philosophical concerns

Broadly speaking, research methodologies are based on philosophical stances. Your own philosophical approach is part and parcel of this self-reflection. There are many philosophical traditions that education draws on, and as a new researcher you can begin to understand about how these ways of thinking relate to your own work. You will come across words that you may have never seen before such as epistemological and ontological, and worry that you will never understand what these mean. A brief explanation may help you get started.

A fundamental way of looking at research is to consider your own ontological position. Cohen and Manion call ontology 'assumptions which concern the very nature or essence of the social phenomena being investigated' (1994: 5). Different ontological positions will inevitably lead to different kinds of research. So in my own research discussions, I have a particular viewpoint around which my research grows and develops – my position is primarily phenomenological, a lovely word in itself. This means I view people as social actors within differing, but valid, representations of reality and this leads to a research approach that focuses on the individual rather than one that generalises from a large amount of data about a whole population. You will see how the idea of a personal leadership journey fits neatly into this research position. Mason (2002) helpfully stresses the importance of realising at the start of the research process that alternative ontological positions tell different stories. Your own assumptions may not be obvious to you now but will become more apparent as you consider the practical tasks of research.

Epistemological assumptions are all about how you view knowledge. For me it is straightforward in the sense that I see knowledge as 'personal, subjective, and unique'. This connects to my ontological assumptions about the nature of reality and leads clearly to the ways in which I would wish to collect and analyse data. The perspective that I adopt in research will be reflected in my methodology, as it ties into my assumptions about human nature, people and the environment and the way that I might describe this as collecting data through personal accounts, interviews and observation. Other researchers may adopt what is a more positivist approach, which is concerned with scientifically describing what we can observe and measure. There are other stances researchers take, but you may need to refer to a book that has a specific focus on this aspect. I hope this helps you examine how any research you read was framed, and the point of view from which it was written. Often, it may seem that research is full of unrecognised codes, but that should not put you off. You can go away and read up on all these words in more detail and apply them to your work, of course, but first you may just want to get started. Try this activity to begin with.

Activity 32

Here is a small piece of research that I carried out a few years ago. Read the overview and think about how you would answer the questions that follow:

As part of a project on vocation and volunteering, I decided to carry out some small-scale research with governors in England that dealt particularly with their motivation. Other research into governance is much larger scale, and relevant to this area (Adams and Punter 2008; Balarin et al. 2008). It is particularly interesting to see the differences in responses now several years on from these studies in a very different policy environment for governors in 2012. For this research a questionnaire was sent out to just under 500 governors in one small local authority to seek their views about why they originally became a governor, what keeps them going as a volunteer governor and what they view as the key challenges for school governors in 2012 and onwards. The response rate was good, with just over a third responding. Of those, 60 per cent were female and 90 per cent of the total were from the primary sector. The latter figure is high because the questionnaire was distributed via a local authority governor's service, and most primary schools in the area still retain the governor service. The average age of the group was between 40 and 60, with 40 per cent having been governors for over five years. Thirty-eight per cent of the sample had become governors relatively recently, in the last two years. Governors responded in great detail to the survey. The piece of writing I then wrote was structured around three areas: initial motivation, keeping motivated and challenges for the future.

1. Is there anything important about the way the research was carried out that I have not mentioned above?
2. What would you do next if you came across this overview?
3. Are there any criticisms you could make based on this overview?

In this brief overview of my governance survey, there is a great deal of detail left out. Often journal articles will only be able to give you some of the important detail. However, in education, you can often look at the original research reports online, especially if they were funded by a national charity. You will probably have noted that the survey mentioned above was weighted towards primary and female. This was because the local governor service gave them out, and many secondary schools are now independent of local area authority in England. Problems of access and how to overcome them are some of the issues that you have to think about when designing even a small piece of research.

Starting out

Once you have found an issue that you would like to research, even before you start, it must be doable and a have clearly defined purpose. That way, if you are working in education full time, you are more likely to complete the research in a clear and meaningful way. In your early planning, it is wise to make sure that your work is exactly that, a planned attempt. Start small and pick out a problem that is current to your professional life or perhaps a burning question you would like to answer. Keeping the ideas neat and tidy is very difficult when you start, and time spent honing your questions is time well spent. For example, you may be interested in the question 'How effective is the teaching of phonics for children's reading?' but this is far too wide to investigate effectively. You might want to start with one of several other possible questions: 'What does the literature say about approaching reading using phonics?' This has the advantage of being a research study that is all about reading the evidence and sorting out the key points. It could also prepare you for another question such has: 'How useful has our local phonics training been for our staff in school?' which would lead you towards a small evaluation where you might conduct a small survey through interviews and/or questionnaires. It is more common than you might think for people to start too broadly. Focus your idea and the results will be better, especially if you can make your question clear and able to be investigated.

Activity 33

Jot down in your journal some ideas for research. Have you got a burning question that you want to find the answer to? Try and break it down into smaller questions. Then ask yourself how doable as a project it is. What parts of it might get very complicated?

When you start out, you may find working with someone else on a problem will give you confidence in what you are doing and how you are doing it.

The next issues are often practical ones. You need to make sure you are well organised and that your evidence is carefully collected and recorded. There are many books out there which are just about this aspect of research. Your system should be clear so that it could be checked by someone else who was working on the same problem if needed. It almost goes without saying that any research must take into account ethical considerations, especially if you are intent on researching your own place of work. Ethical concerns are often forgotten in the rush to gather data.

Ethics

I mentioned at the start of the chapter that a key concern should be that your research must not damage anyone. There can be many sensitive issues that can arise within research, and if you are aware of basic ethical codes before you begin, then the chances of problems arising later, while not definitely resolved, are certainly mitigated. One code that you may find particularly useful is that of the British Educational Research Association (BERA, 2011), which can be found on their website. Looking at ethics will help you make sure that all relevant parties to the research are well informed, clearly consulted and any necessary paperwork or approval (for example, if you were working in or with another school) is carried out well in advance of your research starting. Ethical issues are often neglected by beginning researchers but are very important. For example, there are issues of power involved which you need to take into account if you are in a leadership role. Is it appropriate for you as, say, a head of a subject area to investigate some aspects of the subject delivery yet not others? What issues might arise? You can see already that there are subtle aspects to even a small piece of work which may require your skills not only as a communicator in general but in negotiating what happens and when. For example, I always involve those I interview in seeing my final written account and make it clear that I am open to amendments that make it a fair and accurate reflection of their views. I also discuss clearly at the start any issues around where the research might be reported, how it could be reported, and any concerns they might have over confidentiality. With the people you interview, you want to make sure that they are clear about your research, how it is going to be used and what steps you are taking to maintain confidentiality. This is called informed consent.

As a new researcher, you want to be able to look back at the evidence you have collected to see that it is as reliable, authentic and representative as is possible. If you are inexperienced, you may well want to start simply and build up your expertise. There are many books which will take you through the various stages of a research project (Bell, 2010; Briggs et al., 2012; Delamont, 2002; Middlewood et al., 1999), and I would recommend you have a careful look at some of the recommended books before you start so you are prepared for some of the dilemmas that might arise as you go into the research arena.

Trying it out

For a small project, once you have identified the area, reading around the subject is your first task. This is not only to inform you generally but also to help you get the best out of the questions you may be asking. If you have the opportunity, talk to an educational librarian about the best ways to search for material. Developing your skills with key words and recording can save you huge amounts of time later on. Sometimes, however, an opportunity may suddenly arise that means you just want to get started.

Vignette

Sandy, a deputy principal in Scotland, was interested in why people wanted to lead schools and had been asked to give a talk at a conference about her leadership. She wondered whether wanting to become a leader was something that had always been there for principals as children, whether they had been influenced by people they had worked with or wither there were other reasons. She spent some time researching on the web and in the library of her local

(Continued)

(Continued)

college before she got started, and became quite interested in the idea of auto-biographical writing, which led her to more reading about the lives of people who had become teachers and teacher leaders. It seemed to her that there were similar ideas coming up in her reading and so she made a careful note of them as she went along. She then decided to sit down and write her own life story, and asked her friend Kath to read it and see if any of the themes from the literature appeared. She was surprised to see that they did. It seemed to Sandy that in the time available and with her particular interest interviews would be useful, as many of the books had talked about life histories. Taking her expertise into account, she decided to ask two colleagues if she could interview them and they agreed. She then discovered that writing the questions for the interview was trickier than she thought, so she went back to her reading and adapted some questions from a questionnaire that already existed in one of the books about life history she had read. After two interviews of about two hours each, she sat down and transcribed them herself. It was only afterwards she discovered that she could have bought the service of a transcriber or used voice recognition software. She then used her themes to analyse her data. From this, she was able to give a useful and informative talk at the conference, and it inspired her to sign up on a course at her local university in beginning research for teachers.

This is an example of a small project that helped develop Sandy's expertise and confidence. She could perhaps have gone for an even smaller project to develop more slowly. At each stage, Sandy sat down and reviewed what she had done and asked what was the best way forward. For example, she considered using the Internet to conduct a survey of her colleagues locally. Then she realised that she wanted depth and practice at interviewing and a survey would not give her a chance to ask questions as she went along. It would, however, be useful if she wanted to extend her project to larger groups of people. Sandy's project may well have been successful because it combined a reason to do the research (her talk) with an interest that she had already (people).

Sometimes, though, your interest will arise out of what the organisation needs or from a need to make some particular change in the professional practice that is carried out within that organisation. It may also be that you wish to do some research work collaboratively with colleagues.

Working with and from research

Hopefully the short introduction that you have now read may go some way to convincing you that you are able, perhaps with a little more reading and investigation, to undertake a small research piece. To end this chapter, however, it is worth looking at how research can have wider benefits for the wider team or teams in your organisation, or even outside your own area. The example used is based upon a real-life investigation carried out in Africa.

Vignette

Dari wanted to carry out a small investigation into teaching and learning. Because he was working for the Ministry of Education in his country looking at Science, he was interested in the practices that affect students' Science learning and performance in primary schools. He began his thinking by writing an overview to himself of the current context of the teaching in the country, and then went on to thinking about the reading he needed to do around student practices in primary science. He tried to make sure that his reading was directly relevant to issues of teaching practices in Science generally and any information he could discover about his own country in particular. He was conscious that literature discussing a completely different context, such as Singapore or Canada, may have some issues of relevance to him, but that the on/off civil war in his own country made his context very different as well. He built up a summary of the relevant literature on how children learn and on the teaching and learning approaches adopted. From this reading about theories he mapped out five hypothesis which he set out to test in several schools. He was initially overwhelmed by the data generated from parental and student questionnaires and took the decision to discard some of this information to ensure that the research remained manageable within the given timescale.

When he wrote it up for his workplace, he made sure that he gave a detailed contextual account of the factors affecting students' learning in and beyond science, and focused on three aspects of classroom practice in particular which he saw would be useful in terms of policy in the future. He then went on to test out these aspects in other schools and continued to analysis the results, with the aim that this would eventually be used to scope policy in the country as a whole.

Your work may not be country-wide, but there can be wider benefits from even a small piece of research within school. Some schools have been able to build small research communities, where skills are developed and practice shared, sometimes with the help of an outside facilitator, but often with in-house challenge and support. The next chapter is for those of you who wish to increase your knowledge even more. If you want to explore further before reading on, I would suggest getting hold of one of the books at the end of this section that will help you consider further your own research in educational settings.

15

Further study – choices and challenges

> This chapter will:
>
> - help you to consider the choices and challenges that returning to study involves;
> - discuss the steps you can take to make study work for you and your educational organisation;
> - look forward to how you might disseminate your newly acquired knowledge.

This chapter may seem like a form of self-indulgence as it will focus on those leaders and potential leaders who want to take their knowledge a step further and pursue postgraduate study at a university. I would argue that further study, instead of being viewed as something taking up yet more of the developing leader's time, should be viewed as a way to refresh yourself and your institution by allowing time for thinking.

The reason that this chapter was conceived was because having worked both in schools and universities and with many Master's and doctoral students over the years, one of the questions that I am often asked is: 'Why should I use my precious free time to study at university?' This chapter looks at what can be gained from studying at a higher level, how it can relate to practice, what you should look for in any further study you might undertake, and the challenges that lie ahead if you decide to take the step. Some of the routes to postgraduate study may vary from country to country, and so this chapter makes some generic assumptions which may need to be tested in any particular context. Overall, the focus will be on developing and managing yourself so that the time spent on study will be most helpful whatever the local way of addressing the work involved.

Choices

The first choice that needs to be made is whether this idea of further study is indeed one that is sensible for you at your particular stage in terms of career goals, personal circumstances and time required. It is particularly easy to underestimate the way that real life, and not just school, can get in the way of study. At the same time, it is also easy to overestimate, and never start to look at the varying options available. The prerequisites for successful study are many and various, and crucially are different depending on stage of career, realistic self-knowledge and support from friends and family.

Stage of career is an interesting aspect with which to begin. Postgraduate study in leadership usually requires students to reflect on their leadership practice, and it is more difficult to do that in great depth if you have only been a teacher for a year or so. This is not to argue that young teachers cannot be effective leaders in educational organisations. Studies have shown the potential of such young teacher leaders (Frost, 2008; Muijs et al., 2013) and have also suggested that collaborative approaches to learning about leadership across subjects, faculties and teams are very beneficial at the early stages of leading, which may mean schools developing more professional leadership learning opportunities (Chapter 4), not necessarily postgraduate study. That chapter also looked at the idea of national qualifications which may or may not be part of postgraduate study and linked to universities. Some teachers will have previous leadership experience gained from industry which they could use, but for the young teacher the question that s/he needs to ask is whether committing to postgraduate study at this early stage of their career is going to be the most effective way of learning from the research and practice that is presented to them. It is a personal reflection that needs to be made, not just concerning the nature of knowledge, although that might be important. You might like to refer back to Chapter 4 and the discussion from Simkins (2005) about leadership knowledge consisting of:

- knowledge-for-practice;
- knowledge-in-practice;
- knowledge-of-practice.

New teachers who aspire to leadership positions may be looking for a certain kind of knowledge. Use the following activity to think more about the issue of how much actual practice you need in order to take advantage of the more theoretical side of leadership.

Activity 34

How does your current knowledge level of leadership practice in educational institutions equip you for study? Note down the key aspects of your work that you think study would enhance.

Having decided that this is the appropriate stage of your leadership career to study further, the next step is to ask some difficult questions. This is because many students over- or underestimate what is needed to study part-time. This chapter makes the assumption of part-time study because it is the norm in most countries. If a student is fortunate enough to be given specific time out of school for study, perhaps with funding, these same questions might apply but not quite so severely. Full-time students are often studying in a different country and may have to consider some of the ideas around support discussed below. Part-time students are often, but not always, returning to study after a considerable gap in time. Their confidence may not be high because, although they might consider themselves competent in their own organisation and leadership, academic essays may be something that they have not tackled for some years. Also, their initial degree may not have been as good as they hoped, and they are not sure whether this bodes well for higher degree study. Look at the case of Mike below and see what you think.

Vignette

Mike was a senior teacher in a secondary school in England who taught Art and Design. He had left school at 15 and had worked in the entertainment industry for over 30 years, leading teams and working all over the world. He had returned to study in his 30s when he obtained a degree by distance education with the Open University. This has inspired him to go into teaching, and latterly he had gained a distinction in his Master's degree from a very well thought of university in England. He enjoyed all this so much, he decided to do a doctorate and was interviewed. During the interview, he became concerned, and when pressed by the panel said that he didn't think that he would be able to study for a doctorate after all. His school had given him some study time to do the degree, his proposal was excellent, and Mike himself was knowledgeable and articulate so the panel were puzzled. On further pressing it became clear that the problem was that, in his own mind, Mike still saw himself as a school failure and not the sort of person who could be a doctoral student. It required an adjustment of his own self-image, even though he had the distinction for his Master's work. The panel were able to persuade him that they were confident he could study for this degree and that the department was committed to work with him to build up any study skills he felt he lacked and to support him. He took the place and was very successful.

That vignette has a happy ending. The happy ending was possible because the panel made the right estimation of his motivation and ability. As well as that factor, Mike had chosen a place where he would be supported within an academic community. Support is also vital for further study.

Studying when you are working is stretching to most people. The more mature a student is, the more life events can get in the way of a focus on study and sacrifices have to be made to keep on task. Master's and doctoral students that I have worked with over the years have run the full gamut of events that could have stopped them in their tracks – from late pregnancy to sick children/parents and their own unexpected ill health. There is a simple answer to the life events problem. The event may be more important than the study, so give it due precedence. If it means the degree cannot be finished, it could well be that the human side is much more important. Leadership students are also often very capable managers, not unsurprisingly, and do not tell their institution until after the events. This book has tried to avoid 'top tips', but if there was one, it would be that students who have personal difficulties need not struggle on in silence. In terms of university administration it is much easier to let it be known before or during a difficult time than afterwards. Time out can then be taken without having a permanent detrimental effect on the study. The very qualities that make an effective adult learner such as dogged persistence also mean that they are not so likely to admit that help is needed. It is often a good idea at an early stage to rustle up a 'study buddy' with whom you can talk over events and ideas but who is not an official part of the course team, usually another student who is at the same stage as you. The mature student also benefits from friends and family support – people who will understand if you disappear into a study for hours on end at weekends and unsocial hours of the night. There are also various useful books to follow on particular types of student such as 'women and postgraduate work' (Leonard, 2001).

Activity 35

Given that there may be three components to your choice – stage of career; realistic self-knowledge; support from friends and family – make a note of your own particular thoughts that are related to these areas. Would any of them be a major obstacle or a positive asset?

The other choices that most leaders have to consider are how to study and then where to study. There is a plethora of choices in most countries of the world. Students can learn face to face, online, by Skype or similar, or a mixture of all of these. Some programmes go to where the student is; others require the student to go to the university. Some do not require physical attendance at all. The first step is to identify the choices in your country and see which fit in both with your work and your preferred way of working. Sometimes, there may be compromises because you cannot get to Place A on a Tuesday evening in term time. There may well be supported open learning options which would lead to a new learning experience. Early on in your choices, it may be counterproductive to pick a venue that is miles away if you know that this may be difficult over time. Having said that, many students do find it possible to drive or walk long distances to take part in their preferred option. There is no one solution, but it is definitely something that should be borne in mind when making those initial choices. Sometimes, choices may be driven purely by the availability of options in the nearby area or cultural preferences. For example, students in North America may be willing to drive considerable distances to meet with people from other educational organisations wanting to study. On the other hand, there may be very good reasons for the study to come to you, e.g. a remote Native American group of students in Canada arranged with the 'local' (four hours' drive away) university that the lecturers would come to them for study weekends. This also allowed all the educational leaders locally to come together and discuss local issues. Time, distance and mode of study are considerations for any mature student wishing to study part-time. Full-time students, who normally live near their chosen place of study, may be able to make a choice which is based more on the reputation of the university and the part of the world in which it is situated. Many students also use past recommendations from colleagues as a guide, and this can be an extremely useful way of finding out what further study is like as well as the particulars of any course or university.

This section was primarily about whether to study for a Master's. Mike's vignette shows that there are very similar questions to be asked if moving on from Master's study to a doctorate in terms of time, readiness, etc. He made the decision to move universities because he wanted to study with a particular expert in his topic. In all such choices, reading around study at the relevant level is important, and there are several excellent books available specifically relating to doctoral study, e.g. Thomson and Walker (2010) and Murray (2002), among many. Views and voices may also be found on blogs, Twitter and YouTube, and I would encourage you to search for relevant media material. Any suggestions here would be futile as this is an ever-changing area, so this is an opportunity to use your own burgeoning research skills to find and use these great resources.

Challenges

The previous section looked at the challenges in making choices. This section examines the intellectual challenges that can arise in further study, which of course will differ from person to person. Below are some comments taken from a real-life Master's course which I have been involved with which illustrate some of these challenges. Some of those aspects which they mention will then be picked up and discussed further.

> Liberating, challenging, informative, absolutely inspirational and refreshingly different. (*Student 1*)

> A new sense of purpose and perspective on my profession; I feel as though I have been re-energized and enthused! (*Student 2*)

> At times I have felt uncomfortable in my relative ignorance; at times I have felt tearful when I have come to a stumbling block which seems insurmountable at the time but I have also felt elated when I have achieved something which I never thought possible and this is probably how most of the pupils at school feel too, so it is a very good learning experience for a teacher! (*Student 3*)

> (Educational Leadership and School Improvement students,
> Cambridge, England)

Student 1 is very positive about the entire experience and the quote encapsulates many students' experience of postgraduate study. In particular, the word 'liberating' suggests that an opportunity has been given to think in a different way about matters pertaining to leadership. This feeling of liberation is often why students are able to rise above any difficulties that might arise in terms of time management etc. because the result is worth the effort put in. Student 2 puts their finger on a part of further study which is often underestimated, that of personal refreshment. This is especially true of those students who have been leaders in education for some time. The pressures of the 'day job' can often crowd out opportunities for self-focused activities and renewal on the job can also come from reflecting on activities outside the job. Unless this sounds like too hard a sell for postgraduate study, Student 3 has been included who provides a counterpoint, as the more uncomfortable side is noted where certainties are replaced by ambivalence which, when resolved, leads to new learning. In particular, they make the connection between their own learning about leadership and their own realisation of some of the difficulties their own students might face. These examples indicate that the challenges faced are many and various, but that most people find them well worth the endeavour.

Activity 36

Write down the three things that most concern you about returning to study, and then write against them the ways that you can mitigate these concerns in a positive way. For example, you may have a concern about writing academic essays and may need to remind yourself that most of your colleagues on the course will be the same and working as critical friends can mitigate that feeling (Swaffield, 2004).

This activity will bring to mind some key concerns, some of which may be intellectual, some practical. Some of the practical ones are often the easiest to address and may help mitigate some of the intellectual concerns as you move yourself into study mode.

Making study work for you

Apart from the intellectual challenges, there are some practical considerations that can be worked with in order to make study work most efficiently and effectively. It might seem like a strange section to find in a book devoted to the developing leader but it does take many students quite a while to balance the practical and intellectual side of study. Thinking, reading and writing may seem to happen naturally for some people, but for most students, they are a process of learning new strategies, applying willpower and setting up regular patterns of work.

With both Master's and doctoral programmes, setting up a study routine is a basic building block. For some this means every day at a certain time; for others the routine may involve sacrificing holiday time for extended periods of study. People will have different ways of doing this according to their personal preferences. What certainly does not work is thinking, reading and writing every now and then. Fortunately for students there are numerous of books about learning to read critically, and for leadership I would particularly recommend Wallace and Poulson (2003) as a book that helps students understand the new way of reading that is required of them at Master's level. There are also many books about writing, some of which will be in the suggestions at the end of this chapter. In terms of writing as a skill, I would agree with Goodson (2012), who makes the important point that you have to develop a writing *habit*. This is as true of me writing this book now as it would be of a postgraduate student starting to write essays! For some writers, habit is integrally connected with place, and I certainly would commend a quiet place to write, with everything on hand that is needed for smooth progress. Older students with young families have also recommended interesting strategies over the years, from moving in for a weekend with the in-laws to renting a cottage on their own during school holidays. Readers will now begin to see why a supportive family was mentioned earlier in the chapter. Once these facilitating structures are in place, you may find you can agree with Goodson's exhortation to 'Proceed with care, expect surprises and enjoy the results' (2012: xv). As Student 3 expressed above, it can also give you insights into how pupils feel in similar situations.

Self-study groups of three and critical friendships can also help intellectually and alleviate the loneliness of the long-distance student. Many universities will set these up, and some schools will have self-support groups. These groups can also be part of the sharing of knowledge as you continue with the learning process. Look back at some of the ideas in the chapter on professional learning to stimulate your thinking about what might work for you.

Finally in this section, it is worth noting that some people will do a Master's degree which is right for them at that time in their life, and never want to take it further for a variety of reasons. However, there will be some people reading this chapter who have already completed a Master's degree and have been bitten by the further study bug. Their minds will inevitably turn to the question of whether they have the time, energy and funds to embark upon a doctorate. Again, there are many books which deal specifically with this subject, but there is space here for some initial thoughts. For a doctorate, there is a huge amount of focus time needed. Full-time doctoral students in education are the lucky exception rather than the norm. Many universities offer part-time PhDs and EdDs which fit in better with the busy working professional. An EdD is particularly suited to educational professionals as the research completed will be very much connected with professional practice in education and supporting theory and practice. EdDs are often a good choice for part-time students because they normally work in cohorts which can help strengthen motivation throughout the work on the degree.

Once accepted, all the advice in this section is relevant, plus a developing ability to run a long race of five to seven years. In that time, personal circumstances may change and you may come up with the doctoral equivalent of the marathon runner's wall – that point when you feel you cannot go on any further. You need to summon up reserves to push through it – doctoral 'walls' are often caused by tiredness and overdoing the late night reading, but they may also be attributed to getting to grips with the real meat of the project and, once passed, they give way to new avenues to explore. The support of family and friends is even more vital than for the Master's degree. Finally, a doctoral student needs to have confidence in their supervisor, with whom they should have a long and productive relationship, as the student gradually becomes more versed in the question at hand than the supervisor. A supervisor should be an expert in your area, which almost goes without saying, but they also need to be someone who you can work with for that long marathon. If the relationship breaks down, it is not always because a specific problem has developed. Brabazon (2013) has suggested that there are some important things a student should consider when picking a supervisor which chime with my own experience. These are all about the student being astute and in control. She suggests that students should be engaged in checking out how many complete theses s/he has supervised and making sure that they get the supervisor they want, not the one the university may be trying to give them. She also advises that it is not always wise to pick the top woman or man in the field; such stars may not have the time to see you. There are several other hints that you may well want to read through but the one that I would draw your attention to is her tenth statement – 'Invest your trust only in decent and reliable people who will repay it, not betray it' (p. 3). At first read, this sounds rather shocking. Why would a university not give you such a supervisor? The point she makes is that your relationship will be one of trust, and your best start and progression depends on finding that good relationship. She notes finally: 'Do not select a supervisor who needs you more than you need him or her. Gather information. Arm yourself with these 10 truths. Ask questions. Make a choice with insight, rather than respond – with gratitude – to the offer of a place or supervision' (ibid.). The overarching principle then is to make a well rounded decision that is about knowledge, but also about relationships, in order to give yourself the best chance of finishing that race.

Sharing the knowledge

One aspect of further study that is too often neglected is sharing the knowledge gained – dissemination in some form. Once you have completed your Master's or doctoral study, there should be something to share with someone apart from the examiners. This section unpicks a little of the worry and maybe the mystique that often surrounds this area, and makes some particular suggestions for taking the ideas that you have forward into other arenas.

Activity 37

Let's assume you have written something. It could be an essay, or a complete Master's or doctoral thesis. You have received favourable feedback on it. Someone may even have written 'This is suitable for publication'. What do you do next?

I imagine some of you are now muttering, 'But I am only just thinking about getting started!' If that is the case, then this is a piece you might want to return to, but the argument against that is – think about this now before you start. Assume that something worthwhile is going to be written. It may be worthwhile for your professional practice, your current situation or more policy or theoretically focused. Whatever the 'it' is, the assumption to hang onto is that the topic was worth studying and writing about, so it is worth sharing. There are several ways to do this. Informally, many postgraduate students share their work through blogging and running seminars at their university or in their educational establishment. Feedback from these events can be very helpful to refine arguments and help the presentation more generally. From such beginnings, seek advice from fellow students and your supervisors about suitable journals for your area and do some research on what those articles look like. If your work is about an issue of professional practice, there are many journals which will be delighted to hear from you. Most editors are helpful to new writers, and will make suggestions to help you improve the work. Doctoral students may want to be slightly more ambitious than Master's students, especially if they are in countries like England where a vast tome is produced after years of work. Other countries such as the Netherlands and Iceland, among many, publish work that forms the doctorate as they research, which seems sensible. If you are working towards a huge piece of writing, try and work out which chapters have something to say that you can offer for publication. Only today, one of my students got his literature review published in a journal. He would be the first to tell you it was not easy, and also he could not just send it straight from the doctoral piece. Work was needed to find the right voice and focus around a specific issue from his research question. Nevertheless, it was a piece worth sharing early in his doctoral work, as it had insight into an under-researched issue.

The common thread to this discussion is that if you are spending a great deal of time on something, it must be worth sharing. Early on, work out how, and make an effort to stick to that plan.

Looking forward

This chapter has attempted to explain why the developing leader should seriously consider further study, probably eventually at postgraduate level. It has argued that the benefits personally to the leader are great, and there are opportunities to share that work with other professionals. Some students will go onto doctorates and some will enter academia. Most, however, will return to working as a leader in an educational organisation of some kind. The next chapter introduces research in your own organisation and looks at some of the aspects that help make such a project effective rather than an extra burden on already busy professionals.

16

Researching in your own organisation

This chapter will:

- outline the key parts of the process of researching as an insider;
- discuss the benefits of such research;
- examine the benefits to the organisation of developing researchers internally that are able to disseminate knowledge elsewhere in the system.

This chapter examines the benefits and challenges of researching in the place you work. If you have not read the previous two chapters, it would probably be helpful to do so before you read this one, as they do provide much of the foundation on which this chapter is based as it looks at practical and ethical issues that can arise when researching as an 'insider' in an organisation. Examples are given of research that has been carried out in such settings and there are opportunities to think about the choices that the researcher has made in each instance.

This chapter does not tell you what you must do or how to do it in simple, easy stages. You should bear in mind how your own national cultural context may or may not impinge on the way you carry out the research. You will need to bring a critical framework to mind as a researcher in your own school, college or other educational organisation to enable you to think more clearly about such tasks and their benefits to the organisation as a whole.

Researching as an insider: ethics

It would be easy to assume that the place where you work would be the easiest place to start researching. After all, you know so much about it already and the people like and trust you, so what is the problem about researching as an insider? It is important to think about this question before you go rushing off into planning a study. There may not be a problem with your insider status, and if there is, there may be ways that you can mitigate it. Read the following vignette.

Vignette

Kobus was a very successful teacher and now principal in South Africa. He had finished his Master's degree and was now embarking upon doctoral study while working. The idea that most fascinated him was that of culture and the organisation. What was the role of the leader in making things happen? Armed with a good deal of reading, he began to map out how he would study this in his own school and a neighbouring school where he knew the principal very well and was therefore sure that she would take part. His reading had suggested various questionnaires that can be used to measure culture, and he thought that some good quantitative data were just what was needed to give the study veracity. He also wanted to interview some of the key senior leaders in each organisation and a sample of teachers at various levels of the organisation. He also wondered whether he should send the questionnaire to parents. When he saw his supervisor, she was not as enthusiastic as him. What problems might he encounter? What might mitigate them, if anything?

His supervisor was concerned that by not thinking carefully about ethical dilemmas in his area of interest Kobus was not taking account of any ethical problems that might concern him. She pointed out to him problems that could arise when researchers don't think carefully about the whole project before starting any sort of data collection. Chapter 14 looked at ethical issues, and one that is particularly important in this case is the principal's power relationship over potential informants. Even if he was able to guarantee participants' anonymity through a questionnaire, there would probably still be reluctance on the part of the participants to tell the whole story. Most ethical guides talk of the principle of informed consent. BERA (2011: 5) puts it very clearly:

> Researchers must take the steps necessary to ensure that all participants in the research understand the process in which they are to be engaged, including why their participation is necessary, how it will be used and how and to whom it will be reported [...] Researchers [...] must consider the extent to which their own reflective research impinges on others, for example in the case of the dual role of teacher and researcher and the impact on students and colleagues. Dual roles may also introduce explicit tensions in areas such as confidentiality and must be addressed accordingly.

This can be a particular challenge when you are engaged in leadership research as you may well be in a situation where it would be only too easy to impinge upon colleagues. They may not like to say no, or feel able to back out, because of your personal relationship, when they should be able to do so at any time in the research. The other point that may make it difficult if your research involves, say, interviews in your own organisation, is to write about it afterwards in a way that keeps the anonymity of the participants. If these principles are made a part of the research from the start, most researchers in their own workplace will be able to adjust what they do to fit the question that they want to look at and keep to ethical stances.

Activity 38

Thinking of your own workplace, are there any leadership and management issues that might present you with an ethical dilemma if you wanted to research them? What would they be? How could you solve them? One head teacher that I worked with thought she had solved the power dilemma of headship by asking a colleague to interview her staff, while he did the same for her in her school. What is the potential difficulty with this solution?

At this point I am not going to give any definitive answers except to note that if power relations cannot be avoided, there may need to be another way to research the question that interests you. For instance, if you are particularly interested in the culture of schools, negotiating access to some other schools where you are not in some sort of power dynamic may be a way forward. It would enable you to look at some of the generic issues and then take them back to your workplace.

Making the familiar strange

This section draws on C. W. Mills's famous assertion that researchers (especially those who work with qualitative data) should make the familiar strange. This can be quite difficult to understand on first thinking about it as an issue. Researchers often talk about this in the context of 'reflexivity' or 'being reflexive'. For example, the start of this book suggested you keep a journal to aid your reflections on the process and as an aid to understanding what your own position is in terms of the ideas that you are reading about. Making the familiar strange when you are looking at your own organisation is partly about your own frame of mind as you begin to think about the research you want to do. Are you able to move yourself into a position where you take nothing for granted as you look at common, everyday interactions? For me, it is rather like the works of one of my favourite authors, Neil Gaiman. In *Neverworld* he takes the familiar streets of London that the hero knows very well – his office routine, his flat, the buses, street life – and turns it on its head when he introduces the idea of a 'London Below' that interacts with the familiar London but is not part of it. Thrust into this alternative universe by accident, the hero has to make sense of the same landmarks and people but seen from the viewpoint of another. This temporal shift is challenging for him, but he begins to ask questions that help him make that shift. When you are working in your own school, college or wherever in education, you will need to approach your research with this shifted viewpoint. As in the Neverworld, you will be privileged to have an insider/outsider viewpoint that presents challenges but allows you, as Mannay (2010: 92) suggests, to experience 'the multifaceted nature of identities, lifestyles and perspectives'. This may be a challenge, but it does have some benefits as well.

The benefits

If you are hoping to research and produce new knowledge or understandings about your organisation, it is going to take time and a great deal of effort. The rewards of carrying out such work must, in the end, outweigh the difficulties that you may encounter, as discussed in the last chapter. There are many areas concerned with leadership and management that could be researched. Before you start, you may find it useful to ask yourself some key questions to help focus in on the most beneficial at this moment in the organisation's history.

Activity 39

Try answering these questions in your journal.

1. What aspect of leadership and management in this organisation would benefit from being looked at?
2. Why?
3. What are the benefits of researching in this area?
4. What do I know already that I can use as a backdrop when planning the research (your personal knowledge, reading you have done, a specific time framework within which this work could best be done)?
5. What are the problems I might encounter (personal, methodological, institutional), and how should I go about planning to overcome them?
6. What is the core of what I wish to find out?

Having decided that there is something worth researching, and before making any decisions, it might be wise to form some initial questions around the subject and discuss them with colleagues who may also have useful points of view. Listening to their points of view will also help with the shift necessary to help make the familiar strange.

The following vignette outlines a fictional situation based on real people working inside their organisations. You may like to apply the questions above, or see if you think that they are beginning to use research in their own organisation as something positive.

Vignette

Gwyneth and Bethan were close colleagues in a large (28 teachers and support staff) primary school in Wales. Bethan had just finished studying for a Master's degree and Gwyneth was interested in how research could benefit their school. Gwyneth thought that if she and Bethan worked together they could use their skills to carry out some research into their own school. They sat down and discussed the options. After some interesting discussions, they both decided that there were three areas that might benefit from research and in which they were both interested and knowledgeable:

- *teamworking;*
- *working with parents in the nursery;*
- *using data more effectively to improve work in the top year groups.*

They knew that they did not have a lot of time for this work, but Bethan felt that her knowledge of qualitative research was good (she had gained a Merit on her Master's work overall) and she knew that Gwyneth was excellent at timetabling work and planning. After more discussion, they brought their ideas to the weekly team meeting so that they could involve all the staff in the final decision as they wanted whatever they did to be of benefit to the whole school. These discussions led to a decision about the area of research. They would focus on teamworking because it would benefit all aspects of the school. After the meeting, Gwyneth and Bethan were able to go away and focus on collecting information which could help to answer the question 'How good are we at working together for the benefit of the pupils?' They also decided that an online survey with no identifying questions would be a useful way to see how their colleagues viewed teamworking at the moment without making them feel they were going to be singled out. The wording of the questionnaire was challenging, but they were able to draw upon some of the work Bethan had already done. From the initial data collected, they brought together the key points for discussion at a further meeting and then decided to extend their work further.

Of course, there is much that the two teachers had to hammer out, and you might like to consider what those particular issues might be. One of the key things that they did get out of the research was a much better idea of how to handle research as a process within their environment. The research also had a surprising benefit in that several of the other teachers became very interested and they set up a small active researchers group to work on topics that would benefit the school.

From these small steps, they were able to build a relationship with the local university that eventually led to the setting up of a teacher network across the surrounding area. The insider research discussed above triggered a much wider grouping locally. However, what became apparent as the research interests grew was that ironically, research on leadership and management needed leadership and management! This was not as difficult to provide as the necessary expertise that would allow them to work with more challenging issues and enable them to disseminate their work within a wider network.

Near and far

Whatever the context, there are many absorbing issues to investigate. Some of these will be definitely inside your place of work; others will be part of a research grouping locally either in other schools or in universities. Some research will cross the boundaries being both inside and outside, for example when looking at the community context or the national policy context. In England, the government has been developing Teaching Schools, some of which have research as part of their remit. In other countries, there are other ways of widening the influence of research. The student voice project in Ontario (http://www.edu.gov. on.ca/eng/students/speakup) draws on students as researchers too. Research need not be an individual task. In the Ontario work, the work on student voice was started at Cambridge University under the aegis of Professor Jean Rudduck (see Rudduck, 2002). There are many examples from around the world of examples of research undertaken by school communities to enhance leadership and learning, and one of the ways to find out more is to be a part of an extended researcher community.

Some educational contexts do make leadership research more difficult than others. Apart from contextual issues that have to do with some of the issues already discussed (time, ethical issues, stress levels), Dimmock and Walker (2000) make a strong case for developing cultural and cross-cultural approaches to leadership research. They argue that much of the educational leadership research makes no real mention of societal culture at a macro level, or the composition of the national culture. In fact they argue that national culture has not been used enough as a basis for the assessment of effectiveness in educational leadership in particular contexts, nor has national culture been utilised for examining what is happening in individual schools. They also make the point that existing models and concepts used in comparative study are very limited. In a globalised world continuing to ignore culture as a key component of educational leadership and management means that both practice and understanding are being curtailed. So, if your own organisation is not a comfortable fit with Western management models drawn from research in countries such as the USA, Canada and the UK, there is an opening for insider research to expand and enhance the knowledge base of educational leadership.

Looking forward

These last three chapters have been all about getting into research – getting your hands dirty in data, as a colleague of mine once said. For me, research should be an enhancement to your leadership practice and an opportunity to develop ideas. It is also where you can refresh yourself by allowing yourself time to think and develop new ideas: thinking time can be in short supply in educational organisations. These few chapters can only cover briefly some of the many aspects of researching in leadership. If they have made you consider taking the first steps into research, there is a list of further reading below.

Further Reading for Section 4

- Bell, J. (2010) *Doing Your Research Project: A Guide for First-Time Researchers in Education, Health and Social Science.* Maidenhead: Open University Press.
  Bell's book is an excellent starter text for the first-timer as it covers all the key areas.

- Briggs, A. J., Coleman, M. and Morrison, M. (2012) *Research Methods in Educational Leadership and Management.* London: Sage.
  A recommended book if you want to go into some of the areas covered in this section in more depth.

- Brundrett, M. and Rhodes, C. (2014) *Researching Educational Leadership and Management.* London: Sage.
  An excellent book if your research focus is leadership and management in particular.

- Delamont, S. (2002) *Fieldwork in Educational Settings.* London and New York: Routledge.
  My particular favourite for the thoughtful reflective researcher.

- Middlewood, D. and Coleman, M. et al. (1999) *Practitioner Research in Education: Making a Difference.* London: Sage.
  The focus on practice in this book makes it particularly apposite for the newer researcher.

- Thomson, P. (n.d.) blog at: http://patthomson.wordpress.com.
  Professor Pat Thomson's blog covers research in the social sciences and tackles issues from ethics to how to write for publication.

Section 5

Moving forward

17

The personal side of leadership

In this chapter I will look at:

- personal constraints and barriers in leadership;
- personal leadership behaviours;
- cognitive, emotional and behavioural skills;
- identity and our many selves.

Just as the book has a personal preface, I want to return to the personal side of leadership in this penultimate chapter. This book has been based upon the premise that developing as a leader and a manager is fundamentally about the personal in all its guises, so in this chapter I will look at a number of particular aspects such as personal constraints and barriers in leadership, personal leadership behaviours, cognitive, emotional and behavioural skills, and identity and our many selves.

Hopefully, you will have discovered different ways of conceptualising leadership as you were reading, been able to reflect upon yourself as a potential or developing leader, and perhaps have come to understand a little more about leadership in educational organisations. Throughout, you will have noted my focus on the subjective and the personal. This chapter examines some of the many aspects of leadership that have had the most influence on me personally. It looks explicitly at the psychological and psychodynamic side of leadership studies, because it is an area I have found particularly useful in my own work and research. I will also return to the area of emotion and leadership which is intimately connected to any work on the personal side of leadership.

My research has an interest in life history and how personal experiences shape our own understandings of leadership and how to lead. Interpreting personal stories and seeking to understand the part they play in individuals' everyday lives in schools is worthwhile, if difficult. This narrative approach fits in with my overall approach to interviews in research in believing that objective truth does not necessarily exist in these sorts of encounters. As Cortazzi (2002) has suggested, stories of personal experiences in education can emphasise 'personal/professional qualities as dedication and devotion, patience and persistence, enthusiasm, struggle and sacrifice, hard work and humour. Narrative research may thus quite naturally find itself tackling the all-important but often research neglected humanity of teaching and learning and of its leadership' (p. 200). More details about my research into head teachers' lives can be found in Crawford (2009), but this chapter will concern itself with that underlying humanity.

Awareness of self and others

As you have read throughout the book, the story behind 'who you are' is important in 'who you might become'. For me it is a combination of the psychological and the psychodynamic approaches to leadership in education that offer the most answers to leading others with humanity. Leadership with humanity is important to any leader who wishes to be ethical in their approach to people. Reading about various high-profile leadership crises in schools in England (concerning either financial mismanagement or poor treatment of staff) has reminded me that what often appears as effective leadership is not good leadership. This view has been influenced by the people I have worked with, the experiences I have had and the reading in this area that I have done. Experience has seemed to validate the usefulness of many of the issues that these approaches bring up. Working with both my own and other people's personalities has seemed a valid approach to take because, as this book has outlined, there are some contexts which are more suited to some personalities than others. This doesn't mean that I am advocating a determinist trait approach; rather I am arguing that by having a clearer idea of your own leadership needs and behaviours, you will be more able to become more capable in most situations.

Psychodynamic approaches to and theories of leadership are many and various and will often approach the subject of leadership from early life experiences, as I have done in some of my leadership work. The important idea that I would argue applies to many leadership situations is that understanding the behaviours both of leaders and of followers allows leadership skills to be developed in a supportive organisational structure. Stech (2013) argues that the primary aim of a psychodynamic approach is to make both leaders and followers much more aware of how their own personality types impact on their work relationships, in particular when people come into conflicts over issues. Stech's view is that understanding can increase tolerance (p. 338). I think that such knowledge can also help change behaviours, if we are willing to tackle difficult issues. Here I would depart from pure psychodynamic theory in that I think that although our behaviours may be deeply embedded in our past experiences, they can be changed and altered to enable capable responses to specific leadership issues. Understanding a little more about where our own behaviours might come from enables change to take place. At the same time, understanding of our own and others' personal work preferences can help align the right person to the correct task for them at any one time. Such an approach focuses on relationships and the transactional nature of leadership, and on developing one's own self-awareness and thus cultivating more self-control and confidence as a leader. It is a way of thinking about leadership than can encourage self-respect throughout the organisation because people are seen to matter, and anyone who holds a leadership position needs to be aware of their own reactions in relationships and aim to develop abilities to extend that awareness of others. The benefit of teams in education is that groups can help utilise positive emotional energy. The downside is that poor team or group work may not have those resources and instead be a focus of distrust and unease. While collective capacity is important when you look at leadership across an organisation, individual awareness is also fundamental to building that capacity.

This approach will not find universal favour. For some people this is because it can seem limited in terms of a theoretical base, with a reliance on research taken from psychiatric experiences. For others, the emphasis on emotional reactions may cause them to think that there is little applicability in educational organisations. This is despite the evidence from more recent psychological research that leaders aim to give the appearance of rationality even under some very difficult emotional pressures. It should, however, remind leaders that both cognitive and emotional knowledge, especially the regulation of emotion, are part of being a leader, especially under pressure.

Emotion and leadership

Much of my writing and research has been concerned with emotion and leadership (Crawford, 2009, 2011), and this book has been threaded with references to those concerns. I find that exploring emotional processes in work settings like schools increases our knowledge and understanding of the transaction between the individual and the environment. In terms of a definition of emotion, from a biological perspective, emotions apply to certain specific, self-referent experiences of both body and mind (Oatley and Jenkins, 2003); they reflect a person's values (Stein et al., 1994) and are primarily cognitive. Bodily changes may or may not give signals that the person involved is emotionally stimulated, because of what is viewed as professionally correct. However, emotions are also socially experienced through your personal narrative; in other words, they are an interactive state, involving a subject, an object and the relationship between that subject and object.

I have found the psychodynamic approach to emotion particularly useful for the educational contexts in which I have worked, but my personal view of emotion and leadership draws on various perspectives. Emotion creates part of the social reality of life in schools and colleges all over the world, because it is human service work, and each and every social encounter can be regarded as some sort of dramatic interaction. Leaders can feel much more accountable for outcomes of all kinds, unlike in a factory where problems can be fixed before reaching the final customer. The psychological concept of regulation and our capacity for self-regulation is an important personal resource for those who work in educational environments. Oatley and Jenkins (2003: 192–3) have noted that the idea of emotional regulation can be puzzling because it refers both to people's emotional patterns (crying frequently over anything and everything) and to the processes that we might use in order to work on our expressions of emotion (trying not to cry by thinking of something amusing). They argued that some people have a personal bias towards experiencing and expressing certain emotions, like the crying in the example above. The reasons for this, they said, could be many including their childhood or their particular genetic makeup. In terms of leadership and education, the significance for me is to do with acceptance and management of your own unique ways of expressing and understanding emotion, which of course returns the discussion to the psychodynamic.

Earlier in the book I drew on emotional understanding of oneself in the context of meeting leadership challenges and the idea of playing a role. When discussing communication I noted that Goffman proposed that every kind of social interaction is like a game in which we take on roles. We can become more or less strongly engaged in a role, with fulfilment more likely to occur when we are fully engaged in a role. As your leadership profile becomes more public, the management or control of emotion does become more important. The strain of 'performance' can have a negative effect on leadership, the joy of performance a positive effect. Hochschild (1979: 21) argued that over time extensive emotional management could lead to loss of the capacity to listen to our feelings, and sometimes even loss of the capacity to feel at all.

Activity 40

In your current leadership position, note down any specific times when you have been conscious of the management of emotion. Would you agree with the idea that extensive emotional management over time can lead to a reduced capacity to listen to our own feelings?

Emotions in organisations can be suppressed or acted upon, depending often on the person's history of similar events and how they have been coped with in the past. Emotions offer a rich and useful source of information about what is happening to a person and about the culture of the organisation. Parkinson puts it this way, when discussing how emotion works:

> The idea is that emotion is private and internal; the reality is that it is intrinsically interpersonal and communicative or performative. However, ideas about emotion can also contribute to the way that emotion is played out and regulated in everyday life. To the extent to which we take our ideas about emotion seriously, they are bound to influence how we react to our own and other people's actual emotions. (Parkinson, 1995: 25)

Emotion in leadership has many aspects. Leaders will harness the communicative or performative side of emotion at different times. They may also need to draw upon personal emotional reserves, and enable their staff to most helpfully express their own feelings and emotions in times of stress or crisis. How leaders make a difference is also a messy process. For me, theories of leadership need to be proactive and insistent on maintaining that without emotion there is no such thing as leadership. Such theories are drawn from one's own personality made up of a complex interaction between identity, memory, temperament and emotion, experience and training.

Development

Experience and training have been covered in some detail in Chapters 4 and 9. The personal aspect that I want to stress in this chapter is that of responsibility for your own development as a leader. Insights about yourself and others may come from various perspectives, and the numerous experiences that you have in work and life more generally, but it is down to you to make sure that you take the opportunities that arise for developing yourself as a leader. I have always been taken by the legendary Nordstrom Rule #1.

Vignette

Nordstrom, an American department store, used to give their new employees a handbook which was a piece of card, 5 inches by 8 inches in size which said:

> *Welcome to Nordstrom. We're glad to have you with our Company. Our number one goal is to provide outstanding customer service. Set both your personal and professional goals high. We have great confidence in your ability to achieve them.*
>
> *Nordstrom Rules:*
>
> *Rule #1 Use best judgment in all situations. There will be no additional rules.*
>
> *Please feel free to ask your department manager, store manager, or division general manager any questions at any time.*

Could you apply this to your leadership development?

I found the story of the Nordstrom rule useful for thinking about how you can choose the right people and bring them on in their development. As a chair of governors, I know I have gone back and re-advertised if I felt the candidate pool was not right for us as a school. As a developing leader, you will need to think about how to build up that best judgement as you assume more responsibility across the organisations you work in. In Chapter 1, I noted that this book would not be going into much, if any, detail about the leadership of teaching and learning, assuming that to be a cornerstone of the reason you want to lead. The Nordstrom rule probably applies there too. Where the personal difficulty for many educational leaders can lie is when changes to education policy cut across the things that they value about education and teaching and learning. In this also, good judgement, personal wisdom and astute leadership are pivotal.

Activity 41

In your journal, note down your current strengths in leadership.

1. What are your current development needs?
2. How will they be achieved?
3. Are there any particular leadership activities that you need to focus on in the next six months?

This is an activity that I carry out on a semi-regular basis. The next six months for me in my own leadership career look very interesting, but also challenging. As Haslam et al. (2011) have suggested, I am setting myself the task of reflecting on what needs to be done to build collective support for changes that are happening; my particular task is to work with others to represent our views to the wider community where I work. Their focus is on reflecting, representing and finally realising our goals as a group; this resonates with me. Again, it is based on a psychological theory but the phrase that I have noted as most important to leadership is about working with the group 'to create a social world in which the group can live according to its values' (Haslam et al., 2011: 213). This emphasis on building and growth is a core competence of a capable leader.

Of the personal and different

As this chapter is focused on the personal, one of the areas that actually first interested me as a Master's student is that of gender and leadership. This has lead to a clearer understanding of some of the issues about 'difference' or diversity in leadership, whether these differences are based around gender, race, disability, sexuality or other issues. People are unique, but the social forces that make up the landscape in which we work can be more or less equitable towards people's differences. There is not space here to have a deep discussion about equality and social justice. For me, an important part of developing as an educational leader and manager has been an understanding of how our own assumptions about differences influence practice. Gender equality and feminist discourse has helped shape the way leadership is conceptualised, particularly in the educational leadership field (Coleman, 2002; Hall, 1996), and the work of Coleman and Hall is a good place to start if you are interested in this particular issue. If you are a woman you might like to consider how far Coleman's assertion (2002: 82) that women can feel exposed as leaders because of preconceptions and expectations that the leader will be male holds true for your context. Women have to develop their leadership skills on many levels, as do men. However, individual, organisational and societal level issues can tend to give women a more challenging time. In many countries the question has moved from 'Can women lead?' to 'Why are women still underrepresented in elite leadership roles?' (Hoyt, 2013: 350). In terms of educational leadership development, the focus has moved in many organisations to mentoring and changes in the organisational culture so that women are not disadvantaged. At the same time, there have been wider changes in countries such as the UK which give both men and women opportunities to take on more domestic or childcare roles, for example by working part-time. With shortages in teacher supply in many countries, schools are proactively looking at how to retain talented women. Some would argue that these kinds of development opportunities are not a panacea and do not tackle more fundamental inequalities which mean that women are consistently underrepresented even in countries where the policy framework would seem to be positive towards women in leadership. Stereotypes and unacknowledged gender bias may be part of the problem in some countries; in others the issues could be more to do with the opportunities available.

The reason diversity has been mentioned now is so that you can return to your journal and see if any of the issues you have raised in it have hidden diversity concerns that you have not acknowledged before. If you work in a cross-cultural context, how competent and capable are you as a leader in issues of diversity? Working with people from many different culture backgrounds may help you to understand better your own cultural assumptions and beliefs. I have found that keeping issues of gender and leadership in mind when planning my development has been both theoretically and practically interesting because there have been times when I have had to confront my own assumptions as well as those of colleagues.

The many selves of leaders

Another area that you may wish to explore, which I think is very pertinent to leadership, is that of identity. My gender identity is part of the many selves that we all co-construct in terms of the social roles that we take on. Part of your development as a leader will be concerned with how your leadership identity matches the tasks you and others set, and vice versa. I am also interested in how and why people might try to reshape their sense of self, derived from anthropological theory (Holland et al., 2001), and how people negotiate their cultural or 'figured' world, as they call it. Their theory of self-formation emphasises how our 'identities' are not fixed; they are changeable and dependent on culture.

Identity and transition have featured in various parts of this book, and although this chapter has drawn mainly on psychological and psychodynamic theories, there are other ways of thinking about your personal identity. The many ways identity has been constructed by leaders is one avenue of research in sociology and social psychology. This work looks both at how identities are managed and constructed by subjective social reality, and by the ways in which leadership development has been influenced in terms of exhorting would-be leaders towards self-improvement (Sinclair, 2012). Sinclair draws out a significant area for leaders – that one of the characteristics of an effective leader is the ability to be reflexive about their own ways of dealing with identity-making, and not to get too absorbed in 'branding' yourself as one sort of leader or another. For me, the idea of a personal narrative draws not only on identity work in leadership development, but also on the power of emphasising your own self-efficacy and developing self-confidence over time.

Having drawn on my personal idea of identity and leadership development, the final chapter of the book will widen out to look at the challenges and opportunities that your development as an educational leader and manager can bring.

18

Leadership challenges and opportunities

This chapter will endeavour to:

- bring together some of the ideas discussed in the light of your personal reflections throughout the book;
- consider how and why *you* develop as a leader;
- conclude the book with a self-review and development exercise.

This book has sought to look at how issues in leadership and management are not just about individual accomplishments but are concerned with the subjective social reality of life in educational settings. The last chapter was partly imbued with my subjective personal view of leadership and management. Some of the issues that have been discussed will apply more to your own development as an educational leader than others.

This final chapter looks back at the book and widens out to look at how you can build your personal development profile to enhance the work you carry out with teams, other new leaders and the school community. As noted earlier there are many leadership preparation programmes and university postgraduate courses worldwide which introduce leaders to models of leadership and management, and there may be one that fits you at a particular point in your career. I have noted how such programmes are influenced by 'the model (explicit or implicit) of leadership which underlies the development work' (Hartley and Hinksman, 2003: 9). The responsibility for your development rests with you. As you develop as a leader you will probably move through various levels of leadership, formal or informal, and be involved in different forms of leadership in many diverse settings. This book has discussed some of the debates around the concept of leadership and/or management in its various forms, in various settings and in other cultures, not just in the UK but internationally. Not everything that the developing leader needs to know has been covered or, I would argue, could be covered. The whole premise of this book is that it should help you go away and investigate those areas which interest you and, at the same time, be more aware of your own personal development in all these diverse contexts that have been discussed.

Some of what follows in this final chapter is based on the personal knowledge I have accumulated over the years working in schools and higher education. Of course, just because ideas have worked for me does not mean you will find them meaningful, but as a developing leader you should be able to take such ideas and work out whether or not there are specific concepts or theories that you can utilise for yourself and the people you work with.

Context, critique and creativity

Earlier in the book I noted that Glatter (2006) called for a refocus within the field of leadership studies to pay much more attention to people and the organisation. Close and Raynor (2010: 222) expanded on this when they wrote: 'The study of educational leadership is about paradox, dilemma and debate, not uncritical skills transmission and simplistic solution-seeking. Glatter has called for a reorientation. It's time we put context, critique and creativity back into educational leadership.' This is quite a challenging sentence for would be leaders. Contextual issues were discussed in Section 2 in particular, but they have also formed a large part of the book's tapestry.

Critique is a key message of this book because, whatever your context, being able to critique policy, practice and key leadership concepts is incredibly important. This is often missed when developing leaders and their capacity are discussed. It is useful to ask yourself what you read as a leader that enables you to think, critique and move your thinking on.

Vignette

I was once horrified at a prestigious school where I was on the deputy head appointment panel. The first 'get them relaxed' question was: 'What book or books have you read lately that have influenced your thinking?' Quite a generic question, you might think. All the four candidates struggled to think of a book, and one replied, 'I don't read much actually.' I was left wondering what they would say if a 16-year-old in one of their own classes gave that reply. No one was appointed. What would you say?

Apart from the fact that it is poor interview technique not to come up with at least something popular/controversial/in the news, the panel were astonished that people who were interested in a senior position seemed uninterested in their own ability to learn as an adult. Creativity in leadership implies not only being able to use your own cognitive, emotional and behavioural skills in ways that enhance leadership practice in educational organisations, but also increase your own ability to develop and grow. Twitter is an excellent example of how educationalists have found a creative outlet for sharing good practice creatively in both a few characters and in blogs. It encourages debate around professional focused issues in many differing kinds of forum. At the same time, such professional spaces can never be a substitute for sustained critical thinking and reflective reading.

Critical thinking can be perceived in many ways, and there are certainly many debates in the literature about exactly what such thinking might involve. One particular way I have found useful for leadership and management thinking. On a module that I once used to run on a Master's course, I used Brookfield (1987) who discussed ways of looking at critical thinking as a learning conversation. Such conversations have specific qualities, and the following is an abridged version of those discussions.

- *Good conversations are reciprocal and involving.* When you are engaged in a very stimulating conversation there are many facets to it. All of the participants in the conversation are really involved in the process of making conversation by either talking or listening. When people talk, there is a variety of ways that are used to keep the conversation involving and reciprocal. For example, people may respond to a previous comment, answer questions, add to earlier arguments they have made, give examples and bring in new ideas to the conversation. Listening is also an important part of a good conversation. If you can, it is helpful to watch a conversation to understand more fully the importance of listening for understanding meaning. Effective listeners listen for meaning and at the same time mentally process the meaning in terms of their own knowledge while also working on their next verbal phrase in the conversation.

- *The course of good conversations cannot be anticipated.* Many managers go into discussions expecting an outcome. In a good conversation, you may know the destination in general but if you are listening and participating fully, the final outcome may be even better than the anticipated one. Brookfield encourages learning conversations to be stimulating and not knowing the exact course is one way.

- *Good conversations entail diversity and disagreement.* This is the part that many students on my course found tricky. Brookfield argues that any conversation where everyone agrees is not really a conversation.

(Based on Brookfield, 1987: 238–41)

What do you think? Brookfield noted:

> The development of critical thinking inevitably entails diversity of opin-
> ion, disagreement over correct interpretations of an idea, rule or behaviour,
> and challenges to existing ways of thinking and acting [...] Unless we can
> accept that others have views very different from ours, and that a multi-
> plicity of interpretations of practically every idea or action is possible, we
> will be unable to contemplate alternatives in our own thoughts and
> actions. (1987: 241)

A non-judgemental attitude or just being open-minded comes to some
people naturally; others have to work at it. Both are useful skills to develop
as a leader and you may want to ask a critical friend how non-judgemental
or tolerant you are. It might also be interesting to ask yourself whether you
think these are suitable attributes in most or all situations. This takes the
discussion back to Chapter 2 and what we value.

Fink (2013) has suggested that self-trust is another important quality
to cultivate. Leadership in education is intensely unpredictable in
many policy contexts. Some of you may work in high trust environments, some in low trust. These can also be high or low accountability
environments. In countries where high accountability is paired with
low trust in teachers or the leadership of schools, it can be even more
difficult to remain firm to your beliefs. Citing the example of the US
president Abraham Lincoln, Fink noted that not all of Lincoln's leadership decisions were good ones, but he was willing to take the blame
and move on: 'It was his dedication to a clear and transcendent moral
purpose, his willingness to encourage divergent opinions among his
advisors, his fine sense of timing and his ability to engender trust that
provide an exemplary model for school and district leaders when they
face consequential decisions' (2013: 17). Certainly, research into educational leadership is particularly firm about the centrality of moral purpose
for leaders (Fullan, 2003). If you think that these are important qualities
to cultivate, then it may be useful to explore further possibilities in terms
of finding out more about the relationships between such qualities and
capable leadership. Making sustained critical thinking and reflective reading part of your professional learning as a developing leader can allow
other benefits such as the ability to make time for your own needs as well
as those with whom you work.

The developing leader and practice

I believe that developing leaders should be able to work in a professional
system which values, challenges and develops them. This is not always
the case, either systemically or locally. Challenges to developing can

come from work life or personal life, and may of course occur at the same time. An overarching reminder to yourself that learning is lifelong may help when challenges seem about to swamp you. Make time for yourself and look for outlets that refresh you. These could be intellectual, social or spiritual. I enjoy reading blogs about education, people management and healthcare. Some of these blogs are more life affirming than others, and it is to those that I turn when in need of an intellectual or emotional fillip. One English healthcare management blog I particularly enjoy is by Lilley, probably because of its slightly irreverent tone. He has suggested that good managers are 'resilient realists', and the following is an adaptation of his seven things for leaders and managers to think about (Lilley, 2014), focused on education rather than healthcare.

1. Whether results are good or bad, remember; most people try to do their best. If things aren't right, figure out why and fix it. Any fool can criticise; root causes are the only pathway to excellence. Most people will do better if you treat them better. 'Constructive criticism' is too easily abused but some advice from a friend is always welcome.
2. Be unfailingly courteous; good day or bad, good week or not, good month or iffy, always end it on a high. There will always be something to celebrate. Make the words 'us' and 'we' the most used in your vocabulary and celebrate together. If staff aren't talking, you are just not listening.
3. Top managers don't do great things; they clear time and space for their people to do great things. In someway everyone, everyday has the opportunity to be a leader.
4. You can't manage anything that you haven't smelt. You have to go there. Camp out in the corridors and classrooms. You need to know what the teachers know – beg them to tell you.
5. Make it your personal goal to outperform everyone; out read them, out last them and always, always, always show up. Get 'spooky-good'. Evidence-based anything is too clunky; evidence-informed is nimble, deft and flexes to change. Learn another skill, spend time on you.
6. Bad managers copy bad managers. Beware of any who only use sports or military metaphors. Talk the language of friendship and family. Recognise that most educational organisations have more women than men in the workplace. Is your place women friendly? How many senior managers and Governing Board members are women?
7. As a leader, protect the front-line, fund it properly, protect it fiercely, make it fun to work there and your problems will disappear.

So far so positive, and many developing leaders will particularly relate to the final point. Lilley ends his blog with some fascinating advice for healthcare workers, which I think could be equally applicable to educational organisations: 'Don't expect anyone to ask you what you think, don't expect anyone to say thank you, don't expect any money for anything, don't expect anything with "strategy" written on it to work.' I would, of course, have to disagree with the last suggestion, although I think I know what he means. Many strategic documents are so unwieldy that they are ignored or bypassed in schools. Strategy, it was noted in an earlier chapter, is also about the culture of the organisation and embedding strategic leadership in the organisation's cultural practices.

Developing as an educational leader and manager is also embedded in the cultural practices of an organisation, while at the same time part of your development may be to work on and change those cultural practices. This iterative process of your own self-review being part of your organisation's development is important to remember. Self-review and development as a solo activity is very unlikely to aid your leadership development.

Self-review and development

In this final activity for the book, I am going to ask you to use any and all the notes that you might have put into your journal. If you have not written much, can't find the latest version on your computer or just are not sure what was important, then use this activity anyway as a means of bringing together your own thoughts about where you are now in your leadership journey and the steps you may need to take to go further. It can also be used as an opportunity to embark upon the difficult process of personal change or as a jumping off spot where you decide that your current leadership role is quite the right place to be right now. Also, I would like you to consider making this part of a self-review process talked about in the earlier chapters. Think about how often it might be useful to complete such a process and where it might fit into any critical friendship opportunities that you might have. Critical friends will certainly be able to help you with feasibility issues in any plans you might make and provide a reality check.

I have designed this final activity to help you bring together your thoughts from reading this book and any concurrent extra reading you may have done. It aims to make you think again about the importance of both theoretical frameworks and practical knowledge in the educational organisation. I will also ask you to note down how you might take particular ideas and apply them as a result of new knowledge gained from such reading and reflection. This is a longer activity than all the other ones in the book so do take your time over it. Pay particular attention to any developmental needs that you flag that you feel are not being met in your current workplace, and what you can do to change that. This does not necessarily mean moving as this may only set back your cultural and social knowledge of an organisation.

Activity 42

1. Refresh your knowledge of your journal jottings to begin with. After that, note down in 500 words or less what you consider to be interesting new ideas you can take away from this book and any related reading you might have done.
2. What are your most immediate development needs? Identify and list them.
3. Now prioritise them.
4. How do they relate to your educational organisation's development plans at the moment? Identify common areas for development.
5. What are the chief benefits to you and your organisation if you are able to develop further as a leader?
6. Are there any particular blocks – financial, time, personal or something else entirely – that could get in the way of achieving some or any of your goals?
7. Set up an Action Plan, with an attached timescale. What do you or others need to do in order for development needs to be meet? List short- and long-term steps you might take.
8. Now write down the one most important thing you need to do and how you will get support to achieve it.
9. Double check how realistic you have been with 1–8!

This activity should give you some helpful guidance about realistic approaches to your own development in the context of your team and the culture of the educational organisation that you work in. At the very least, it should have stimulated some more thoughts about your own professional practice.

The professional and social

Being sustained as a professional is so important it should never be overlooked. There are many ideals and values that keep professionals going, or a personal connection can be important when professional life becomes very difficult for whatever reason. Being more aware of the possibilities of learning as adults (Eraut, 1993) means that you should look out for opportunities to improve your skilled professional behaviour throughout your career. Eraut's suggestions apply firstly to teaching but are very similar to leadership qualities that have already been suggested in the book: gaining feedback, reviewing behaviour, observing others, expanding your repertoire, and using the information you gain from all of these to make the best of your innate qualities. He also noted that thinking skills of a very high order are needed to tackle practical problems, which is one of the capabilities that I have suggested leaders and managers should develop. Self-knowledge of the kind discussed in this book and self-management strategies need to work together to maximise your opportunities.

As with anything involving people, your challenges and opportunities will depend on the culture of the workplace and how the institution views formal development opportunities. Informal personal relations may be more important in some cases in moving you on in terms of your development, but they are made more powerful when they are part of a collaborative culture more generally. Such cultures, perhaps involving professional learning communities as discussed earlier, can help group members articulate group values clearly and keep you focused on development issues and the idea of continuous improvement for both students and staff. The fact that such cultures must be nurtured and reinvigorated over time could be the focus of many genuine critical learning conversations. As part of your leadership development, you may wish to be their instigator and systematically work on changing the culture of a department for example. One of my Master's students made this the focus of his research thesis and, while systematically reading the literature, changed the culture of his department's team meetings towards one of collaboration and continuous learning about the processes of the department. He managed to strike a balance between his need to write a research essay and the need of his departmental colleagues to change some of their practices. In fact, one of the things I noticed about the whole project was how he sought to influence his colleagues and began to lead meetings with collective purpose rather than just manage them so that they finished on time. For him, it was a good balance between the needs of the individual and the learning for the collective. Of course, it was also a great opportunity to try out some of his leadership skills and develop them further.

Leading by example

I hope that you have found some issues in this book to make you think more critically about your own leadership and management and the culture in which you work. Educationalists work in demanding environments, where personal pressure can cause some in leadership positions to behave less than perfectly and, in some cases, at the limits of ethically acceptable behaviour. Although the former may be inevitable every now and again, it is to be hoped that any reader of this book would find the latter deplorable in any leader. At the same time, you might understand some of the issues that have lead them to that situation. In England, there have been several high-profile cases of head teachers massaging their exam results, often because of heavy pressure for the school to achieve certain grades. You might be able to put yourself into that situation and understand, though not condone, the action. There have been some examples of leaders being less than honest with their new-found financial freedoms. In that case, you would, I expect want to draw an ethical line at fraud. If student achievement *and* staff motivation are important, then as a capable but ethical leader you will want to challenge complacency but also support those colleagues who need your advice and professional backup at various points in their careers. Leading by example involves being more than the exceptional head at the front, although it may involve that in some contexts. They can endeavour to model positive attitudes and support others to have a similar view. Being supportive does not mean that leaders do not have to take difficult management decisions about people. Those of you who are very people-focused may find this a more difficult task, at least to begin with, and it may leave you feeling emotionally raw. This brings us back to leaders as supporters who also make sure that they have put in place ways of managing their own support whether through mentoring, union colleagues or particular team members. Without such support, many developing leaders can burn out before they reach the leadership and management work that they are capable of.

Wrapping up

In the preface, I introduced my own story and asked you to consider your own narrative as a developing leader. Leaders in education face a complex world full of competing agendas and differing value systems. As leaders of teaching and learning, leaders bring their understanding of how a classroom works well to leadership roles; they then have to learn to use such understanding most effectively to gain commitment to organisational rather than individual learning goals. For some people, this will be a relatively easy transition, sustained by a professional learning environment. Others will find the transition more difficult for some of the many reasons that this book has suggested. To develop as a leader, you will need all your current knowledge, skills and understanding of educational organisations and the people within them as well as professional understanding of classroom practice. All these are only a start. To develop as a leader and manager you will need to continue being firm and purposeful in your intent to increase your capacity as a leader, drawing on appropriate support. There will be times when you will probably wish you were not leading, but equally times when you are glad that you set out to develop yourself further. I hope that engaging with this book, with its mixture of theoretical text and practical examples, will help you to do this capably in whatever the best way is for you, with your current responsibilities in your particular context.

Further Reading for Section 5

- http://johntomsett.com/
  Reflections on policy and practice from an experienced head teacher.

- *Journal of Cases in Educational Leadership*
  A case study-based journal which is a great way to keep up with current issues and debates.

- http://www.belmas.org.uk
  A society for academics and practitioners interested in research and practice.

- Coleman, M. (2002) *Women as Headteachers*. Stoke-on-Trent: Trentham Books.
  A very interesting book to read if you are a woman aspiring to leadership roles.

References

Ackerman, R. and Maslin-Ostrowski, P. (2004) 'The wounded leader and emotional learning in the schoolhouse', *School Leadership and Management*, 24 (3): 311–28.

Adair, J. (1998) *Not Bosses But How to Lead Leaders: The Way to Success*. London: Kogan Page.

Adams, J. and Punter, A. (2008) 'Finding (and keeping) school governors: the work of the school governors one-stop-shop', *Management in Education*, 22 (4): 14–17.

Anderson, K., Brien, K., McNamara, G., O'Hara, J. and McIsaac, D. (2011) 'Reluctant leaders: why are some capable leaders not interested in the principalship?', *International Journal of Management in Education*, 5 (4): 384–400.

Armstrong, D. (2011) *Administrative Passages: Navigating the Transition from Teacher to Assistant Principal*. New York: Springer.

Ashforth, B. and Tomiuk, M. A. (2000) 'Emotional labour and authenticity: views from service agents', in S. Fineman (ed.), *Emotion in Organizations*. London: Sage.

Balarin, M., Brammer, S., James, C. R. and McCormack, M. (2008) *The School Governance Study*. London: Business in the Community.

Ball, S. (1987) *The Micropolitics of the School*. London: Routledge.

Bass, B. M. (1985) *Leadership and Performance Beyond Expectations*. New York: Free Press.

Bass, B. M. and Avolio, B. (1993) 'Transformational leadership: a response to critiques', in M. M. Chemers and R. Ayman (eds), *Leadership Theory and Research: Perspectives and Directions*. New York: Academic Press, p. 49–90.

Bass, B. M., and Avolio, B. J. (1994) 'Introduction', in B. M. Bass and B. J. Avolio (eds), *Improving Organizational Effectiveness through Transformational Leadership*. Thousand Oaks, CA: Sage.

Bassey, M. (1999) *Case Study Research in Educational Settings*. Buckingham: Open University Press.

Bauch, P., and Goldring, E. (1995) 'Parent involvement and school responsiveness: facilitating the home-school connection in schools of choice', *Educational Evaluation and Policy Analysis*, 17 (1): 1–21.

Begley, P. (2012) 'Leading with moral purpose: the place of ethics', in M. Preedy, N. Bennett and C. Wise (eds), *Educational Leadership: Context, Strategy and Collaboration*. London: Sage.

Begley, P. and Johansson, O. (eds) (2003) *The Ethical Dimensions of School Leadership*. New York: Springer.

Belbin, R. M. (1981) *Management Teams: Why They Succeed or Fail*. Oxford: Heinemann.

Bell, J. (2010) *Doing Your Research Project: A Guide for First-Time Researchers in Education, Health and Social Science*. Maidenhead: Open University Press.

Bennis, W. (1969) *Organisation Development: Its Nature, Origin and Prospects*. Reading, MA: Addison-Wesley.

Bennis, W. and Nanus, B. (1985) *Leaders: The Strategies for Taking Charge*. New York: Harper & Row.

BERA (2011) *Ethical Guidelines for Educational Research*. London: British Educational Research Association.

Bloisi, W. (2003) *Management and Organisational Behaviour*, 2nd edn. London: McGraw-Hill.

Bolam, R., McMahon, A., Pocklington, D. and Weindling, D. (eds) (1993) *Effective Management in Schools*. London: HMSO.

Bolden, R. (2011) 'Distributed leadership in organizations: a review of theory and research', *International Journal of Management Review*, 13: 251–69.

Bolman, L. G. and Deal, T. E. (2003) *Reframing Organizations: Artistry, Choice, and Leadership*. San Francisco: Jossey-Bass.

Bottery, M. (2002) *The Use and Misuse of Trust*. Paper presented at the BELMAS conference, Aston University, Birmingham.

Bottery, M. (2004) *The Challenges of Educational Leadership*. London: Paul Chapman.

Bourdieu, P. (1986) 'The forms of capital', in J. Richardson (ed.), *Handbook for Theory and Research for the Sociology of Education*. Westport, CT: Greenwood, pp. 241–58.

Bourdieu, P. (1991) *Language and Symbolic Power*. Cambridge: Polity Press.

Boyatzis, R., Stubbs, E. and Taylor, S. (2002) 'Learning cognitive and emotional intelligence competencies through graduate management education', *Academy of Management Learning and Education*, 1 (2): 150–62.

Boydell, T. (1985) *Management Self Development: A Guide for Managers, Organisations and Institutions*. Geneva: International Labour Organisation.

Brabazon, T. (2013) *10 Truths a PhD Supervisor Will Never Tell You*. Retrieved 6 November 2013, from: http://www.timeshighereducation.co.uk/features/10-truths-a-phd-supervisor-will-never-tell-you/2/2005513.article.

Briggs, A. J., Coleman, M. and Morrison, M. (2012) *Research Methods in Educational Leadership and Management*. London: Sage.

Briner, R. (1999) 'The neglect and importance of emotion at work', *European Journal of Work and Organizational Psychology*, 8 (3): 323–46.

Brookfield, S. D. (1987) *Developing Critical Thinkers: Challenging Adults to Explore Alternative Ways of Thinking and Acting*. Milton Keynes: Open University Press.

Browne-Ferrigno, T. and Muth, R. (2004) 'Leadership mentoring in clinical practice: role socialization, professional development, and capacity building', *Educational Administration Quarterly*, 40 (4): 468–94.

Brundrett, M. and Rhodes, C. (2014) *Researching Educational Leadership and Management*. London: Sage.

Bryant, M. (2003) 'Cross-cultural perspectives on leadership', in N. Bennett, M. Crawford and M. Cartwright (eds), *Effective Educational Leadership*. London: Sage.

Burke, Joseph C. (ed.) (2005) *Achieving Accountability in Higher Education: Balancing Public, Academic, and Market Demands*. San Francisco: Jossey-Bass.

Bush, T. (2008) *Leadership and Management Development in Education*. Melbourne: Hawker Brownlow.

Bush, T. (2009) 'Leadership development and school improvement: contemporary issues in leadership development', *Educational Review*, 61 (4): 375–89.

Bush, T. (2011) *Theories of Educational Leadership and Management*, 4th edn. London: Sage.

Bush, T. and Glover, D. (2003) *Leadership Development: Evidence and Beliefs*. Nottingham: NCSL.

Carli, L. and Eagly, A. (2011) 'Gender and leadership', in A. Bryman, D. Collinson, K. Grint, B. Jackson and M. Uhl-Bien (eds), *The Sage Handbook of Leadership*. London: Sage.

Carr-Stewart, S. and Steeves, L. (2009) 'First Nations educational governance: a fractured mirror', *Canadian Journal of Educational Administration and Policy*, 97: 1–10.

Clarke, S. and Wildy, H. (2010) 'Preparing for principalship from the crucible of experience: reflecting on theory, practice and research', *Journal of Educational Administration and History*, 41 (1): 1–16.

Close, P. and Raynor, A. (2010) 'Five literatures of organisation: putting the context back into educational leadership', *School Leadership and Management*, 30 (3): 209–24.

Cohen, L. and Manion, L. (1994) *Research Methods in Education*. London: Routledge.

Cohen, M. D., March, J. G. and Olsen, J. P. (1972) 'A garbage can model of organizational choice', *Administration Science Quarterly*, 17: 1–25.

Coldron, J., Crawford, M., Jones, S. and Simkins, T. (2014) 'The restructuring of schooling in England: the responses of well-positioned headteachers', *Educational Management Administration and Leadership*, 42 (3): 387–403.

Coleman, M. (2002) *Women as Headteachers: Striking the Balance*. Stoke-on-Trent: Trentham.

Coleman, M. (2012) 'Leadership and diversity', *Educational Management Administration and Leadership*, 40 (5): 592–609.

Conger, J. A. (2011) 'Charismatic leadership', in A. Bryman, D. Collinson, K. Grint, B. Jackson and M. Uhl-Bien (eds), *The Sage Handbook of Leadership*. London: Sage.

Cortazzi, M. (2002) 'Analysing narratives and documents', in M. Coleman and A. Briggs (eds), *Research Methods in Educational Leadership and Management*. London: Paul Chapman.

Cowie, M. (ed.) (2011) *New Primary Leaders: International Perspectives*. London: Continuum.

Cowie, M. and Crawford, M. (2008) 'Being a new principal in Scotland', *Journal of Educational Administration*, 46 (6): 676–89.

Cranwell-Ward, J. (1987) *Managing Stress*. London: Pan Business.

Crawford, M. (2002) 'The charismatic school leader – potent myth or persuasive effect?', *School Leadership and Management*, 22 (3): 273–87.

Crawford, M. (2003) 'Inventive management and wise leadership', in N. Bennett, M. Crawford and M. Cartwright (eds), *Effective Educational Leadership*. London: Sage, pp. 62–74.

Crawford, M. (2004) 'Leadership and emotion in the primary school – reflections from four primary headteachers', *Education 3–13*, 32 (1): 20–5.

Crawford, M. (2007) 'Let's start at the very beginning: setting up a new secondary school', *Management in Education*, 21 (3): 14–18.

Crawford, M. (2009) *Getting the Heart of Leadership: Emotion and the Educational Leader*. London: Sage.

Crawford, M. (2011) 'Rationality and emotion in education leadership – enhancing our understanding', in C. Day and J. C. Lee (eds), *New Understandings of Teacher's Work*. London: Springer, pp. 207–17.

Crawford, M. (2012) 'Overlapping social spheres: the social domain of schools, parents and the community', in M. Brundrett (ed.), *Principles of School Leadership*, 2nd edn. London: Sage.

Crawford, M. and Cowie, M. (2012) 'Bridging theory and practice in headship preparation', *Educational Management Administration and Leadership*, 40 (2): 175–87.

Delamont, S. (2002) *Fieldwork in Educational Settings*. London and New York: Routledge.

Dimmock, C. and Walker, A. (2000) 'Developing comparative and international educational leadership and management: a cross-cultural model', *School Leadership and Management*, 20 (2): 143–60.

Dimmock, C. and Walker, A. (2005) *Educational Leadership: Culture and Diversity*. London: Sage.

Downs, C. W. and Adrian, A. D. (2004) *Assessing Organizational Communication*. New York: Guilford Press.

Draper, J. and McMichael, P. (1998) 'Making sense of primary headship: the surprises awaiting new heads', *School Leadership and Management*, 18 (2): 197–211.

Duignan, P. A. and Macpherson, R. J. S. (1992) *Educative Leadership: A Practical Theory for New Administrators and Managers*. London: Falmer Press.

Duke, D. (1987) *School Leadership and Instructional Improvement*. New York: Random House.

Dutton, J. E., Spreitzer, G. et al. (2006) 'Composing the reflective best self portrait: building pathways for becoming extraordinary in work organizations, *Academy of Management Review*, 30 (4): 712–36.

Edwards, A., Lunt, I. and Stamou, E. (2012) 'Inter-professional work and expertise: new roles at the boundaries of schools', in M. Preedy, N. Bennett and C. Wise (eds), *Educational Leadership: Context, Strategy and Collaboration*. London: Sage.

Elmore, R. (2008) 'Leadership as the practice of improvement', *Improving School Leadership*, 2: 37–67.

Eraut, M. (1993) 'The characterisation and development of professional expertise in school management and teaching', *Educational Management and Administration*, 21 (4): 222–32.

Everard, B. and Morris, G. (1996) *Effective School Management*, 3rd edn. London: Paul Chapman.

Fineman, S. (2003) *Understanding Emotion at Work*. London: Sage.

Fineman, S. (2008) *The Emotional Organization: Passions and Power*. Oxford: Blackwell.

Fineman, S. (ed.) (2000) *Emotion in Organizations*. London: Sage.

Fink, D. (2013) *Trust in Our Schools: The Missing Part of School Improvement?* (personal communication).

Foot, H. and McCreaddie, M. (2006) 'Humour and laughter', in O. Hargie (ed.), *The Handbook of Communication Skills*. London: Routledge.

French, J. R. P. and Raven, B. (1959) 'The bases of social power', in D. Cartwright (ed.), *Studies in Social Power*. Ann Arbor, MI: Oxford University Press, pp. 150–67.

Frost, D. (2008) 'Teacher leadership: values and voice', *School Leadership and Management*, 28 (4): 337–52.

Fullan, M. G. (1991) *The New Meaning of Educational Change*. New York: Teachers College Press.

Fullan, M. G. (1993) *Change Forces: Probing the Depths of Educational Reform*. London: Falmer.

Fullan, M. G. (2001) *Leading in a Culture of Change*. San Francisco: Jossey-Bass.

Fullan, M. G. (2003) *The Moral Imperative of School Leadership*. Thousand Oaks, CA: Corwin Press.

Furnham, A. (2006) *The Psychology of Behaviour at Work: The Individual in the Organisation*. London: Psychology Press.

Gabriel, Y. (2000) *Storytelling in Organizations: Facts, Fiction, and Fantasies*. Oxford: Oxford University Press.

Gill, R. (2011) *Theory and Practice of Leadership*. London: Sage.

Glatter, R. (2006) 'Leadership and organisation in education: time for a reorientation', *School Leadership and Management*, 26 (1): 69–83.

Goddard, J. T. (1998) *Of Daffodils and Dog Teams: Reflections on Leadership*. Paper presented at the British Educational Management and Administration Society (BEMAS), Warwick, England, September.

Goffman, E. (1990) *The Presentation of Self in Everyday Life*. London: Penguin.

Goldring, E. (1986) 'The school community: its effects on principals' perceptions of parents. *Educational Administration Quarterly*, 22 (2): 115–32.

Goleman, D. (1995) *Emotional Intelligence*. New York: Bantam.

Goodson, P. (2012) *Becoming an Academic Writer: 50 Exercises for Paced, Productive, and Powerful Writing*. London: Sage.

Gordon, M. F. and Seashore Louis, K. (2009) 'Linking parent and community involvement with student achievement: comparing principal and teacher perceptions of stakeholder influence', *American Journal of Education*, 116 (1): 1–31.

Gordon, R. M. (1974) 'The aboutness of emotions', *American Philosophical Quarterly*, 11: 17–36.

Greenfield, T. (1988) 'The decline and fall of science in educational administration', in A. Westoby (ed.), *Culture and Power in Educational Organisations*. Milton Keynes: Open University Press.

Greenfield, T. (1991) 'Re-forming and re-valuing educational administration: whence and when cometh the phoenix?', *Educational Management and Administration*, 19 (4): 200–17.

Greenfield, T. and Ribbins, P. (1993) *Greenfield on Educational Administration: Towards a Human Science*. London: Routledge.

Gronn, P. (2000) 'Distributed properties: a new architecture for leadership', *Educational Management Administration and Leadership*, 28 (1): 317–38.

Gronn, P. (2003a) 'Distributing and intensifying school leadership', in N. Bennett and L. Anderson (eds), *Rethinking Educational Leadership*. London, Sage.

Gronn, P. (2003b) *The Work of New Educational Leaders: Changing Leadership Practice in an Era of School Reform*. London: Paul Chapman.

Gronn, P. (2009) 'Leadership configurations', *Leadership*, 5 (3): 381–94.

Gronn, P. (2011) 'Hybrid configurations of leadership', in A. Bryman, D. Collinson, K. Grint, B. Jackson and M. Uhl-Bien (eds), *The Sage Handbook of Leadership*. London: Sage.

Guskey, T. R. (2000) *Evaluating Professional Development*. Thousand Oaks, CA: Corwin.

Hall, V. (1996) *Dancing on the Ceiling: A Study of Women Managers in Education*. London: Paul Chapman.

Hammersley, M. (ed.) (1993) *Educational Research: Current Issues*. London: Paul Chapman.

Hannah, M. T. and Freeman, J. (1984) 'Structural inertia and organizational change', *American Sociology Review*, 49: 149–64.

Hargie, O. (ed.) (2006) *The Handbook of Communication Skills*, 3rd edn. London: Routledge.

Hargreaves, A. (1997) 'From reform to renewal: a new deal for a new age', in A. Hargreaves and R. Evans (eds), *Beyond Educational Reform: Bringing Teachers Back In*. Buckingham: Open University Press.

Hargreaves, A. and Fullan, M. G. (2012) *Professional Capital: Transforming Teaching in Every School*. London: Routledge.

Harris, A. (2008) *Distributed Leadership in Schools: Developing the Leaders of Tomorrow*. London: Routledge.

Hartley, J. and Hinksman, B. (2003) *Leadership Development: A Systematic Review of the Literature – A Report for the NHS Leadership Centre*. Coventry, University of Warwick.

Haslam, A. S., Reicher, S. D. and Platow, M. J. (2011) *The New Psychology of Leadership: Identity, Influence and Power*. Hove and New York: Psychology Press.

Haydon, G. (2007) *Values for Educational Leadership*. London: Sage.

Hess, U. and Kirouac, G. (2000) 'Emotion expression in groups', in M. Lewis and J. Haviland-Jones (eds), *Handbook of Emotion*, 2nd edn. New York: Guilford Press.

Hochschild, A. (1979) 'Emotion work, feeling rules, and social structure', *American Journal of Sociology*, 85 (3): 551–75.

Hodgkinson, C. (1991) *Educational Leadership: The Moral Art*. Albany, NY: State University of New York Press.

Hofstede, G. H. (1991) *Cultures and Organisations: Software of the Mind*. London: McGraw-Hill.

Holland, D., Lachicotte, W., Skinner, D. and Cain, C. (2001) *Identity and Agency in Cultural Worlds*. President and Fellows of Harvard College.

Hosie, P., Sevastos, P. and Cooper, C. L. (2007) 'The "happy productive worker thesis" and Australian managers', *Journal of Human Values*, 13 (2): 151–76.

Howson, J. and Sprigade, A. (2011) *26th Annual Survey of Senior Staff Appointments in Schools Across England and Wales*. TSL/EDS.

Hoyle, E. (1988) 'Micropolitics of educational organizations', in A. Westoby (ed.), *Culture and Power in Educational Organizations*. Milton Keynes: Open University Press.

Hoyt, C. (2013) 'Woman and leadership', in P. Northouse (ed.), *Leadership: Theory and Practice*, 6th edn. London: Sage.

Huczynski, A. and Buchanan, D. (2001) *Organizational Behaviour*. London: Pearson Education.

Ingvarson, L. (2005) *Getting Professional Development Right*. Online at: http://research.acer.edu.au/professional_dev/4.

James, C., Brammer, S., Connelly, M., Fertig, M., James, J. and Jones, J. (2010) *The 'Hidden Givers': A Study of School Governing Bodies in England.* Reading: CfBT.

Katzenbach, J. and Smith, D. (2003) *The Wisdom of Teams.* New York: HarperCollins.

Kelchtermans, G., Piot, L. and Ballet, K. (2011) 'The lucid loneliness of the gate-keeper: exploring the emotional dimension in principals' work lives', *Oxford Review of Education, iFirst*, January, pp. 1–16.

Kelly, A. and Saunders, N. (2010) 'New heads on the block: three case studies of transition to primary school headship', *School Leadership and Management*, 30 (1).

Kilduff, M. and Balkundi, P. (2011) 'A network approach to leader cognition and effectiveness', in A. Bryman, D. Collinson, K. Grint, B. Jackson and M. Uhl-Bien (eds), *The Sage Handbook of Leadership.* London: Sage.

Lave, J. and Wenger, E. (1991) *Situated Learning: Legitimate Peripheral Participation.* Cambridge: Cambridge University Press.

Law, S. and Glover, D. (2000) *Educational Leadership and Learning.* Buckingham: Open University Press.

Lencioni, P. (2002) 'Making your values mean something', *Harvard Business Review*, 80 (7): 113–17.

Leonard, D. (2001) *A Woman's Guide to Doctoral Studies.* Buckingham: Open University Press.

Levicki, C. (2001) *Developing Leadership Genius.* London: McGraw-Hill Educational.

Lilley, R. (2014) 'It's OK to be proud of what you do', *NHSManagers.net* Newsletter, 6 January (accessed 7 January 2014).

Luthans, F. and Avolio, B. J. (2003) 'Authentic leadership development', in K. S. Cameron, J. E. Dutton and R. E. Quinn (eds), *Positive Organizational Scholarship.* San Francisco: Berrett-Koehler.

Luthans, F. and Youssef, C. M. (2007) 'Emerging positive organizational behavior', *Journal of Managment*, 33: 321–49.

MacBeath, J. and Kirwan, T. (2008) *Identifying Links Between ECM and Improvements in School Standards.* Nottingham: NCSL.

MacBeath, J. and Townsend, T. (2011) 'Leadership and learning: paradox, para-digms and principles', *International Handbook of Leadership for Learning Part 1.* New York: Springer, pp. 1–25.

McClelland, D. (1988) *Human Motivation.* Cambridge: Cambridge University Press.

Mannay, D. (2010) 'Making the familiar strange: can visual research methods ren-der the familiar setting more perceptible?', *Qualitative Research*, 10 (1): 91–111.

Mason, J. (2002) *Qualitative Researching.* London: Sage.

Middlewood, D., Coleman, M. and Lumby, J. (1999) *Practitioner Research in Education: Making a Difference.* London: Sage.

Mintzberg, H. (1979) *The Structuring of Organisations.* Englewood Cliffs, NJ: Prentice Hall.

Mintzberg, H. (1990) 'The manager's job, folklore and fact', *Harvard Business Review*, March–April, pp. 163–76.

Morgan, G. (1998) *Images of Organisations.* New York: Sage.

Muijs, D., Chapman, C. and Armstrong, P. (2013) 'Can early career teachers be teacher leaders? A study of second year trainess in the Teach First Alternative

Certification Programme', *Educational Management Administration and Leadership*, 41 (6): 767–81.

Murray, R. (2002) *How to Write a Thesis*. Maidenhead: Open University Press.

Nelson, S., De La Colina, M. and Boone, M. D. (2008) 'Lifeworld or systemsworld: what guides novice principals?', *Journal of Educational Administration*, 46 (6): 690–701.

Nestor-Baker, N. and Hoy, W. (2001) 'Tacit knowledge of school superintendents: its nature, meaning and content', *Educational Administration Quarterly*, 37 (1): 86–129.

O'Keefe, D. (2006) 'Persuasion', in O. Hargie (ed.), *The Handbook of Communication Skills*. London: Routledge, pp. 323–34.

O'Neill, J. (2003) 'Managing through teams', in L. Kydd, L. Anderson and W. Newton (eds), *Leading People and Teams in Education*. London: Sage.

Oatley, K. and Jenkins, J. M. (2003) *Understanding Emotions*. Oxford: Blackwell.

Ogawa, R. T. and Bossert, S. T. (eds) (1997) *Leadership as an Organisational Quality*. Buckingham: Open University Press.

Onguko, B., Abdalla, M. and Webber, C. (2012) 'Walking in unfamiliar territory: headteachers' preparation and experiences in their first year in Tanzania', *Educational Administration Quarterly*, 48 (1): 86–115.

Opfer, D., Pedder, D. and Lavicza, Z. (2010) 'The role of teachers' orientation to learning in professional development and change: a national study of teachers in England', *Teaching and Teacher Education*, 27: 443–53.

Parkinson, B. (1995) *Ideas and Realities of Emotion*. London: Routledge.

Parry, K. W. (2011) 'Leadership and organization theory', in A. Bryman, D. Collinson, K. Grint, B. Jackson and M. Uhl-Bien (eds), *The Sage Handbook of Leadership*. London: Sage.

Pascal, C. and Ribbins, P. (1998) *Understanding Primary Headteachers*. London: Cassell.

Pollitt, C. (2007) 'New Labour's re-disorganisation', *Public Management Review*, 9 (4): 529–43.

Ribbins, P. (1995) 'Understanding contemporary leaders and leadership in education: values and visions', in J. Bell and B. T. Harrison (eds), *Visions and Values in Managing Education*. London: David Fulton.

Riley, K. A. (2012) 'Reconfiguring urban leadership: taking a perspective on community', in M. Preedy, N. Bennett and C. Wise (eds), *Educational Leadership: Context, Strategy and Collaboration*. London: Sage.

Riley, K. A. (2013) *Leadership of Place*. London: Bloomsbury.

Riley, K. A. and Louis, K. S. (2004) *Exploring New Forms of Community Leadership: Linking Schools and Communities to Improve Educational Opportunities for Young People*. Nottingham: NCSL.

Roberts, B. (2002) *Biographical Research*. Buckingham: Open University Press.

Roberts, L. M., Dutton, J. E., Spreitzer, G., Heaphy, E. D. and Quinn, R. E. (2005) 'Composing the reflected best self portrait: building pathways for becoming extraordinary in work organizations', *Academy of Management Review*, 30 (4): 712–36.

Roberts, N. C. and Bradley, R. T. (1988) 'Limits of charisma', in J. A. Conger and R. N. Kanungo (eds), *Charismatic Leadership: The Elusive Factor in Organizational Effectiveness*. San Francisco: Jossey-Bass.

Robson, C. (2002) *Real World Research*. Oxford: Blackwell.

Rudduck, J. (2002) 'The transformative potential of consulting young people about teaching, learning and schooling', *Scottish Educational Review*, 34 (2): 123–37.

Ryan, K. and Feller, I. (2012) 'Evaluation, accountability, and performance measurement in national education systems: trends, methods, and issues', in M. Preedy, N. Bennett and C. Wise (eds), *Educational Leadership: Context, Strategy and Collaboration*. London, Sage.

Salovey, P. and Mayer, J. D. (1990) 'Emotional intelligence', *Imagination, Cognition and Personality*, 9: 185–211.

Salovey, P., Hsee, C. K. and Mayer, J. D. (2001) 'Emotional intelligence and the self-regulation of affect', in W. Gerrod Parrott (ed.), *Emotions in Social Psychology*. London and New York: Taylor & Francis.

Schön, D. (1983) *The Reflective Practitioner*. Harper Collins.

Sergiovanni, T. J. (2003) 'The lifeworld at the center: values and action in educational leadership', in N. Bennett, M. Crawford and M. Cartwright (eds), *Effective Educational Leadership*. London: Sage.

Silins, H. and Mulford, W. R. (2009) 'Transformational leadership and organizational learning in schools', in M. S. Khine and I. M. Saleh (eds), *Transformational Leadership in Educational Excellence: Learning Organisations in the Information Age*. Rotterdam: Sense, pp. 139–64.

Simkins, T. (1999) 'Values, power and instrumentality: theory and research in educational management', *Educational Management Administration and Leadership*, 27 (3): 267–81.

Simkins, T. (2005) 'Leadership in education: "what works" or "what makes sense"?', *Educational Management Administration and Leadership*, 33 (1): 9–26.

Sinclair, A. (2012) 'Being leaders: identities and identity work in leadership', in A. Bryman, D. Collinson, K. Grint, B. Jackson and M. Uhl-Bien (eds), *The Sage Handbook of Leadership*. London: Sage.

Sorenson, G., Goethals, G. R. and Haber, P. (2011) 'The enduring and elusive quest for a general theory of leadership: initial efforts and new horizons', in A. Bryman, D. Collinson, K. Grint, B. Jackson and M. Uhl-Bien (eds), *The Sage Handbook of Leadership*. London: Sage.

Southworth, G. (1995) *Looking into Primary Headship*. London: Falmer.

Southworth, G. (2011) Connecting Leadership and Learning. In J. Robertson and H. Timperley (eds), *Leadership and Learning*. London: Sage.

Sparrowe, R. T. (2005) 'Authentic leadership and the narrative self', *Leadership Quarterly*, 16: 419–39.

Spillane, J. (2006) *Distributed Leadership*. San Francisco: Jossey-Bass.

Spillane, J., Healey, K. et al. (2011) 'A distributed perspective on learning leadership', in J. Robertson and H. Timperley (eds), *Leadership and Learning*. London: Sage.

Starratt, R. J. (2003) 'Democratic leadership in late modernity: an oxymoron or ironic possibility?', in P. Begley and O. Johansson (eds), *The Ethical Dimensions of School Leadership*. Dordrecht: Kluwer.

Stech, E. (2013) 'Psychodynamic approach', in P. Northouse (ed.), *Leadership: Theory and Practice*, 6th edn. London: Sage.

Stein, N. L., Trabasso, T. and Liwag, M. (1994) 'The Rashomon phenomenon: personal frames and future-oriented appraisals in memory for emotional events', in M. M. Haith, J. B. Benson, R. J. Roberts and B. F. Pennington (eds), *Future Oriented Processes*. Chicago: University of Chicago Press.

Stoll, L. (2011) 'Leadership and learning', in J. Robertson and H. Timperley (eds), *Leadership and Learning*. London: Sage.

Stoll, L., Bolam, R., McMahon, A., Wallace, M. and Thomas, S. (2006) 'Professional learning communities: a review of the literature', *Journal of Educational Change*, 7: 221–58.

Swaffield, S. (2004) 'Critical friends: supporting leadership, improving learning', *Improving Schools*, 7 (3): 267–78.

Thomson, P. and Walker, M. (eds) (2010) *The Routledge Doctoral Students' Companion: Getting to Grips with Research in Education and the Social Sciences*. London: Routledge.

Timperley, H. (2011) 'Leading teachers' professional learning', in J. Robertson and H. Timperley (eds), *Leadership and Learning*. London: Sage.

Tuckman, B. (1965) 'Development sequences in small groups', *Psychological Bulletin*, 63 (1): 53–64.

Tuckman, B. and Jensen, M. (1977) 'Stages of group development revisited', *Group and Organization Studies*, 2 (4): 419–27.

Vermunt, J. D. and Endedijk, M. D. (2011) 'Patterns in teacher learning in different phases of the professional career', *Learning and Individual Differences*, 21: 294–302.

Wallace, M. and Poulson, L. (2003) *Learning to Read Critically in Educational Leadership and Management*. London: Sage.

Weick, K. E. (1976) 'Educational organizations as loosely coupled systems', *Administration Science Quarterly*, 21 (1): 1–19.

Weick, K. E. (1979) *The Social Psychology of Organising*, 2nd edn. Reading, MA: Addison-Wesley.

Weick, K. E. (1995) *Sensemaking in Organizations*. Thousand Oaks, CA: Sage.

Weick, K. E. (2001) *Making Sense of the Organization*. Oxford: Blackwell.

Weindling, D. and Earley, P. (1987) *Secondary Headship – The Early Years*. Cheltenham: NFER Nelson.

Western, S. (2012) 'An overview of leadership discourses', in M. Preedy, N. Bennett and C. Wise (eds), *Educational Leadership Context Strategy and Collaboration*. London, Sage.

Westoby, A. (ed.) (1988) *Culture and Power in Educational Organizations*. Milton Keynes: Open University Press.

Wildy, H. and Clarke, S. (2008a) 'Charting an arid landscape: the preparation of novice primary principals in Western Australia', *School Leadership and Management*, 28 (5): 469–87.

Wildy, H. and Clarke, S. (2008b) 'Principals on L-plates: rear view mirror reflections', *Journal of Educational Administration*, 46 (6): 727–38.

Woods, P. A. (2005) *Democratic Leadership in Education*. London: Paul Chapman.

Woods, P., Bennett, N., Harvey, J. A. and Wise, C. (2004) 'Variabilities and dualities in distributed leadership: findings from a systematic literature review', 32 (4): 439–57.

Yip, J., Ernst, C. and Campbell, M. (2011) *Boundary Spanning Leadership*. Greensboro, NC: Center for Creative Leadership.

Index